AUSTRALIAN TELEVISION CULTURE

Other titles in the series

Australian Television
Programs, pleasures and politics
Edited by John Tulloch and Graeme Turner

Dark Side of the Dream
Australian literature and the postcolonial mind
Bob Hodge and Vijay Mishra

Fashioning the Feminine
Girls, popular culture and schooling
Pam Gilbert and Sandra Taylor

Featuring Australia
The cinema of Charles Chauvel
Stuart Cunningham

Framing Culture
Criticism and policy in Australia
Stuart Cunningham

From Nimbin to Mardi Gras
Constructing community arts
Gay Hawkins

From Pop to Punk to Postmodernism
Popular music and Australian culture from the 1960s to the 1990s
Edited by Philip Hayward

Myths of Oz
Reading Australian popular culture
John Fiske, Bob Hodge, Graeme Turner

Resorting to Tourism
Cultural policies for tourist development in Australia
Jennifer Craik

Stay Tuned
The Australian Broadcasting Reader
Edited by Albert Moran

Temptations
Sex, selling and the department store
Gail Reekie

Australian Cultural Studies
Editor: John Tulloch

AUSTRALIAN TELEVISION CULTURE

Tom O'Regan

LONDON AND NEW YORK

for Rita

First published 1993 by Allen & Unwin

Published 2020 by Routledge
2 Park Square, Milton Park, Abingdon, Oxon OX14 4RN
605 Third Avenue, New York, NY 10017

Routledge is an imprint of the Taylor & Francis Group, an informa business

Copyright © Tom O'Regan, 1993

All rights reserved. No part of this book may be reprinted or reproduced or utilised in any form or by any electronic, mechanical, or other means, now known or hereafter invented, including photocopying and recording, or in any information storage or retrieval system, without permission in writing from the publishers.

Notice:
Product or corporate names may be trademarks or registered trademarks, and are used only for identification and explanation without intent to infringe.

National Library of Australia
Cataloguing-in-Publication entry:

O'Regan, Tom, 1956– .
 Australian television culture.
 Includes index.
 ISBN 186373 527 5.
 1. Television broadcasting—Social aspects—Australia.
 2. Television programs—Australia.
 3. Communication and culture—Australia.
 4. Australia—Popular culture. I. Title.
 306.4850994

Set in 10/11.5pt Sabon by Graphicraft Typesetters Ltd., Hong Kong

ISBN-13: 9781863735278 (pbk)

General Editor's Foreword

Nowadays the social and anthropological definition of 'culture' is probably gaining as much public currency as the aesthetic one. Particularly in Australia, politicians are liable to speak of the vital need for a domestic film industry in 'promoting our cultural identity'—and they mean by 'cultural identity' some sense of Australianness, of our nationalism as a distinct form of social organisation. Notably, though, the emphasis tends to be on Australian *film* (not popular television); and not just *any* film, but those of 'quality'. So the aesthetic definition tends to be smuggled back in—on top of the kind of cultural nationalism which assumes that 'Australia' is a unified entity with certain essential features that distinguish it from 'Britain', the 'USA' or any other national entities which threaten us with 'cultural dependency'.

This series is titled 'Australian Cultural Studies', and I should say at the outset that my understanding of 'Australian' is not as an essentially unified category; and further, that my understanding of cultural is anthropological rather than aesthetic. By 'culture' I mean the social production of meaning and understanding, whether in the inter-personal and practical organisation of daily routines or in broader institutional and ideological structures. I am *not* thinking of 'culture' as some form of universal 'excellence', based on aesthetic 'discrimination' and embodied in a pantheon of 'great works'. Rather, I take this aesthetic definition of culture itself to be part of the *social mobilisation of discourse* to differentiate a cultural 'élite' from the 'mass' of society.

Unlike the cultural nationalism of our opinion leaders, 'Cultural Studies' focuses not on the essential unity of national cultures, but on the meanings attached to social difference (as in the distinction between 'élite' and 'mass' taste). It analyses the construction and mobilisation of these distinctions to maintain or challenge existing power differentials, such as those of gender, class, age, race and ethnicity. In this analysis, terms designed to socially differentiate people (like 'élite' and 'mass') become categories of discourse, communication and power. Hence our concern in this series is for an analytical understanding of the meanings attached to social difference within the *history* and *politics* of discourse.

It follows that the analysis of 'texts' needs to be united from a single-minded association with 'high' culture (marked by 'authorship'), but must include the 'popular' too—since these distinctions of 'high' and 'popular' culture themselves need to be analysed, not assumed.

Tom O'Regan's *Australian television culture* takes the work of television critics beyond the analysis of particular 'high' or 'popular' cultural texts (or programs) to, in his words, 'the dissemination of television and its political and social disposition in space and time'. His book is innovative in articulating the relationship between the familiar differentiations noted by Cultural Studies (of gender, sexual preference, ethnicity, aboriginality, etc.) and the economic and cultural geographies that construct 'Australia'. O'Regan organises his text 'to show how the different cultural and spatial levels of television—its international, national, regional and local dimensions; and its minoritarian, ethnic, indigenous and "established Australia" manifestations—interconnect in a synergistic and competitive fashion in Australian television services. Australian television is a heterogeneous site at which these various tendencies cohere.'

O'Regan's emphasis on 'coherence' as well as 'heterogeneity' is another important feature of this book. He emphasises both the conflict and the continuity between these different cultural and spatial levels; arguing, 'These continuities and discontinuities, consensus and antagonism between (and within) the different parts of the service provide Australia's television culture with its characteristic shape. A culture is necessarily made up of contradictory, antagonistic, disconnected and connected elements; Australia's television culture is no different.' Nevertheless, as we can see from the adjectival weighting of O'Regan's sentence ('contradictory, antagonistic, disconnected'), the sense of cultural clash and conflict, the quest by social groups for self-definition and power, remains strong. The book ends, for example, with the view that 'For many Aboriginal broadcasters, self-determination in Aboriginal television is seen as an important component of the broader struggle for the power and right to determine Aboriginal cultural, political and economic futures.'

FOREWORD

Culture, as Fiske, Hodge and Turner say in *Myths of Oz*, grows out of the divisions of society, not its unity. 'It has to work to construct any unity that it has, rather than simply celebrate an achieved or natural harmony.' Australian culture is then no more than the temporary, embattled construction of 'unity' at any particular historical moment. The 'readings' in this series of 'Australian Cultural Studies' inevitably (and polemically) form part of the struggle to make and break the boundaries of meaning which, in conflict and collusion, dynamically define our culture.

JOHN TULLOCH

Contents

Foreword	v
Abbreviations	ix
Acknowledgements	xi
Contributors	xiii
Glossary	xiv
Introduction	xix
1 Australia's television culture	1
2 High communications policy in Australia	22
3 The rise and fall of entrepreneurial television, 1986–92	40
4 Television's double face: Of imported and local programming	59
5 Television and national culture	80
6 National television in the new cultural order	98
7 SBS-TV: Symbolic politics and multicultural policy in television provision (*with Dona Kolar-Panov*)	121
8 SBS-TV: A television service (*with Dona Kolar-Panov*)	143
9 An Aboriginal television culture: Issues, strategies, politics (*with Philip Batty*)	169
Endnotes	193
Bibliography	197
Index	209

Abbreviations

ABA Australian Broadcasting Authority (the ABT's successor)
ABC (US) American Broadcasting Company
ABC Australian Broadcasting Corporation
ABCB Australian Broadcasting Control Board (the ABT's predecessor)
ABT Australian Broadcasting Tribunal
AFC Australian Film Commission
AFL Australian Football League
AFTRS Australian Film, Television and Radio School
AGPS Australian Government Publishing Service
ALP Australian Labor Party
ATSIC Aboriginal and Torres Strait Islander Commission
AUSSAT company operating domestic satellite, now Optus
BAPH Brisbane, Adelaide, Perth and Hobart
BBC British Broadcasting Commission
BRACS Broadcasting in Remote Aboriginal Communities Scheme
CAAMA Central Australian Aboriginal Media Association
CBS Columbia Broadcasting System (US)

CLC Communications Law Centre, Sydney
DAA Department of Aboriginal Affairs
DOTAC Department of Transport and Communications
EBR Entertainment Business Review
ESB English-speaking background
FACTS Federation of Australian Commercial Television Stations
FCC Federal Communications Commission (US)
FFC Film Finance Corporation
GATT General Agreement on Tariffs and Trade
ITV Independent Television (Britain)
NBC National Broadcasting Company (US)
NESB non-English-speaking background
NIMAA National Indigenous Media Association of Australia
RCTS Remote Commercial Television Service
RTA Regional Television Australia
SBS Special Broadcasting Service
SBS-TV Special Broadcasting Service Television Network
SMBA Sydney, Melbourne, Brisbane, and Adelaide
TAIMA Townsville Aboriginal and Islander Media Association
TPC Trade Practices Commission
UHF ultra high frequency
UTS University of Technology, Sydney
VCR video cassette recorder
VFL Victorian Football League
VHF very high frequency

Notes
Australian dollars used throughout, unless otherwise indicated.
One billion = 1000 million

Acknowledgements

I owe a large debt to co-authors, Dona Kolar-Panov (on SBS-TV) and Philip Batty (on Aboriginal television). Dona and Philip expanded my horizons and gave this book a depth it would not have had otherwise.

Many other people contributed to the shape of this book. My interest in Australian television had its beginnings as a graduate student at Griffith University in the late 1970s and was shaped by my teachers and friends at Griffith and elsewhere at that time, particularly Albert Moran, Sylvia Lawson, Stuart Cunningham, Mick Counihan, Paul Willemen and Meaghan Morris. Stuart Cunningham urged me to collect my essays on television into a book, worked on publishers on my behalf, and then read the manuscript. Especial thanks in the preparation of this manuscript go to Toby Miller who read drafts of each chapter a number of times and provided detailed critical advice. Rita Shanahan and John Hartley also read and commented on it all. A number of people gave me useful comments on different parts of the book: Jock Given, Cathy Robinson, Jonathan Levy, Steve Mickler, Mudrooroo, Ien Ang, Allan Brown, Peter Morris, Peter White, Humphrey McQueen, Peter Cook, Henry Mayer, Graham Shirley, David Watson and Denise Corrigan. Others helped more indirectly: Michael Leigh, Penny Taylor, Tim Rowse, David Noakes, John Darling and Mitzi Goldman.

A Murdoch University Special Research grant and Outside Studies Leave enabled me to finish the book. I am grateful to the university for this support. Throughout this project I have been assisted by some wonderful librarians at Murdoch University and the Film &

Television Institute (WA) who helped overcome the tyranny of distance. I also owe a special debt to my colleagues in the Communication Studies Program at Murdoch University and especially the Program Chair Irma Whitford and the Deputy Chair Alec McHoul who both encouraged and helped me to 'get on with it'. Finally, thank you to Elizabeth Weiss of Allen & Unwin and to series editor John Tulloch, for their support of this book.

This book is dedicated to Rita whose support I always had, despite the burden it placed on her at a time when we had just had twins.

The third part of 'Australia's Television Culture' appeared as 'Inventing Australian Television' in *TV Times*, eds D Watson and D Corrigan, Museum of Contemporary Art, Sydney. It is published with permission of the Museum of Contemporary Art.

Two longer versions of 'High Communications Policy in Australia' appeared as 'Towards a High Communication Policy' in *Continuum* 2, 1 (1988/89); and in *Media Information Australia* 58 (November 1990). The shortened and revised version contained here is published by permission of *Continuum* and *Media Information Australia*.

An earlier version of 'The Rise and Fall of Entrepreneurial Television, 1986–1992' appeared originally in *Screen* 32, 1 (1991) and is published by permission of the editors of *Screen* and its publisher, Oxford University Press.

An earlier version of 'Television's Double Face: Of Imported and Local Programming' appears in *Film Policy: An Australian Reader*, Institute for Cultural Policy Studies, Griffith University, 1993. It is republished here by permission of Albert Moran.

For copyright clearances for the use of particular quotations I would like to thank: the Museum of Contemporary Art (Sydney) and Anna Maria dell'Oso for permission to republish an extract from her article 'White Man's Dreaming' published in *TV Times*, eds D Watson and D Corrigan, Museum of Contemporary Art, Sydney, pp 18–22; *Entertainment Business Review* for permission to quote extensively from its article 'Focus on the Television Industry: How Seven, Nine and Ten are Coping with the Industry's Transition to Maturity' which appeared in *Entertainment Business Review*, 4 November 1991: and finally thanks to *Variety* for permission to reprint figures on global television prices from *Variety* April 1991, copyright 1991 by Cahners Publishing Co.

Contributors

Tom O'Regan is Senior Lecturer in Communication Studies at Murdoch University, Perth. He is co-editor with Albert Moran of two reference works on Australian cinema: *An Australian Film Reader* (Currency 1985) and *Australian Screen* (Penguin 1989); and is co-editor of *Continuum: The Australian Journal of Media and Culture*.

Philip Batty is currently the Director of the National Aboriginal Cultural Institute (TANDANYA) in Adelaide. He was communications consultant to the Western Australian Aboriginal Media Association in Perth, co-founder of the Central Australian Aboriginal Media Association in 1980, co-authored the licence application for Imparja TV and was Deputy Managing Director of the CAAMA group of companies which included Imparja.

Dona Kolar-Panov is a PhD student at Murdoch University studying ethnic video and television dynamics amongst Croatian and Macedonian communities in Perth. Her research is supported by an Australian Overseas Postgraduate Research Scholarship.

Glossary of Terms

bicycling the physical distribution of film or videotape between television stations.

blockbuster refers here to principally (Hollywood) movies which have been major box-office successes in the cinema and whose television broadcast in prime time usually attracts considerable audiences.

broadcast (as opposed to narrowcast) television services are those which attract a mass audience from across the social spectrum—people of different age, gender, ethnicity, class and geographical location.

cable television the distribution of a television signal by means of cable.

coaxial links a point-to-point interconnection system carrying video signals based on the coaxial cable (a cable consisting of two conductors and a solid wire running down the centre of a hollow tube to carry the television signal).

coverage or service area the area within which adequate reception of a television's signal is possible.

DBS (direct broadcasting by satellite service) a service designed to allow signals from a satellite to be received directly by individual earth stations in the viewer's home.

deregulation refers to a process of deleting or softening specific rules imposed on broad-casters by regulators. It is based on an assumption that 'the competitive give-and-take of the market place can satisfy most regulatory goals without the need for government rules and bureaucratic supervision' (Head and Stirling, 1990: p 445).

downlink the signal from a satellite to receiving equipment on earth (as opposed to the uplink).

ENG (electronic news gathering) a term used for an audio-visual system permitting all stages of production from shooting, editing to screening to be carried out by means of electronic equipment (video, microwave etc).

equalisation the process of extending the metropolitan television environment of three commercial stations, the ABC and SBS-TV to large parts of regional Australia.

footprint of a satellite the geographical area on the surface of the earth where signals transmitted from a satellite can be received.

free-to-air a terrestrial broadcasting system offered free to consumers.

globalisation see discussion of this term in Chapter 6.

infotainment a hybrid of information and entertainment familiar from quiz, variety and increasingly applied to news and current affairs programming.

MDS (multipoint distribution service) a means of delivering a video signal using a micro-wave transmitter. Special receiving equipment is needed to convert the signal for a conventional television service.

microwave links the terrestrial telecommunication system utilising radio waves above 1GHz used to relay television signals.

mini-series limited episode drama serial usually screened in 2 to 4 parts of over an hour each, over consecutive nights or weeks.

narrowcast (as opposed to broadcast) television services are those geared to smaller, more selective audiences. SBS-TV is, for example, is the narrowcast national broadcaster (see chapter 8).

national broadcaster the Australian term given for the publicly-funded broadcasters—the ABC and SBS-TV. They are national because they are federally-funded and in the case of the ABC there is a commitment to a national reach.

networking used in Australia to refer to cooperative distribution, program purchase, and program funding arrangements between a number of stations (historically, the Sydney, Melbourne, Brisbane and Adelaide stations).

networks the Nine, Seven, Ten, ABC and SBS operations. These provide a schedule of daily programming which is relayed around the country to affiliated stations (in the case of Nine, Seven and Ten) or to 'sister' stations (in the case of the ABC and SBS).

off prime time day-time, early evening and late night time slots of television broadcasts where there are less viewers and it is less expensive to advertise than in prime time (6–10pm).

pay-TV any television service which is supplied for a fee.

point-to-multi-point used here to refer to the way in which the satellite system for television program distribution can provide a point-to-multi-point system in which the same transmission could service any number of recipients within the satellite footprint so long as they have downlink equipment.

point-to-point used here to refer to the way the microwave telecommunications system for television program distribution is based on connecting particular points up into a national grid (such that programs from Sydney need to be delivered point-to-point from Sydney to Brisbane; Brisbane to Cairns; Sydney to Melbourne).

prime time 6–10pm television broadcasts. Called prime time because it is the time when television viewers are most numerous and so is the time in which it is most expensive to advertise.

regionals non-metropolitan television stations (including Hobart and Darwin).

serial drama programs usually half an hour or one hour in length where the large number of episodes tell a continuing story.

series a program usually half an hour or one hour in length with a large number of episodes. When used for documentary it means a documentary program which continues the same format from week to week; in drama it refers to an on-going program where many of the characters, situations and locales remain the same but each episode tells a discrete story.

specials or special event programs one-off programs presented and usually heavily promoted as a special event by the television station. They include live concerts and other variety formats and sometimes mini-series and blockbuster movies.

syndication a process by which a program is licensed for a fee to a station for exhibition in that market.

telethon day- or weekend-long television variety format with the aim of raising money for charity. It is usually staged by metropolitan television stations for their local coverage area.

translator a television station which receives a signal from a distant station, amplifies it, and rebroadcasts it in an unaltered form on a different channel.

transponder the part of a satellite which accepts an uplink signal, alters its frequency, amplifies it and then beams it back to earth.

UHF (Ultra High Frequency) that part of the radio wave spectrum between 300MHz and 3GHz which includes the bands used for SBS-TV and many regional broadcasters since equalisation.

uplink the signal from earth to a satellite for subsequent downlinking.

VHF (Very High Frequency) the part of the radio wave spectrum between 30 to 300MHz which includes the bands used for FM radio and most metropolitan television services in Australia.

Introduction

Television critics are usually concerned with programs (Tulloch & Turner 1989; Stern 1982). Rarely do they concern themselves with the dissemination of television and its political and social disposition in space and time. By contrast, policy makers and the Australian Broadcasting Authority deal with the shape and running of 'television services'. The 'television service' of these regulators and policy makers is redisposed for television criticism in this book. In the more inclusive understanding promoted here, the television service is made up of policy, regulation, politics, criticism, industry and programs. These sites mould Australia's television culture.

Australian television culture consists of distribution and broadcasting strategies, institutional structures, and the different activities involved in creating, regulating, screening, criticising and otherwise producing and watching television in Australia. There is the diverse cast of stations at some distance from each other in the Australian Broadcasting Corporation, ABC-TV, the different commercial networks and affiliated stations, the Special Broadcasting Service, SBS-TV, and the various Aboriginal television initiatives. There is Australian television's mix of international, national, regional and local programming. There are the different regulatory techniques of the broadcast, company and competition regulators and the policies of the industry subsidy support structures. All these take effect in particular political, economic, demographic and geographic contexts. The interaction and non-interaction, the cohesion and lack of cohesion of these different aspects of the service gives Australia's television culture its particular shape.

The term 'culture' is used in its sociological, not aesthetic, sense. Culture's typical meaning as 'a way of life' becomes 'the ways we do things with television in Australia'. The concept of culture addresses the heterogeneity of television in terms of its diversity of elements and functions in ways that notions of industry, policy and text do not. This concern with Australia's television culture sets this study apart from policy approaches and from much television criticism. Unlike broadcasting policy making and regulatory supervision, the cultural approach is taken up with the interaction of the different parts of the television service in addition to those aspects of concern to regulators and policy makers. And unlike most television criticism which is concerned with the programs themselves here the programs are embedded in a broadly conceived television culture.

Australia's television culture is distinctive but shares much with British, US, Canadian and New Zealand systems. Its distinctiveness is best understood as a point somewhere between two seemingly opposed positions: Australian television as a particular *invention* of television and Australian television as simply an *imitation* of the transnational form of television. Taken singly they are insufficient as explanations for the Australian television service; taken together they disclose Australian television's equivocal nature and origins, with its characteristic uncertainty about originality and sameness being foundational. These two positions may seem mutually exclusive but are, nonetheless, complementary. Some aspects of Australian television are original, others are a copy or close adaptation, while others —perhaps the majority—are a mixture of originality and adaptation.[1]

The problem of deciding what is innovation and what is not can be seen with respect to multicultural policy. This policy is responsible for the development of SBS-TV. As Ken Ruthven has recently pointed out[2] we can never be certain whether multiculturalism in Canada, Australia and the US are variations of the same basic configuration or are different configurations whose only common element is that the same word appears in each context. The word 'multiculturalism' came to Australian cultural and communication policy making from Canada and had its lexical origins in the US, but Australian policy makers took multiculturalism in a particular direction by virtue of Australian demographic, ethnic, immigrant and existing national cultural policy configurations. Thus SBS-TV is a multicultural television service unlike its Canadian and US counterparts in some of its locally produced programming, its program mix (which sources roughly half its programming from outside the English language), its scheduling formats, and its diversity of programming sources. Yet SBS-TV also screens US, Canadian and British programming created out of their multicultural and cultural pluralist orientations, and it uses programming formats and ideas adapted from these same sources.

Much the same problem of deciding whether we are dealing with an invention or an imitation confronts us when examining our other central television institutions: public service broadcasting in the ABC and commercial television in the commercial networks and the stations affiliated with them. These were certainly reconfigured and taken some distance from Anglo-American models, but they variously resemble their British and US counterparts through their programs, program concept purchase, and administration. The alternatives of Australian innovation in *Neighbours* and *Perfect Match* (see Oram 1988; Turner 1989 pp 30–37) and propensity to copy in *Wheel of Fortune*, ultimately turn on how Australian television simultaneously tailors imported programs and concepts (policies, program formats and regulatory techniques) and how, by virtue of its many similarities with Britain and the US, Australian television hits upon similar kinds of programming and responses to television. The argument is that Australian television functions in an *interdependent* fashion within a larger transnational television system.

Geographers and regulators use terms such as local, regional, national and international to deal with the geographical dimension to cultural formations. This vocabulary is important to this book. Australian television is shaped by domestic geography and demography; it has a cultural geography.

The local is used to designate the *geographically* local. Thus, the local means Adelaide news broadcasts with Adelaide-based news readers, the local service area of Sydney for its terrestrial broadcast signal, Melbourne advertisers targeting a Melbourne television audience and so on. (It is not used here, as is sometimes the case, to refer to the authentic or the communitarian, see Jacka 1988, p 127.)

The 'regional' refers to intermediate geographical scales larger than the local but smaller than the national—the scale of the different Australian states or non-metropolitan country areas (such as when the television industry talks of the 'regional stations' as opposed to the 'metropolitan stations'). There are regional advertisers such as Queensland-based advertisers constituting the Queensland audience as their market; there are farm-based advertisers advertising only on the 'regionals' (stations which serve non-metropolitan areas), there are the different State versions of, for example, the ABC's current affairs program the *7:30 Report*; and there are the different regional audience identities as, for example, Tasmanians or non-metropolitan Australians.

The national level refers to Australia-wide programming, networking, advertising, broadcast regulation, audiences and services (from Nine's *A Current Affair* to *60 Minutes*; from the Seven, Nine and Ten networks to SBS-TV; from ads for Meadow-Lea to Commodores; from Australian content to national program standard regulations). It also refers to audience identities constituted at a national level (as e.g., Australians), and to the Australian public in whose name regulators regulate and broadcasters broadcast.

The international scale involves program and program concept imports, the international program makers for whom Australia is a valuable export market, multinational advertisers, international agreements regulating satellite, copyright and the television trade, and the internationally constituted audiences developed for imported English-language programs (on the ABC, the commercials and SBS-TV) and for imported non-English language programs (especially on SBS-TV).

All these scales are integral to each other, with their interaction shaping Australia's television culture. 'Internationalism' in the sense of an engagement with and interest in the rest of the world is then as much a part of Australia's television culture as are 'localist' and 'nationalist' sentiments.

As in all economic and cultural geographies, there are core and peripheral centres of television: Sydney and Melbourne, with their 43 per cent of the Australian population, constitute the core of Australian television in ways that make Brisbane, Adelaide, Perth and Hobart (BAPH) peripheral; yet BAPH stations are in turn a 'core' for their peripheries in Townsville, Whyalla, Albany and Launceston. Sydney and Melbourne are, in turn, peripheral to the centres of the larger transnational television system—Los Angeles, New York, London, Paris, Tokyo, Rome, Hong Kong etc.

To these different geographical levels should be added a series of cultural differentiations operating across each. The principal ones developed here are: the indigenous or Aboriginal, the ethnic (e.g. Australian Greeks) and the minoritarian (e.g. gays) as opposed to the 'mainstream', and the ethnically 'unmarked' Australian (e.g. the 'Aussie'—sometimes seen as the 'Anglo-Celtic'). These levels cut across the local, regional, national and international levels, persist at each level and configure them in different ways. This book is designed to show how the different cultural and spatial levels of television— its international, national, regional and local dimensions, and its minoritarian, ethnic, indigenous and 'established Australian' manifestations—interconnect in a synergistic and competitive fashion in Australian television services. Australian television is a heterogeneous site at which these various tendencies cohere.

INTRODUCTION

As a rule, critics and lobbyists take up pragmatic and political positions within Australian television, and organise irreconcilable oppositions between these different cultural levels. Out of political and practical necessity, they pose international against national levels (Jacka 1991, passim); local against national (Moran 1982, p 89–102); and ethnic and indigenous levels against (Anglo-)Australian (UTS 1990, p 148). We use these neat binaries to organise our criticism, our understanding of television, and our polemical activity. But such logics of television criticism and policy hide fundamental continuities and consensus within the system. These also accentuate *perceptions* of discontinuity and conflict in it. Viewers, after all, do move easily between the local, regional, national and international components of television's evening schedule; they also move readily between being a member of a minority for one program, an 'ethnic' in another, and part of the Australian and/or international 'mainstream' in another. In Australian television services, the relationship between the different cultural levels is much more fluid and interpenetrated than these oppositions allow. Australian television is a mosaic of sites, levels, issues, and developments. These continuities and discontinuities, the consensus and antagonism between (and within) the different parts of the service provide Australia's television culture with its characteristic shape. A culture is necessarily made up of contradictory, antagonistic, disconnected and connected elements; Australia's television culture is no different.

Consider the relationship between imported and local programming on Australian television (see chapters 1 and 4). The economics of the Australian television service is predicated on a changing mix of local and imported programming. Viewers routinely negotiate a mixed program schedule. Program schedulers need to make programming from a range of different sources and genres cohere. Those supporting Australian content provisions are in their creative practice interpreters and rewriters of program imports and imported concepts. Cultural and communications policy formation has been not only concerned with developing an Australian content supplement but also with diversifying imports. This has always been an important task for the national broadcasters, the ABC and the SBS.

The post-1986 changes in Australian television adjusted the relationship between national, regional and local levels of television, bringing television into line with broader business and political changes which privileged the international and national levels at the expense of the local and regional. The rise and fall of the television entrepreneurs in the late 1980s (see chapters 2 and 3) paralleled similar national business developments, with the financial insolvency of two commercial networks in the late 1980s placing pressures on the local production industry.

Similarly, the mixed relationship between television and national culture cannot be simply read off the different geographical scales. Nationwide programming does not just equal the national, international programming does not just represent an internationalism, and local programming may only sometimes promote a localism antagonistic to the national. Rather, national cultural formations are formed at the intersection of international, national, regional and local scales. There is, for instance, a contiguity of international programming and national culture and identity in Australia by virtue of our broader cultural area identity as a predominantly Anglophone and Western European culture; and local and regional programming often complements national culture and identity through defining Australia federally, integrating the local 'here' into the national 'we'. Indeed, domestic disputes over national projects and interests are more disputes over which kinds of 'national' projects should be ascendant rather than attacks on national projects in themselves (see chapter 5). National culture issues, paradoxically, continue to be important to the emerging television order of globalisation, deregulation, multiculturalism, and changing geopolitical alignments (see chapter 6).

So too those aspects of the service at its margins (at least in financial, policy, and audience terms)—such as multiculturalism and Aboriginal issues—are part of and not apart from the Australian television system. SBS-TV and Aboriginal television initiatives may act from time to time as a counter-space within television, but these initiatives are connected to, implicated within and an intrinsic part of a broader Australian television culture. For all this SBS-TV is, still, an innovative 'minoritarian' television service and a particular political initiative in a multi-ethnic force-field; and Aboriginal television initiatives are part of the contemporary Aboriginal aspirations and policies of self-determination and social justice.

This book with particular contributions from my co-authors, Dona Kolar-Panov (on SBS-TV) and Philip Batty (on Aboriginal television) attends to these developments at some length. It does so for a number of reasons. Both sites are little examined as television services and are, moreover, innovations in television despite their marginal nature and small audiences. Additionally, multiculturalism and Aboriginal issues are becoming increasingly important issues for the television service as a whole and not just for SBS-TV and the Aboriginal initiatives in question. Programming, regulation and policy, employment, government production subsidies and scheduling are continuing to be affected by Aboriginal and multicultural issues, demands and projects. And multicultural and Aboriginal issues can be expected to affect notions of national identity and national culture by pushing them to become less Anglo-Celtic and more open to Aboriginal involvement.

This book sets itself a task of connecting up the divergent tendencies, strategies, levels and sites of the television service into a coherent picture of a multifaceted and interconnected television culture. To accomplish this synthetic task, policy analysis, cultural and economic geography, economic and industry analysis, political science, and cultural and media studies are combined. This is, admittedly, an unusual undertaking for cultural studies. Yet, it is firmly within a cultural studies remit in that it is concerned with the interconnections of the media system and that system's embedding in wider social, geographical, political and economic formations.

Finally, this study is presented as a support for—not a denigration of—television criticism. It follows Sandra Hall's (1976; 1981) lead and presents an argument about Australia's television culture—the industry, the scheduling, the regulation, the politics, and the program production—which is designed to assist criticism and debate about programs as well as provide better ideas about the service. Like Hall, I explain how Australian television services are organised and how this helps explain why Australian television looks the way it does; why television industry political economy moves along certain well-defined corridors; why the programs take the form they do and are taken up by audiences and reviewers in particular ways. This focus means there is less on programs, but I would like to think that it offers a means for viewers and critics to turn to programs and therefore television criticism all the more empowered.

1 Australia's television culture

On many counts Australian television's characteristic form can scarcely be claimed as its own. By the time television was introduced in 1956 to Sydney and Melbourne, its form had become stabilised as a free, governmentally regulated, broadcast service for a well-defined geographic area. The US had pioneered commercial television, and the British established public service and later mixed broadcasting environments (with the commercial ITV and the BBC). US and British programming models were on hand to instruct Australian program production and have continued to do so to this day. US and British programs also dominated that half of Australian television schedules taken up with imports. Given the minimal Australian contribution to television drama in the 1950s, to feature films until the 1970s feature revival, and to limited episode television drama until the mini-series boom of the 1980s (production of which has greatly declined since), these imports tended to define particular program categories. In the process they have become integral features of the Australian television landscape. Contemporary innovations such as indigenous television were first developed in Canada (Barker 1984; Brisebois 1990). Australian television audiences, in terms of their viewing habits and uptake of television are not markedly different from those in the US and Britain. They tune in and out of programs, advertisements and limited episode serials in similar ways to UK and US audiences (Barwise & Ehrenberg 1988, pp 5-7) with the percentage of Australian households with the VCR roughly matching US, UK and Canadian figures.[1]

But if television services around the world share many technological and distribution features, these services still need to be tailored to the environmental, social, commercial, cultural and political conditions of the country in question. Television policy, regulation, programs, broadcasting, scheduling, criticism and buying take distinctive national routes (see chapters 2 and 3). The general transnational form of television represented by the US and the UK became indigenised in Australia. If this ensured there would always be close family resemblances between Australian and US and UK television, it also made Australian television subtly and distinctively different.

To understand Australian television's distinctiveness it will be necessary to look to the use made of the same television technologies, the nature of the public and commercial broadcasting mix, the local trajectories of domestic and imported programming (see chapter 4), the relation between television and national culture (chapters 5 and 6), the nature and direction of local television criticism, and of the exhibition and distribution networks for television (its market settings, and its regulations controlling television's introduction, viewing area, number of licences, and new television services).

Australia's national broadcasters (ABC and SBS) and its commercial stations are different from their British and US counterparts. Australian television indigenised imported programming concepts, often taking them some distance from their US or British original. It developed its own drama concepts with reference to Australian cultural forms and adjacent US and British programming. Audiences customised and broadcasters framed the imported programming in an Australian informational and cultural context. Similar sorts of television regulation in Australia and the US led to different outcomes. Television technologies—like videotape and satellites—were used to different ends. By the same token multicultural and indigenous television evolved their own shapes in SBS-TV (see chapters 7 and 8) and Aboriginal television initiatives (see chapter 9).

Given Australia's poly-ethnic society, the geographic dispersal of television markets, and the different television environments across the country, it is important to allow for the internal diversity of the Australian experience of television. Television viewing was different in regional Australia to the metropolitan centres (until 1990–91 most of regional Australia—making up some 30 per cent of the viewing audience—had only one commercial television station and the ABC). It was also different for ethnic groups at some cultural distance from mainstream Australian society (chapters 7 and 8). This is shown for instance, in that regional Australia and immigrant groups had a higher uptake of the VCR during the first half of the 1980s than did the rest of the Australian population (Connor Report 1985, p 405). Such cultural disparities led in the 1980s to regional television equalisation and the 'minorities initiatives' of SBS-TV and Aboriginal television.

COMPARING TELEVISION CULTURES

Australian television should be regarded as distinct from—not worse or better than—UK and US television. US and Australian commercial television regulations governing ownership and control have mostly borne a distinct family resemblance to each other. Each prohibited ownership above a stipulated number of television station licences until the mid-1980s. In Australia the limit was two stations, in the US a limit of five VHF stations and seven stations overall. Both had localism doctrines encouraging local ownership, programming and control of television stations. Their regulation initially permitted cross-media ownership of radio, press and television franchises in the one service area and prohibited the ownership of more than one television station in a given market. Subsequently, both regulated against cross-ownership; the US in 1970, Australia in 1986. As part of a deregulationist agenda both moved after 1985 to clear up the glaring anomalies created by the limitation on station ownership rule—which, in the Australian case, saw owning Townsville and Cairns licences treated as equivalent to owning Sydney and Melbourne licences. The US raised the number of station licences permitted to twelve and set a ceiling on the audience share any one group could have at 25 per cent of the nation's population (Head & Sterling 1990, p 452); Australia adopted an audience share of 60 per cent of the nation's population, scrapped station ownership limitations expressed in numbers of stations, and simultaneously introduced cross-media ownership rules.

Despite these similarities the outcome on the ground was different. Because US networks pioneered television services they retained the control over the television service they had exercised in radio (Barnouw 1975, pp 22–96). Yet Australia's major radio network, Macquarie, failed to gain the place in television it had expected (McKay 1959). In Australia, newspaper companies—not radio companies—dominated the principal broadcasting markets and benefited from the station licensing process. By 1953 in the US, local television stations were little more than rebroadcasting outfits as networks provided affiliates with 'a reasonably full schedule of sponsored evening programs' (Summers & Summers 1966, p 96). The development of coaxial and microwave links was critical to US networking (New York and Chicago were linked in 1949 and East and West coasts were linked in 1951 [Summers & Summer 1966, p 76]). These links enabled the three networks (CBS, NBC and ABC) to reach over 95 per cent of homes with television by the mid-1950s (Head & Sterling 1990, p 69). By contrast, Australian commercial television networks (Seven, Nine and Ten) did not obtain this audience coverage until the advent of three commercial stations in the major regional Australian markets between 1990 and 1991. It was only then that Australia's commercial networks offered a national schedule simultaneously broadcast around Australia, and something approximating US network affiliation came to Australia. Significant differences remained, as Australia's non-network-owned stations retained control over advertising but now had less control over their schedule than did their US counterparts.

Station independence has been the norm for most of Australian television history. Stations in Australia never surrendered their control over advertising to networks or to advertisers. Networking arrangements between Sydney, Melbourne, Brisbane, and Adelaide (SMBA) were cooperative arrangements between independent stations, with each contributing towards both the purchase and production of programs according to their market size (Walker 1967, pp 293–294; Moran 1985, p 22). Such arrangements only started to be formalised in this way during 1963 and 1964 (some seven years after television's introduction). Up until the mid-1980s programs were mostly distributed by transporting film prints and videotapes—sometimes the same copy, sometimes a multiple copy—from station to station, usually by aeroplane (called program bicycling or syndication) for later broadcasting at the convenience of local stations. The use of this more loosely organised and cheaper form of program distribution meant co-axial and microwave linkages were not as critical to the development of television services as they had been in the US. Consequently, they took time to develop (Sydney and Melbourne were not linked until 1962, and it took another eight years to complete the east–west connection to Perth). Like US television, Australian television screened much the same programs nationwide. However it did not schedule them at the same time or on the same day. This only changed in the five major capital cities (Sydney, Melbourne, Brisbane, Adelaide and Perth) during 1988 and 1989 and in most regional television markets between 1990 and 1991 (see chapter 2).

Characteristically, the US television industry distinguishes between the more loosely organised syndicated programming distribution structure used for repeats and items of regional interest, and the more tightly organised nationally networked daily schedule of programs. The Australian equivalent of this programming mix is the distinction between imported and locally produced programming. Local programs needed to be networked around SMBA to cover immediately a sufficient proportion of production costs for programming to be viable, while imported programs (with their lower purchase costs) did not (they could be profitably sustained through syndication). Because roughly half the schedule was made up of imported programming (mostly US on the commercials, British on the ABC, and European on SBS) Australian television could purchase this half of its programming requirements on a station-by-station basis from US distributors, not the Australian networks. This market structure enabled commercial stations to remain for many years relatively independent from each other. The situation was only reversed with changes in the regulations governing ownership and control, and the advent of satellite program distribution.

In the US, the networks were less tied to the stations than in Australia. Although the US networks—CBS, NBC, and ABC—owned television stations in the most profitable and largest markets, this never amounted to the significant levels of ownership of the system possible in the Australian system. In the US, ownership of five VHF stations amounted to, at most, access to 23 per cent of the total US audience; a figure the three major networks roughly owned each (Reel 1979, p 43). Even with the 1985 regulatory changes in the US, this situation continued. In Australia there was no real separation between network and stations. Networks were controlled by the Sydney and Melbourne stations because the Australian two station ownership rule in force from 1956 to 1986 permitted two then, after the third commercial station in 1965, three groups to control 43 per cent of the entire Australian viewing audience through controlling licences in Sydney and Melbourne. When total audience reach regulation was developed in 1986 enabling an upper limit of 60 per cent of the viewing audience, this control was further reinforced. The 1986 regulations permitted ownership of two of the three next largest Australian cities—Brisbane, Adelaide, and Perth—in addition to Sydney and Melbourne. It was this extension of ownership which drove US-style national networking and scheduling in Australia in the late 1980s. By contrast, lack of common ownership drove the network–affiliate relations characteristic of US television history.

Even the same hardware led to different outcomes. For instance, US television introduced videotape so that East and West coasts could see the same programs at the same time irrespective of time zones. US television evolved—indeed, was principally sold to advertisers—as a broadcasting medium with identical network program scheduling across the country. In Australia, videotape was one of the factors which enabled stations outside Sydney and Melbourne to remain relatively independent in terms of their identity and their control of program scheduling. It helped them maintain separate profiles before advertisers while broadcasting the same programs. It held back the extensive use of telecommunications infrastructure on a routine basis. The ABC was encouraged to use these telecommunication facilities while the commercials did not make nearly so much use of them. (In similar fashion the ABC was encouraged to restructure its operations around AUSSAT in the mid-1980s.) Not until the late 1970s with the advent of greater commercial television interest in nationally packaged sporting events and current affairs television—notably Australian rules football with *Victorian Football League* (now *Australian Football League*), *World Series Cricket*, *The Mike Walsh Show* (later *The Midday Show*), and *60 Minutes*—did commercial television make extensive use of telecommunications facilities.

Differences can be also observed with broadcast satellites. In the US, broadcast satellites helped diminish the power of the networks. These enabled local stations to better develop their own news and information structures, conferring upon themselves relative informational independence from network feeds leading to a regionalisation of news broadcasts (Fields 1987, p 84). With greater station independence from the networks syndication became of greater importance to stations. Additionally, a combination of cable television and satellites launched new television services such as CNN, Home Box Office and the Nashville Network. These new services eroded network shares and hastened the development of a long-awaited fourth broadcast television network (Rupert Murdoch's Fox). In Australia, the satellite justified the extension of the metropolitan television environment of three commercial stations, the ABC and SBS to regional Australia in a process called 'equalisation'. Regional commercial operators—like RTQ 7 in Rockhampton in Queensland, which had been the only commercial station operating in its service area—were forced into network affiliation and turned their stations into relay facilities for network scheduling. The domestic satellite was critical to Australian networks asserting their national dominance. Current affairs feeds were concentrated into centralised operations in Sydney and, to a lesser extent, Melbourne. The era of *A Current Affair*, *Real Life*, *Lateline* and *Hinch* had arrived. The importing sources available to commercial television contracted as the independent buying organisation Regional Television Australia folded as a direct consequence of equalisation; the ABC reduced its operations in Brisbane, Adelaide, Perth, and Hobart (BAPH is the industry acronym for these metropolitan centres) and its regional operations (in Rockhampton and Townsville). Unlike in the US, new television services using the satellite (like Pay TV) were held back to permit equalisation. The Hawke government shelved Pay TV in 1983; the moratorium on its provision ended in 1991, with 1992 and 1993 (then) dominated by policy changes but little commercial development (see Cunningham 1992, pp 104–36).

Australia's mixed public and commercial broadcasting arrangements also differed from those obtaining in Britain. Unlike the BBC, the ABC was cast into a secondary role. The British situation—until the late 1980s—insisted upon the 'equality' of the commercial and public broadcasters. The British regulated commercial broadcasting through a policy of complementarity with, rather than competition to, the BBC, and this helped ensure that public and commercial broadcasters resembled each other. British broadcasting policy did this by restricting the number of commercial licences, doubling the number of BBC channels to two, and creating closely supervised regional monopolies in commercial television. In Australia, the ABC was always competing against two and then three commercial stations in the major population centres. Under these conditions the Australian national broadcaster did not occupy the central position that the BBC did, with government spending on non-commercial television and radio services per capita being less in Australia than in Britain and Canada—Geller put the 1989 figures at Australia $25, the UK $30, and Canada $36, with Australia still spending slightly more than Japan ($18), and five times more than the US ($4.56) (Geller 1990, pp 115–16, Australian dollars). The Australian arrangement, whereby commercial stations can pick up product after its ABC screening and achieve greater ratings with it, would be impossible in Britain. Yet this is what happened to *Mother and Son* in 1987. Screened on the ABC, it rated between 14 and 18 in Melbourne; its subsequent Ten Network screening saw it rate in the 20s (ABT 1991a, p 154). In these circumstances, the ABC developed a characteristic identity crisis. It sought to be competitive with the commercials to justify taxpayer expenditure, but this drew criticism for chasing ratings and therefore aping the commercials. Expected to provide a complementary service, the more it takes this route the more it draws criticism for failing to 'speak to the people of Australia' to justify taxpayer expenditure on such a low rating network. The ABC was always and peculiarly susceptible to 'reform' compared to its British counterpart. By contrast, Australian commercial broadcasting's highly competitive market (initially in SMBA, later in Perth and the regionals), and with powerful media proprietors heading the major television companies (Hall 1976; Chadwick 1989), made commercial television operations, as in the US, more politically 'off limits'.

The commercials also functioned differently in Australia. They adjusted to the ABC's presence; Seven was close to the ABC in many areas (it would successfully show British commercial television programs) and Nine to the commercial and entertainment side, while Ten struggled for an identity. Sometimes it found it to the more commercial side of Nine with *Number 96*, and sometimes to the quality side of Seven with its involvements in the Kennedy Miller mini-series including *The Dismissal*, *Bangkok Hilton*, and *Bodyline* in the 1980s.

Moreover, the nomenclature was different. The ABC and SBS (after its 1980 introduction) are termed 'national' broadcasters, the stations not primarily government-funded are 'commercial' or 'local' stations. In Britain, the BBC was always the 'public (service)' broadcaster and the commercials 'independent television'. In Australia, the ABC was initially expected to be the national network while the commercials were to be local (commercial) stations, as in radio. Rhetorics of the 'public interest', the 'social good' and the 'state' preoccupied UK debates. In the Australian context, where commercial market segmentation dynamics developed largely outside interventionist government settings, and the public broadcaster adjusted itself to a secondary role, the rhetoric took on a less 'civic' and more 'nation-building' character. Concepts of 'an Australian look', 'Australian content' as nurturing Australian culture, and ideas about the important place of television in national life promoting national identity emerged as central policy reference points. With more television in the UK and Europe, less interventionist governmental regulation there, a diminished—even secondary—role for the public broadcaster, and the sovereignty issue forced by the reality of the European Community, the same 'national' tropes as in Australia are now emerging there to displace rhetorics of the 'public interest' from centre stage.

Television criticism took a particular direction in Australia. Take the television violence controversies in the US and Australia from the late 1950s to the mid-1970s. Because these controversies were associated in Australia with imported product, the *importing* of that product became a political issue in Australia; in the US, the issue was one of influencing Hollywood's generation of product. Controversies over the same programs in Australia carried an additional weight in that Australian kids were not just being affected by violence, they were also being Americanised. Social and educational elites in Australia found themselves supporting Australian production as a quality alternative to exploitative US programming with its ambiguous moral and social values. Quality television meant non-US television drama (British and Australian). This legacy can be seen in programs such as *A Country Practice*, *Flying Doctors*, *Bellbird*, *Certain Women*, *GP*, and *Homicide*, which treat social problems less sensationally than do some US programs, with their producers priding themselves on their social responsibility. In the US, calls for quality television were calls for the adoption by US producers of British styles of television production in a less advertiser-driven television service (the consequence can be seen in the 'quality' US television of *Mary Tyler Moore*, *Hill Street Blues* and *Northern Exposure*).

Critiques of the concentration of power in television, and the need for a greater diversity of programming, were associated with different projects in the US and Australia. Before 1976, public critics of the existing structure of the Australian television service called for greater independence of the regulatory agency, better funding of the ABC (to enable it to be an antidote to the commercials), one less commercial television station (in order better to underwrite 'quality' Australian programming), stiffer Australian content rules, and greater public control of commercial networking through the adoption of a British-style Independent Broadcasting Authority structure as a means of achieving economies of scale and reducing network power (McClelland 1974). At the same time in the US, critics were associated with anti-network, locally orientated public television funded by local communities, the limited breaking up of network monopoly of prime time by access rules to redress the imbalance in the relationship between networks, program suppliers and television stations, and support for more, not less television as a means to create program diversity (Baughman 1986, pp 153–65). Thus similar concerns about media concentration and ameliorating television's perceived social effects in Australia and the US became attached to different programs.

In a similar fashion, 'minorities' issues in the 1980s were handled differently in both countries. Australia created an additional national broadcaster—SBS—to handle ethnic minority issues; while the US left it to the market with additional commercial television operations for Hispanics developing in the SIN network and cable television. There are differences in the public culture of each: Australians do not share the deep hostility to state intervention and institutions of Americans and do not so quickly associate at a public policy level solutions to social problems with market solutions.[2]

Like the French and British, Australian and Canadian lobbyists invoke national and cultural traditions to legitimate local content rules. But no Australian or Canadian content lobbyist entertains the Japanese–French–Anglo ambition of stipulating allowable foreign content on domestic screens; rather they promote levels of local content, proposing such content as a supplement to the international product. Success in Australia and Canada is measured by getting to certain levels of local program capacity and by bringing prices paid for imported (US) programming under control. By contrast the French and British target the entire schedule. They try to create local programming to match and displace program imports. Australian and Canadian responses are thus defensive, the English and French offensive. Notions of protecting the nation's culture are associated with different programs of action. Australian and Canadian responses are developed in a context where international programming and outlooks are firmly present, where local drama production is outward as much as inward looking, and in which policy explicitly provides a framework within which international program imports can develop (often at state expense as in ABC and SBS schedules, or the programs from France's La Sept network on Canadian Cable and Radio Canada).

Comparing Australian with British and US television is part of the rhetoric of television in Australia. This talk is facilitated by Australia's comparative isolation from the humdrum realities of both systems. 'American' and 'British' television comes to mean particular aspects of these systems for Australian debate. There was, for example, great enthusiasm for the British Channel 4 model in Australia in the late 1980s (Evans 1989, pp 37–42) which led me to form an image of Channel 4 that watching the service in England did not live up to! I had been, of course, idealising that service, projecting the benefits of its application in an Australian context that I knew well. Naturally I was disappointed to find, as in all television services, that only isolated programs appealed to me, that the production values were roughly equivalent to those on Australian television, and that British ways of producing interesting and internationally orientated television were not those familiar to me from SBS-TV and the ABC.

AUSTRALIA'S MEDIUM-SIZED TELEVISION SERVICE

Some kinds of television are more famous than others. British and US television constitute 'Television' in ways that Australian, Canadian and Dutch television services do not. Both US and British television have a distinctive form, their television fare is exported widely, and they have come to represent two poles of the televisual experience, public service television and commercial television. Both constitute models to aspire to—and to resist—within other television systems. The British model is one of public service broadcasting alongside carefully regulated commercial broadcasting, managed so as to promote the centrality of a public service broadcasting ethos for both sectors and the separation of broadcasting from the government of the day. In the US context, multi-channel commercial television services operate with few governmentally imposed entry barriers, alongside an under-funded public television service.

However, British and US television are generally unrepresentative of television in that they mostly: create their own product; have limited imports; fill a relatively 'pure' model of public service television and commercial television respectively; have a culturally valued status within the international system (the UK supplying the best 'highbrow' television, the US supplying the best 'popular' programming); and produce programs with high production values by virtue of their market size, their export market potential and the international pre-eminence of the English language.

The less famous Australian, Canadian, and Dutch television services are not at the centre of definitions of television, in that these nations import program concepts and programs (usually drama, documentary and musical entertainment, with imports making up a substantial proportion of their schedules); they do not have extensive or valuable export markets; their local product is not so much critically valued with reference to itself as with reference—often negatively—to 'imports'. When exported, such local programming is rarely as popular or as critically respected internationally as are British and US programs (also available in those same markets). Sometimes programs exports may even suffer from problems of 'program' identification; Australian programs often gets confused in export with British and US products.

These television services typically fail the 'ideal' represented by US and British television for audiences, lobbyists, policy makers and critics alike. Australian television, for example, fails the public service television ideal in that political intervention rather than 'arm's length' separation from the government of the day dogs the public service broadcaster (Harding 1979), while the operations of the regulatory body and broadcasting policy are prone to political intervention (Armstrong 1974; Chadwick 1989). It fails the commercial television ideal of a relatively unregulated, multichannel television environment with minimal barriers to entry and competition in that there are stricter licensing controls and forms of social regulation through content provisions (McGuinness 1990, p 22). And it fails the originality test by being so reliant upon British and US television in the form and direction of its program development (Bridges 1991).

Australian television is a medium-sized Western television service operating in the English language. Servicing 17 million people, it is not large enough to support local programming across the schedule as can the huge US and Japanese television markets. Nor is it large enough to support the scale of local production in higher budgeted movie and limited episode serial television as can the large countries of Europe (France, Germany and Italy). Like other medium-sized systems operating in the OECD with populations between 6 and 25 million, Australian television affords imported programming a much more important place than do larger countries. High-rating imported product routinely includes series and serial television in addition to blockbuster films (in French, German, and Italian television, blockbusters are the high-rating imported product). Imports rate more consistently than in larger countries and have a greater prime time presence. Because of this the international program trade with Australia is regular and predictable. Television markets like Australia, Canada, Holland, Sweden, and Austria are natural markets for imported programming. Such markets develop long-term arrangements with overseas broadcasters and producers. In Canada, US programming carries a common North American culture; in Austria, Germany's programming is part of the broader German-language cultural area; in Australia, US programming on commercial TV and British programming on the ABC are central to its definition as an Anglophone television service.

Australia's broad reliance upon imports across its schedule sees it pay more for imported programming per viewer than do larger television markets. The Australian Tariff Board estimated in 1973 that in terms of international relativities Australian TV was paying in 1971–72 some 20 per cent more for its imports than its market size in the English language warranted (Tariff Board 1973, p 30). Chapter 4 shows that on *Variety*'s program prices for half-hour drama series, when averaged for 1990, Australia pays some four times more per viewer than does the UK and France. Yet Australia is larger than the Scandinavian countries, Belgium, Holland, Austria, New Zealand and Singapore, and is capable of producing more local programming than they can and of developing its own export markets.

Because Australia's indigenising dynamics have definite limits owing to its market size, imports routinely occupy both pivotal and filler spaces in prime time (6–10 pm) and off-prime time alike. Yet those imports as a whole tend to attract less significant viewing from audiences than their half of all broadcasting time would suggest. Overall, Australian programs are decidedly more popular than the imports although individual US and UK series and movies do attract some of the highest individual ratings. In markets like Australia's, lower cost local production is important. This prioritises 'infotainment', news and current affairs, and sets clearly defined upper limits to local participation in higher budgeted television such as documentary series and one-offs, made-for-TV films, and high-budget limited episode

TV serials. Participation in those categories is often dependent in Australia (as in Canada, New Zealand and the Netherlands) upon state subsidies and/or tax concessions. Chapter 4 explores further this relationship between imported and local programming on Australian television.

Programming within the English-language market mostly flows from the centres of the English language (the US and Britain) to its Australian, Canadian, New Zealand and South African margins. There are some flows the other way, and some between these smaller countries. Australian programs have long been shown on British television in off-prime time slots and now in prime time with *Neighbours* and *Home and Away*; some Australian programs gained US network release (the series *Skippy* and the mini-series *A Town Like Alice*), with a great many more obtaining screenings in the television syndication and Pay TV markets in the 1980s. Australian television is well represented on New Zealand screens in a one-way relationship: Australia sells, New Zealand imports. Australian programs are less routinely sold into Ireland, Canada and Europe (particularly The Netherlands and Germany). Typically, Australian exporters seek British and US sales because of the higher prices these markets pay and the wider international circulation guaranteed by success there. Often this means distribution by the Hollywood majors, as when the 1970s television series *Spyforce* was distributed internationally by Paramount television and sold in packages with US series. New Zealand, Irish and Canadian programs are an occasional program source for the ABC and SBS. The ABC screens the mini-series *Angel at My Table* as a New Zealand co-production, occasional New Zealand movies like *Smash Palace*, and the Canadian series *Degrassi High*, and 'Canadian' films are screened on the commercials (films such as Cronenberg's oeuvre and *Bird on the Wire*). In this context, Australian co-productions—a measure of television interrelationships—typically involve British groups first, then US groups, then New Zealand, then Canadian and other European partners.

As with other countries which constitute a minor fragment of the language-speaking group within which they participate, Australian television's import profile centres imported programming. This centring impacts upon the forms of local television, criticism of it and of television generally.

A DISTINCTIVE TELEVISION CULTURE?

Sir: I am an American visiting Australia and, although I am charmed by this country and enamoured of the people, there is one facet of life here to which I take great offence. It is in the direct theft in television of American concepts.

I understand the importance of American programming itself to please an audience, but what disgusts me is the adaptation of American televisual ideas without even changing the names. Programs such as *Let's Make a Deal, Family Feud, Australia's Funniest Home Videos,* and several more are plucked directly from the US market.

I was prompted to write this letter on the discovery that Steve Vizard had won a Logie award for most popular personality for his program, *Tonight Live*. This program could not more directly be a copy of its American counterpart, *Late Night with David Letterman*, and it shocks and offends me that Vizard can win awards without acknowledging proper credit to the creators of the concept which has brought him fame.

It seems from the time that I have spent in this country that Australians are quite self-conscious about a belief that they have little artistic culture of their own. The solution to this, I'm afraid, is not to 'borrow' from another culture, but to develop one's own artistic ideas.

James Bridges
18 March 1991, (*Sydney Morning Herald*)

Bridges's complaint is that Australian television is derivative. It is at once too American and (in its inept imitation and concept 'theft') not American enough. Such Australian derivativeness has also been assigned a positive value by some cultural critics. For them Australian cultural production generally—and not simply television—is positively unoriginal in that the Australian 'imitation' disadvantages the standing of the 'original' program or concept (Morris 1988, pp 241–9).

The cultural derivativeness both positions assume is sustained by the close family resemblance between Australian and US and British social, cultural and political formations. In television this means a likeness in programming, scheduling and production models. The close affinity is further underscored by the significant presence of US and British programs on Australian screens. These conditions encourage a sense amongst audiences, schedulers and program purchasers that the Australian product is to a significant extent interchangeable with US and British product. Not surprisingly then, Australian programs tend to be akin to US and British programs—whether or not imitation was intended by producers or thought to be an issue for viewers.

The program concept purchase arrangements for quiz, sports, variety and current affairs formats that Bridges finds so disturbing are not theft—they are, after all, mostly paid for—but are part of a broader system of commonalities and cultural exchange (which is not simply one way) between the US and Australia. Nor is this exchange even across formats. In infotainment and sporting formats Australian innovation through concept purchase is possible as infotainment programming needs to be localised; the US original simply will not do. American baseball league games are not going to displace test and one-day cricket with Australian participants. Yet such arrangements are more difficult in drama programming because the US and British original has a ready Australian market. Consequently, Australian drama relies on innovation through producers adjusting—and audiences adjusting to—local program and cultural traditions with common international formats evident from contemporaneous US and British imports.

Bridges's contention that the Australian program is a poor copy of a US original and his image of Australians as having no idea that what they were producing was not the 'real article' both assume the standing of the US original and use it as the yardstick against which local programs are to be judged. But local programs—even format remakes—do necessarily redispose the original (just as the original program is itself a combination of previous formats only some of which are US). That Bridges can find Australian programs both too 'American' by their imitation and not 'American' by not striking out on their own suggests an Australian disposing of materials which is sufficiently different for recognition of difference to be noted but sufficiently similar for such difference not always to be recognised as something in its own right and to be valued as such. Australia's television culture continues to provide critics and audiences with many such opportunities to label Australian difference as flaws and misconstrue commonalities in both cultures as evidence of endemic Australian unoriginality.

Another American, cultural analyst and author Eric Michaels, has shed further light on these issues (1990a, pp 62–3). Sick and alone in Brisbane at Christmas 1987, he wrote in his posthumously published diary *Unbecoming* that although he could watch the same US shows as his distant friends in Texas, the experience afforded him no sense of community with them. Australian program scheduling practices bore no relation to any US logic he understood. Unlike US television, which ensured programming continuity during the summer so that the population did not go off 'grabbing the shotguns and potshotting in the street' (p 62). Australian television did the exact reverse. Like the rest of the population *it* seemed to go on holiday: its programming became erratic, with new programs introduced, continuing programming becoming shelved, and its personalities being pensioned off for the summer. Michaels, used to network repeats over summer (see Barwise & Ehrenberg 1989, pp 45–6), had to work to find and follow the programs he wanted; and then when he found them there was also a problem with *how* they were presented. It was impossible for this expatriat American to 'go home'. In exasperation, Michaels concluded

> Australians have no idea: they think they're watching the same television as the Yanks... They imagine they're becoming Yanks. And you're not allowed to tell them that they're actually becoming something much more like Filipinos. (1990a, p 62)

Like the Filipino, the Australian audience watches a lot of US television, both countries' television imports many US program concepts and faces the same need to frame imported programs successfully, and both countries have political, historical and cultural ties with the US. But the Australian, like the Canadian—and unlike the Filipino—has the fantasy of becoming American through exposure, not realising that such fantasies are themselves indicative of a local use of imported materials.

Michaels's problems were not due to Australian scheduling incompetence, but were due to an Australian approach to scheduling, program presentation, to the holiday and summer seasons. These resulted in a different kind of general regard for the medium. Arguably Australians take television much less seriously than do Americans (though they watch nearly as much). In Australia television is more of a diversion. As Elizabeth Riddell (1968, p 28), television critic for the *Daily Mirror*, put it: 'For television to determine our character or attitudes we would have to take it seriously.' When television was launched as an important domestic technology in the late 1940s and early 1950s in the US, it was worried over much more than when launched in Australia later as a consumer good. Compare Lynn Spigel's (1990, pp 73–97) account of the domestication of television in the US with John Hartley's and mine (1992, pp 202–17).

Though it has not made Australians more (US) American, or more British per se, their exposure to US and British programming over more than three decades has endowed them with a specifically Australian imagining of the US and of Britain. This invention may have little to do with those countries' indigenous realities. The French have a word for their imaginary America created through exposure to US culture: *Americanité*. Australia's imagining of 'America' is, I am sure, similarly fantastic. So, though Australian audiences may share many of the same cultural resources as the Americans and British, it does not follow that they read their programs in the same way, attach the same value to them, or use them for the same purposes. As Riddell described it, 'a weekly injection of *Peyton Place* is not going to turn a Richmond dairy farmer into an Idaho potato grower' (1968, p 27).

The accusation that Australian television is derivative means only that local programs can be viewed as similar to other US and British programs. Sometimes this similarity is formalised as when program concepts—such as *60 Minutes*—are bought and redisposed for the Australian market.[3] Sometimes it stems from the 'borrowing' and 'redisposing' of pre-existing materials that is characteristic of *all* popular art (Routt 1982). Sometimes it stems from the fact that Australian producers hit upon similar formats and solutions to problems as their US and British counterparts. Australian television drama producers turn to US, British and (since SBS) European programming formats in addition to local ones for inspiration. *Homicide*, for example, owes its existence to both Crawford Productions' and Australian radio's venerable history with police and detective serials, and to the success of *The Untouchables* on Australian television.

At other times, the similarity between Australian and US and British programs resides in the minds of viewers, who often assume, for example, that Australia shamelessly 'borrows' its quiz show formats. Yet the Australian tradition of quiz show production (first on radio, then on television) is longer and more extensive than Britain's, and nearly as long as North America's. And the same can be said for variety. Even the Australian 'outdoors' series and serials owe as much to an Australian popular fiction tradition going back to the nineteenth century as they do to US westerns and British 'period' television.

However, there is a crucial difference. Australian audiences (and critics), when they are disposed to criticise their home-grown product, tend to compare their local output with the US and British output on offer. In this way audiences and critics routinely weigh the Australian production tradition against contemporaneous US and British programs. By contrast, when US audiences (and critics) criticise their programming, they tend to do so with reference only to US product. In this way a US production tradition assimilates new programming into itself. This is because television in the US *means* US-produced television (until recently this has been also the case in Britain). Thus US and British audiences are provided with many more co-ordinates with which to consider their programming (including US television drama remakes from imported concepts) as a seamless continuation of their respective traditions. This close identification of television with the 'home-grown' also helps explain why US and British producers do not normally go outside their respective production traditions to look for new ideas; and why when they do—as with US remakes of British comedy—the result is promoted (and perceived by audiences) as a development of the local production tradition.

Nowhere are these differences more elaborated than in the

international trade in concepts. Without experience of the 'original', US audiences have had no way of seeing that many of their contemporary situation comedies were either concept remakes of British shows, or 'rewrites'. (It started with *All in the Family* as a concept remake of *Till Death Us Do Part*.) Australian viewers, though, spot the concept remake right away because they have often watched the 'original' (this makes it difficult to remake concepts in Australian drama explicitly). Perhaps this goes some way to explaining how aberrant local comedies have to be to succeed with local audiences: *Kingswood Country* and *Mother and Son*, the bizarre *Norman Gunstan Show* in the 1970s, *The Paul Hogan Show*, and that extraordinary political satire without, I believe, any international peer, *The Max Gillies Show*, in the late 1980s. It also suggests how, in order to work for domestic audiences, local drama series must differentiate themselves from, and also be similar to, their British and US competitors. Suzanne Norton argues that Australian serial drama occupies 'the middle ground between the American and the British soap operas', incorporating 'many of the elements characteristic of both':

> The Australians concentrate more on action in their stories [than the British] which deal primarily with relationships, yet hang on to elements of everyday life. Even though the accent is on relationships, they tend to be less sensual than the American soaps and use humour more in the British manner. (Norton 1985, p 18)

Such differentiation has, if anything, been responsible for Australia obtaining a niche in the Anglophone market, producing 'moderately budgeted soaps' (alongside the US's 'high-cost melodramas' and Britain's 'high-budget costume drama' (Collins 1990, p 211).

In Australia the concept trade tends to be in US and to a lesser extent British concepts so long as the 'original' is not available. It therefore tends to be in quiz and games shows, current affairs (*60 Minutes*) and news formats, sports (*Wide World of Sports*) and variety formats (*Tonight Live*).

Australia is a good place to watch television. It always has been a place from which to watch US and British television programming. Since SBS, it's also been a good place to watch a fair amount of world television. Australian television services are not as parochial and inwardly focused as British, US, and Japanese services. For Australians, locally produced programming gives one more program choice, providing one more vantage point from which to be critical of the programming mix. The import component also explains why Australians are not as serious about their television as are Americans and Britons. How can you be as 'serious' about imported programming whose processes of construction exclude your participation save as an 'audience'? Unlike Britons and Americans, who believe they make the best television in the world (British professionals & critics often smugly phrase theirs 'as the least worst television in the world'), Australians typically labour under few delusions about their product being consistently the 'best'. Indeed there is often a good deal of disrespect for local programs and a tendency to be more generous in estimations of imports. This is because critics of local programs can use imports as a yardstick against which Australian programs fail to measure up in addition to their normal critical tropes.

But there is more to the identification of Australian television's 'Americanness' than the presence in commercial and ABC television's schedules of US product. It is also that Australia (along with Canada and the US) is another imagined 'America'. The promise of Australia is of a latter-day 'America'. Certainly waves of Australian immigrants from Ireland, Croatia, Vietnam, Italy, England and Lebanon (to name a few) saw Australia, Canada and the US as interchangeable destinations. This was as true for my Lebanese relatives who came here in the early 1970s as it was for my Irish ancestors in the nineteenth century.

There were and still are good reasons for this interchangeability of destination. Some are structural. They are predominantly English-speaking 'settler cultures' in which indigenous people were displaced. Each has traditions of dealing with many immigrant ethnicities. Each offers the promise of citizenship rather than guest worker status to immigrants. Each sees its culture as emergent and mixed, producing a new society. None demands as stringently as do the more traditional 'nations' that change be constructed in accordance with 'primordial' national traditions. Each has a version of the 'bush' and the frontier which predisposes each to the 'western' and similar kinds of conceptions of the wilderness and the environment. Each shares common elements in political, legal and constitutional arrangements. And for the immigrant there are—at least in the first generation—likely to be relatives in more than one of these three 'Americas'. When added to the pre-eminent place of the US in international audiovisual trade, these conditions help explain why the US—the major vision of 'America'—should have in Australia and Anglophone Canada its best television export markets.

In addition, Hollywood and British drama provide a point of continuity for migrants (see chapters 5 through 9). As the major suppliers of international programming within the world system, the US and Britain export to most of the countries from which Australia draws its immigrants. For the migrants who will have already watched

Hollywood and British programming, the Australian screening of this programming provides for points of continuity. Given the degree of Australian cultural proximity to the US and Britain, this programming probably assists 'integration' more than is commonly recognised, in that it provides rough maps of Australia, its values, and its institutions.[4] Additionally, SBS-TV's provision of Italian, French, Chinese, and German programs furnish additional forms of continuity for particular ethnic communities not as publicly available in the US.

Australian-made programs are also important to ethnic communities as an informational and entertainment resource. Australian productions provide information about the life of the 'host' culture. They often serve as a reference point in the maintenance and transformation of ethnic identities. For example, parents use Australian programs to instruct their children on the differences between Australian social and cultural practices and those of their ethnic fragment, just as their children use those same programs to negotiate their own relation both to their parent's culture and the broader 'host' culture (see Turnbull 1992, passim).

Television programs help transform ethnicities in a dynamic way facilitating the creation of hybrid identities and cultural formations such as the Australian Croatian and the Australian Italian. Typically, Australian programming as 'host programming' sits beside international programs in a dynamic interrelationship facilitating the self-management by immigrant communities of their mixing into the broader Australian society. This mix has probably aided more than hindered the effective social and cultural integration of ethnic minorities.

Simultaneously different and the same; this is the peculiarity of the television service as it is of debates about it (Routt & Bertrand 1989, p 4). What is different for some about Australian television is what is the same for others; what is culturally similar is also that program which is dissimilar; one person's original Australian program is another's fake. Simultaneous difference and sameness structure Australian understandings of what is produced and imported. It produces anxiety about lack of originality and the effect on Australians of what is imported; just as it promotes vigorous assertions of originality, identity and Australian competence to produce television to an international standard.

The difference and sameness dynamic also means that the criticism of Australian television does not have to pass through Australian production traditions to authorise itself or to understand that work. Thus, Nick Roddick wrote glowingly of Australian television from the moment he landed in Australia (Roddick 1985). Criticism can simply use the contemporary imported content as the yardstick. This creates a relatively open informational culture. This is a structure for Australian television, and by implication its culture, which requires little previous experience and expertise for participation. If this can be positive in that it is so inclusive, it is also negative in that ignorance about Australia, its television and its production traditions are often structured into Australian television debates and production processes.

Critics and audiences routinely ignore the fact that Australian television is only a medium-sized market and criticise it for failing to measure up to what can be expected of large country television services. But local productions cannot afford the budgets of US and UK television nor easily match the US and UK product at their own game. Local product must instead be differentiated from imports to carve out a market niche for itself in its own domestic market.

Nonetheless, there is something positive and healthy about a television service which permits diverse people, including typically (but not exclusively) those British, Irish and North Americans who 'just got off the boat', to feel no reticence in voicing their opinions about and contributing to developing Australian television. So it was with Dave Allen, Kamahl and Trisha Goddard. So it was with our Yanks— Bob Dyer, Marcia Hines, Tommy Hanlon and Don Lane. And so it has been for the countless British and North American television producers, directors and critics who have shaped so much Australian television. Only in the 1980s has the same courtesy been extended to first-generation non-English-speaking background (NESB) immigrants in SBS-TV, second-generation NESB immigrants with Jana Wendt, and to Aborigines, with Stan Grant as host of *Real Life*. Australian television drama is beginning to mainstream ethnic identities in *GP* and *A Country Practice*. The television mini-series of the 1980s routinely redisposed many ethnic Australian identities. And, increasingly, Southern and Eastern European and Asian personalities are appearing on television.

From the arguments put in this chapter, Australian television is a particular invention of television in the international television system. This invention has advantages and disadvantages stemming from limitations which are both self-imposed and structural to it as a medium-sized television service operating in the English language, and as a service for a new society formed by the interaction of many settler and indigenous cultures.

2 High communications policy in Australia

There was a watershed in Australian television services in November 1986. The immediate cause was the regulatory change shifting the ownership policy from a two television stations limit to a limit of 60 per cent of the total Australian television audience (initially it was 75 per cent but was scaled down to 60 per cent to get the bill through the non-Labor-controlled Senate). Counterbalancing this extension in allowable market reach, the legislation restricted cross-media ownership of press, television and radio. Within weeks, television, the press and radio underwent the most dramatic change in its state and operating conditions since the advent of television (ABT 1988, pp 7–11, 21–39; Schultz 1989, 68–84). These changes, when taken in conjunction with adjacent political and commercial developments, follow a pattern described by James Carey (1981, p 84) as a 'high communications policy'.

Carey coined this term to describe the development of communications in the US. There, constitutional sanction, active policy, and commercial culture favoured the delivery of messages and information across time and space in the most competitive way possible by removing social and regional obstacles to transmission. Carey sees the US as having single-mindedly 'pursued an almost exclusive policy of improving communications over long distance' (hence a 'high communications policy'). The US did so because it saw 'communication as a form of power and transmission' capable of binding together a continent ('space binding') and different ethnic groups (immigrant and native) often within the same locality (binding a community through time). The pursuit of such a high communications policy transformed both 'the effective units of culture' and 'social organisation' through:

> ...a progressive shift from local and regional units to national and international ones, though not without considerable struggle and conflict. Individuals were linked into larger units of social organisation without the necessity of appealing to them through local and proximate structures. Communication within these local units became less critical for the operation of society and less relevant to the solutions of personal problems. (Carey 1981, p 84)

Carey argues that the growth of long distance communication such as railways, telegraphs, telephones, roads, radio, television and satellites 'cultivated new structures in which thought occurred—national classes and professions—new things thought about—speed, space, movement, mobility—and new things to think with—increasingly abstract, analytic, and manipulative symbols' (Carey 1981, p 84).

Regulatory, commercial and technological changes within Australian media after November 1986, when taken in conjunction with changes in business, politics and government regulation, reshaped the culture of television in Australia towards a high communications policy. Audience boundaries were altered. A space-binding emphasis in television advanced apace, redrawing cultural and political boundaries, reconfiguring state and regional geographical scales, and encouraging the further development of centralised corridors of information. The kind of corridors of information that Carey speaks of in the US context, where *adjacent* states and centres communicate with each other effectively via New York (Carey 1981, p 82), were now occurring on the same scale in Australia.

THE SITUATION BEFORE 1986

Before the 1986 changes, Australia had a version of a high communications policy in television and communications, but it was not pursued assiduously. Broadcasting policy and practice placed obstacles to an unmediated delivery of programs nationwide. As noted previously, many programs—such as drama, elements of news and current affairs, quiz, and variety—were distributed nationally but in a loosely integrated way, as commercial stations screened the same firstrun Australian television drama, but not at the same time, nor on the same day, nor with the same episode being screened (often there was as much as an eighteen-month or two-year time-lag between screenings of the same episode of a program). Networking was limited by local control over the scheduling of programs and advertising. With SMBA networking being a cooperative arrangement and with common ownership limited to two of the four markets, there was no urgent imperative to integrate advertising, program production and scheduling.

Additionally, outside SMBA, regional stations and the smaller state and territory capitals (Hobart, Darwin, Canberra) operated as the sole commercial station in their market and, in Perth, as one of two commercial stations. It was to the commercial advantage of these stations not to lock themselves into a national networking system (O'Regan & Hiltula 1985, pp 75–82). Regional stations used their monopoly, and in Perth's case duopoly, positions to drive down prices and cushion themselves from direct network control (ABT 1984, p 55). This enabled them to retain control over their schedules and advertising profits. Compare this to the US situation where network payments to affiliates lagged behind increases in network income by as much as 44 per cent per year (Gomery 1984, p 63). By the late 1970s, Perth and some regional stations were among the most profitable television companies in the country (Brown 1986, p 144). Broadcasting policy limited ownership to two stations and the localism doctrine provided the rhetorical and structural basis for commercial television. The localism policy protected the financial viability and corporate integrity of television stations outside Sydney and Melbourne. It ensured that licences initially went to local groups, discouraged regionals from entering into formal networking arrangements, and encouraged the limited development of program production for local audiences (ABT 1984, pp 29–30, 36–37, 55).

Sydney and Melbourne stations dominated the system but the regional and peripheral capital city stations had relative autonomy. Sydney and Melbourne's influence was conferred by the 43 per cent of the Australian viewing audience both markets commanded. Also, the ownership of stations in both Sydney and Melbourne by Packer's Nine Network after 1960 and Murdoch's Ten Network after 1979 gave them considerable power over other cooperating stations in their network. When coupled with the loose networking arrangements in SMBA, this meant that the SMBA 'networks' tended to dictate what programs were brought into Australia and the kind of Australia-wide programs that were produced, but without having direct control over the stations showing this material.[1] This was an Australian communications system in which control was at the level of what was to be screened but not over the scheduling or the profits from screening.

Before the domestic satellite, program delivery was mostly through program bicycling; when simultaneous programming was used, it was delivered via the terrestrial microwave and cable links. This system worked on payment for each point-to-point transmission. It provided incentives for users to minimise transmission costs by utilising alternative and cheaper delivery systems—such as air-freighted videotape—for all but the most time-sensitive of programs. The more a station used the terrestrial links, the greater its expenses. Contrast this with the situation after the launch of the AUSSAT satellites in 1984–85, where the fixed cost of uplinking and satellite time could be spread over a potentially infinite number of receiving stations, thereby encouraging the use of the single transmission by multiple users: that is, networking, the *sine qua non* of high communications.

The pre-satellite program delivery system needs to be understood not only as a technological outcome but as a delivery system suited to the television business milieu with its cooperative networking in SMBA, its station independence, its regulatory policy settings favouring localism and limited television ownership, and its actively disconnected Perth, Hobart and regional television markets. All these factors retarded the development of simultaneous programming, and of delivery systems and pricing policies to support it. Nevertheless, the cost of transmission between distant centres was moving downwards even before the launch of the domestic satellite, and with this came a greater use of the microwave links for programming on the ABC and the commercials. From the latter half of the 1970s these links were used for time-sensitive programs such as *World Series Cricket, 60 Minutes* and *Victorian Football League.* One reason the introduction of the domestic communications satellite was so long after the technology became available was that there was no obvious commercial demand for it as a vehicle for intra-Australian television services delivery. Thus AUSSAT came on stream many years after overseas satellite feeds had become the norm for news broadcasts; with Indonesia having one operating before Australia.

Alongside these television arrangements was a telecommunications policy which gave a central place to social policy objectives alongside economic ones (Barr 1985, p 116). Communication flows between major centres helped subsidise the rural exchange network and business communications the private telephone system (Barr 1985, pp 127–8). This policy discouraged inequalities in service delivery and therefore the creation of information-poor groups. However such protection and cross-subsidisation of communication corridors helped distort both the markets and metropolitan development.

TELEVISION IN TRANSITION

All this started to change in the 1980s and particularly after 1986. The initial catalyst was the prospect of the domestic satellite (Hazlehurst

1990, pp 9–22). It opened a can of worms for broadcasting policy (Chadwick 1989, pp 3–25), encouraging a fundamental rethinking of existing policy settings including ownership and control, audience boundaries, program deliveries, connections between places and the number of stations sustainable in broadcast markets. Because AUSSAT permitted point-to-multipoint distribution, its broadcast area (footprint) constructed a geographically diverse audience getting the same service in terms of quality and cost of reception. AUSSAT thus promised to revolutionise existing telecommunications arrangements for the delivery of broadcasting messages between stations in that, provided it was used heavily, savings were to be had in the sending and receiving of broadcast messages. AUSSAT would also enable the extension of television services to outlying towns, homesteads, camps and communities outside the reach of existing terrestrial television services (estimated at 2 per cent of the population, see Brown 1988, p 177) enabling a national television and radio coverage. Indeed this last was a major initial selling point for AUSSAT (Barr 1985, pp 141–3). It led to the development of policy frameworks for remote commercial television (the RCTS service) and the ABC which saw a commercial service and an ABC service beamed to remote communities and stations across Australia after 1985. The high-powered satellite signal permitted direct broadcasting to remote audiences who accessed the service through a small satellite dish. To take account of time zones across the continent and to respect state boundaries four remote services were created (western, central, north-east and south-east—only the first three of which developed as fully fledged broadcasters). The large proportion of Aborigines included amongst the remote population led directly to the recognition of the particular communication needs of Aborigines in broadcasting.

AUSSAT threatened vested interests. By putting on the agenda more television in regional markets, it compromised the commercial monopoly enjoyed by regional television. No longer could the regionals argue that the cost of delivery was holding back as comprehensive a service to regional Australia as that enjoyed by capital cities (Brown 1988, pp 175–87). Telecom, which had heavily invested in alternative terrestrial technology, saw a competitor eroding its monopoly and market share. Satellite delivery and the increasing importance of simultaneous programming threatened the integrity of BAPH television stations vis-a-vis central program providers as the satellite would help Sydney and Melbourne stations to dominate the Australian system further. All found it difficult to swim against the tide.

Additional television services in regional areas were inevitable from the late 1970s once bipartisan support for them developed. The only issue bitterly fought over to the last was whether adjacent regional stations should be broadcasting into each other's markets or whether additional services should be provided through supplementary licences granted to the regional stations. Perth stations could no longer plausibly argue that Perth's size and the high cost of service delivery to the western third of the continent inhibited a third commercial station. By the mid-1980s it had more people than Adelaide, which had been operating three commercial stations since 1965; and at last, a federal government, the Hawke Labor Government, was prepared to support actively the granting of a third commercial licence in Perth.

Federal governments also felt it strategically and politically necessary to launch an Australian domestic satellite. Policy makers met regional and BAPH concerns through promising changes in the ownership and control regulations so as to enable regional operators to get bigger. The Hawke government supported plans to bring three commercial stations to regional television markets by 'aggregating' adjacent regional television markets into larger and therefore more viable single markets. Called 'equalisation' (for equalising regional television services with metropolitan services), this policy involved turning some thirty regional television service areas on the eastern seaboard, where only a commercial and an ABC station were then available, into four discrete markets. The ABC and three commercial stations would be progressively introduced from 1990 ending in 1992. (WA, SA, Tasmania and the Northern Territory were omitted from the equalisation plan on the grounds that their regional populations were insufficient to support three commercial stations.) For some of the larger cities in regional markets a fifth public network, the SBS, would also be made available. The third commercial station in Perth and equalisation promised the incorporation of Perth (then 6.3 per cent of the population) and most of the regional television audience (34 per cent of the population) into the SMBA networks (Brown 1988, p 177). Policy had thus created powerful commercial incentives for SMBA networks to take up a more aggressive position in the television system.

Suddenly simultaneous programming was not only routinely possible but desirable from policy and industry points of view. Satellite space was leased to the ABC and the SMBA networks, the heavy users of point-to-multipoint television transmissions. This biased the television system towards the simultaneous delivery of programming undercutting the air freighting of videotapes for program distribution. This in turn drove a greater standardisation of the television system, initially in the larger capital city markets and later in regional markets in the wake of equalisation. The overturning of the two-station rule in favour of a 60 per cent market share encouraged the further integration of SMBA, Perth and regional stations (it was easier to tell a subsidiary station how to program than an independently owned one!). Thus the seemingly intractable obstacles within commercial television to simultaneous networking were removed between November 1986 and 1990: station independence, diversified ownership, single (or in Perth's case two) commercial station markets, and non-networking.

The launch of the domestic satellite also acted as a catalyst to reconfigure ABC and SBS television operations. Satellite useage was forced upon a reluctant ABC for the delivery of its television and radio services both to new remote audiences and existing audiences. With declining government funding, this resulted in nothing less than a governmental edict to restructure ABC operations to 'take advantage of the satellite' at the expense of its existing federal structure. ABC regional television production ceased in Rockhampton and Townsville as the satellite redrew the map of broadcasting in Queensland in 1984–85, bypassing those centres and cutting them off from their hinterland in favour of a Brisbane-based broadcast signal. With the second wave of ABC cutbacks in the late 1980s, BAPH operations were reduced further. Even the ABC's rural network came to be based on what could be called the new principle: a commonality of interests no matter where you are on the continent, so long as you are outside the major metropolitan conurbations. Thus the ABC increasingly came to use interstate segments in both the news and current affairs area—partly because there were not the same funds available for local production, and partly because the link was there, paid for and needed to be used.

For the other national broadcaster, SBS-TV, the satellite provided an opportunity to break out of its Sydney and Melbourne confines and begin to achieve quasi-national coverage in the larger metropolitan and regional cities. Federal funds were made available for this service area extension. Highly centralised to begin with, SBS-TV had no semblance of a federal structure to break up. SBS-TV represented *in extremis* a tendency for BAPH operations to consist of no more than a bank of computer-controlled VTRs recording and then automatically rebroadcasting. SBS-TV was undoubtedly reacting to budgetary pressures. But SBS-TV also saw its audience as sets of nationally and internationally based constituencies (Hartley 1992, 200–1). Its programming relied on a narrowcasting to principally ethnic and cultural segments of the population.

The advent of AUSSAT changed Telecom. With potential competition from satellite delivered telephony in mind, Telecom concentrated resources on the competitive fibre optic cabling between major urban centres as a means of retaining long-term control over profitable STD routes, potential Pay TV provision and market share for its existing land lines for television transmissions. AUSSAT acted as a circuit breaker, legitimating the integration of services, ensconcing a commercial (rather than social) focus and pushing Telecom to adopt competitive technologies and pricing structures.

Federal government investment in and ownership of AUSSAT over the 1980s (it was privatised in 1991 and became part of the Optus group) provided government with additional incentives to make the satellite work. This need to make a very expensive satellite system pay was exacerbated in the mid-1980s by devaluation, large foreign debt, and determination to reduce government expenditure and debt. Policy initiatives such as equalisation, the thrusting of AUSSAT useage on the ABC, the extension of the SBS-TV network and the change in the ownership and control regulations all promoted satellite useage. Additionally, the Hawke government encouraged greater non-broadcast use of AUSSAT through its Video and Audio Entertainment and Information Services (VAEIS) provisions while stopping short of permitting domestic Pay TV. Thus Sky Channel, the main VAEIS operations, was set up as a sports and entertainment service available to clubs and hotels but not to individual homes. Such policy changes were not, however, sufficient to 'make AUSSAT pay its way' (see *Communications Update* 1990 n. 52 pp 3–5).

The impact of these changes upon existing services, whether national or commercial, was profound. Commercial television moved in the same networking direction as had the SBS and the ABC. Regional current affairs programming initially disappeared from Brisbane, Adelaide and then Perth screens in the late 1980s. Such programming later re-emerged in the 1990s but were scheduled earlier and were decidedly less high profile than were the national current affairs programs. This move toward networked programs was also due to the need to service the large debts incurred by companies attempting to take advantage of the new ownership and control regulations by getting larger, and after 1990 to a deepening recession which mandated industry rationalisation. Using network feeds enabled job shedding in regional, BAPH and ultimately Sydney and Melbourne stations. Symbolically this change was well represented by the transformation of television continuity. As late as early 1989, the metropolitan commercial stations celebrated their regional existence in television continuity as local images were presented with lyrics and graphics declaring 'Love you Brisbane' (or Perth or Melbourne etc). Such regional identifications of the service were replaced by more abstract continuity using Australian map designs, in Network Nine's case linking together the major cities.

The changes have accentuated a trend for 'local programming' to mean 'Australia-wide programming', rather than its previous ambiguous meaning as both regionally based output for regional audiences and Australia-wide output. Some local programs for regional constituencies continued in news broadcasts, local television advertising, and various community events like telethons (using network drama stars and personalities). This programming maintained regional stations' identities and retained some of the stepped communication flow whereby the state capitals filtered broadcast flows and decisions into states (familiar from the pre-1986 era). But, increasingly, local and regional identifications found their place within a network of national images and image-making

With national integration through networking, a new form of localisation developed, most dramatically in winter sports programming and for sports best placed to take advantage of quasi-national competition. The development of the National Basketball League, Australian Football through the Australian Football League, and Rugby League's attempt to win back Queensland and New South Wales support for the code as a prelude to its national expansion permitted 'local' teams' games to be viewed on television at home, often with a local commentary team. Thus a new sort of parochialism emerged defined in relation to other city teams; the meaning of the 'local' shifted. The Perth enthusiasm for its teams (the West Coast Eagles in Australian Rules and the Wildcats in basketball) demonstrates the new localism.

Producers and stations based in Brisbane, Adelaide and Perth still supplied the national networks with low-cost children's and some specialist programming, but such 'out work' contracted in the late 1980s in favour of a better 'national coverage' in individual programs. In current affairs programs like *A Current Affair*, production piecework was developed in peripheral capitals and regional centres through multipurpose stringers providing research for satellite interviews, the images, production crews, and some roles for locally based reporters. Similar strategies have been successful in programs such as *Gardening Australia, Holiday* and *Burke's Backyard*. This inclusive strategy has also seen producers set an episode or two of drama series in one of the peripheral cities or broadcast a week of a current affairs or variety show such as the *Midday Show* or *Hinch* from one of them. Sometimes, as with mini-series and movies such as *Jackaroo* and *Fran*, this has meant producing out of one of these cities for the national grid.

In encouraging these programming changes, policy has made Australian television markets less context-sensitive than previously. There has been a partial shift away from the local and regional community towards more national and international community mind-sets. Under a high communications policy, the checks and balances which were a feature of the media for the past 30 years have been removed. The frenetic scrambling for positions inflated television asset values and program costs. (Such costs were to some extent offset by the larger pool of stations contributing to network coffers.) And there has also been a turnover in industry management and in assumptions about television, its conduct and its limits. Within weeks of the change in broadcasting policy, two of the largest and most stable media groups in the country—Herald and Weekly Times and Packer's television and satellite holdings—had been carved up and had ceased to exist. All of these changes occurred, only to be replaced later by a new austerity in the wake of the inevitable 'bust' (See O'Connor 1989, pp 28, 30, and chapter 3).

CHANGES IN AUSTRALIAN CAPITALISM

The change in broadcasting policy would not have been as likely if the economic instruments outside the media had not been moving in a similar direction. The 1980s saw the rapid consolidation, takeover and merger of corporations: in retail (with the Coles–Myer merger), brewing (with Fosters and Bond Brewing), mining (with BHP's takeover of Utah and other companies), banking (with mergers of banks and building societies leading to fewer regionally based financial institutions) and the share market (with the linking together of stock markets and their integration within international markets). The 1990 corporate and financial sector collapses strengthened, rather than fractured, this consolidation of national market power. A New Zealand group gained control of Bond Brewing, thereby creating a large Australasian brewing enterprise, and the major banks appear to be the winners out of the collapses of regionally based financial groups. Australian corporate sickness ultimately assisted international integration as levels of foreign ownership of companies grew. Stable, longer term foreign investors took advantage of the national market integration the better to match their Australian and international operations. So too, in the wake of corporate collapses, uniform corporate laws and federal instrumentalities overseeing business regulation were demanded by Victoria's Cain Labor and NSW's Greiner Liberal governments in 1989. Such ceding of state responsibility for the corporate sector to the commonwealth was unprecedented.

The sensational media changes, led by the dominant medium of television, brought the mass marketing sector of the media into line with these emerging conditions of Australian-based business. This is the classic chicken-and-egg situation: changes within the media already happening before the November 1986 announcement encouraged national market coordination. Before 1986 the move towards efficiency in the sale of television minutes to advertisers had proceeded apace, with regional stations banding together with other regional stations and metropolitan stations with other metropolitan stations in cooperative arrangements to sell time to national advertisers. Within television program production there was a move towards national simultaneous programming with the emergence on a national scale of Australian football, *World Series Cricket*, *60 Minutes* and *Sunday*.

Thus we can speak at a number of different levels of a process of reconfiguring at work in both the form of programming and the make-up of television markets. Networking, in promising that everywhere is the same place, is enacting the same kind of space-binding marketing strategy as Elders and Bond had used to create Fosters, Swan Premium and XXXX as national and international beers. Despite the national coverage that satellite interviews from around the continent provide, regional identities cannot afford to be totally ignored. XXXX's stranglehold on market share in Queensland was eroded through Bond management's inappropriate national marketing strategies and corporate practices which cut across longstanding local and regional arrangements. Similarly, attempts to 'share' common news services between cities created problems in the late 1980s for the Seven Network and the ABC. Some concessions and adjustments need to be made to suit local market conditions. One such concession in Perth was the development in the early 1990s of a half-hour weekday local current affairs program, *Perth Extra*, broadcast prior to the evening news. (Sydney audiences, too, got the local *Sydney Extra*.) But concessions of this nature do not compromise the increasing evolution of a Sydney and Melbourne corridor of information and the reconstruction of core–periphery relations—a move from the loose integration of the past towards full-scale integration.

Accompanying the new approaches to broadcasting communication has been a revolution in business communication. Evidence can be seen in the regearing of business markets towards national interconnection. This can be variously seen in the national networking of real estate information; the telephone-computer linked cattle and sheep sales by description on a state and national basis; and the move to make corporate communications between centres cheaper (this by either bypassing Telecom or else eliminating the cross-subsidising by business of the private and rural user).

Such networking has facilitated a similar reconfiguring of markets as in the television business. For business, like television, point-to-multipoint distribution (and its concomitant national organisation and networking) has become the norm. If networking favours the national advertiser, the ability to organise national slots encourages the development of national markets and diminishes the importance of more context-sensitive regional ones. The transformation of regional markets under equalisation created larger, more amorphous regional markets. Thus non-metropolitan Queensland stretching from the wheat belts of the south-west to the cane farms of the far north was developed as one market (as too was regional Victoria), and regional New South Wales became two markets (northern and southern).

Similar changes occurred in the wake of the development of the Remote Commercial Television Service in Western Australia. There the whole of regional Western Australia became a single commercial television market, as existing markets in Geraldton, Kalgoorlie, Bunbury and Albany and new markets in the Kimberley and Pilbara became amalgamated into the one market.

NATIONALISING POLITICS

Such nationalising of business and media affected politics. But, equally, political and legislative thinking were already moving in a similar direction. The election of the Hawke Labor government in 1982 and Labor governments in most Australian states ensured that the most centrally organised of the major political parties and the party most convinced of the value and importance of national institutions and structures held office through the 1980s. Its political agenda was shaped by integrating state and federal priorities and where necessary—mostly related to environmental and Aboriginal issues—imposing its will upon the states. The ALP's centralised structure had been a political liability, under the new conditions it became an advantage. Its structure and orientations made it a suitable instrument for the changing dynamics of Australian capital to find political and legislative expression. But the conservative side of politics was equally affected. The 'Joh for PM' campaign of the early 1980s saw Joh Bjelke-Petersen—a major supporter of states rights in the 1970s and the National Party premier of Queensland from 1968 to 1987—become for a time a plausible national candidate employing Canberra and ex-Canberra advice and personnel. State governments, in conditions favouring integration rather than separation, were significantly less important to a nationally geared company than they once had been. Their role has not been totally eclipsed, however, as they remain important for the resource and commodity sectors, both of which can expect favourable treatment from state governments more prepared to look after state rather than national interests.

The televising of politics was affected by local programming coming to imply Australia-wide programming from a centralised source. The contraction or withdrawal of regionally based current affairs and news services pressured political coverage to go national and this led in another way to a nationalising of politics. The Sydney-based *A Current Affair* provided the model in its use of the satellite for Sydney interviews of people in other parts of Australia, carefully constructing its truly national look. In Perth, its opposition in the late 1980s was TVW 7's *State Affair*, which was the platform for Seven's ratings dominance at the time. It needed to provide a semblance of a national coverage. The problem facing *State Affair* going the same route was in part the lack of the critical audience mass to amortise the added cost of putting together and organising satellite interviews. Facilities in other states had to be booked, technical expertise to be developed, the cost of interviewing and research escalated and the style of interviewing changed. The state-based programs simply did not have the same funds to compete in terms of the standard of imaging—or to buy national exclusives of a magazine style, such as an interview with parents of Siamese twins. Not surprisingly then, Perth's TVW Seven's *State Affair* was replaced by *Hinch* networked out of Melbourne in January 1989.

From a network perspective of the maximum use of production resources, the pre-AUSSAT/network situation—which maintained extensive regional competences in news journalism and current affairs—was inefficient. Expensive equipment and personnel were tied up in the BAPH states producing material for a fraction of the Australian viewing public. However, the result was programs which constructed state rather than national audience identities. In the process, what evolved was a state-wide mediation of local, national and international stories through their respective capital cities. This led to parochial content. But it also marked out the ways in which pre-network television was inextricably wedded to the states' objective of maintaining a separate political position on the Australian continent. Networking diminished state filtering, substituting for it an unmediated access to state stories from a national viewpoint.

With the dimininished importance of state boundaries to business and the erosion of the state-based filtering of messages, state politics became understood on a national stage. Queensland National Party conferences, the Fitzgerald Inquiry into police corruption and the 1989 Queensland election were extensively covered on television across

Australia in ways that would have been unthinkable a short time before. With this came a disturbance of the often comfortable political hegemony that the previous system permitted in peripheral states like WA, SA and Queensland. State governments did not become irrelevant. But these new media conditions, when coupled with the explicit and pronounced nationalisation and internationalisation of business, have bypassed them significantly in determining the conditions under which business operates and political agendas are set on the continent. State governments are now more centrally concerned with their national and international integration.

SHIFTS IN CONCENTRATIONS OF COMMERCIAL POWER

The new legislation hastened ownership concentrations within particular media while reducing the concentration across different media. The 1986 changes favoured horizontal business expansion across space as conglomerations developed which explicitly linked operations across distance, and so across geographically dispersed communities. This was at the expense of the vertically integrated media outlets in particular cities and regions of the past. With as few as three large operators within the different spheres of press, radio and television emerging there has been a move away from large and small diverse media holdings to even larger single media holdings.

The result was an historic dislocation of the press, TV and radio sectors. A decline in media cross-ownership and the rise of integrated and highly developed national markets within media led to different relations within and between media and between Australian and international media industries. Cross-media ownership had enabled the old corporations—Packer's Consolidated Press, the Herald and Weekly Times, and Fairfax—to rely upon press interests to subsidise their other media interests if needed (Souter 1981, pp 509–16). It encouraged complementarities between print and broadcasting rather than direct competition and limited print reporting of controversies regarding the shape and direction of parent company's television services. The new conditions broke up such 'monopoly localism', favouring competition between radio, press and television.

The television market was transformed. As aggregation, common ownership and the third commercial station in Perth eliminated the regional buyers' market for programs, regional and Perth stations could be expected to pay more for programming. Now the networks purchased programming for the whole Australian market and expected it to be screened in most of it (the only exceptions being remote and marginal service areas which only received the ABC and one commercial television service).

The concentration of ownership and the new power of the networks encouraged direct negotiations for the entire national market. This placed the three commercial networks in the kind of position that Australian-controlled cinema exhibitors once were. While these new groupings have unprecedented market power in terms of their size, reach and overall percentage of the Australian market, this power is conferred at a local rather than international level. As far as international distributors are concerned, the rise of large single-medium corporations within the Australian industry is a mixed blessing. Pressure can be applied directly, without the checks and balances provided by either cross-media ownership or the decentralised regional and Perth stations. Thus intense competition for US programming was now felt by all the television stations rather than just the SMBA stations. In the process, a significant cushion against full international pressures being exerted on parts of Australian television was removed. It would not be as easy now, for example, for SMBA television stations to go on 'strike' (Davidson 1968, p 22) as they did in the mid-1960s to reduce the cost to them of US series and serials after a period of disastrous competitive bidding for US programming.

The changes towards a high communications policy saw the Australian television industry further integrated with the international television system. Competition within SMBA markets for US programming of all kinds before the changes was not new. After 1982, demand for US programming increased as more US informational and variety programs were broadcast—particularly after Channels Nine and Seven in Sydney obtained direct satellite links to studios in the US, and by 1984 Murdoch's international operations were becoming inreasingly important to his Channel Ten stations in Sydney and Melbourne. The intense competition for US programs peaked between 1987 and 1989, with all Australian commercial networks signing output deals with US studios and the Seven network affiliated with a US network. Given Australia's medium size in terms of population and its markets, a degree of cross-media ownership may have been helpful in providing a bargaining position and cross-subsidisation of Australian material.

SHIFTS IN THE FOCUS OF REGULATION

Accompanying these changes was a new pattern of broadcast regulation and policy development consonant with a high communication policy. In the new policy dynamic, the ABT (and its successor from 5 October 1992, the ABA) lost its role as the central institution overseeing television policy. Its place in broadcasting policy development was taken by federal departments (first the Department of Communications, then the Department of Transport and Communications (DOTAC)). With this shift came a changing of the guard and a sweeping aside of most of the policy work done in the late 1970s and early 1980s (Armstrong 1988, p 3).

In contrast with the previous bottom-up and interactionalist policy development of the ABT, departmental policy development was determinedly top-down and centralist. Advice-taking shifted from public inquiries and tribunals to commissioned consultancies and departmental policy development in policy papers and invited submissions (Armstrong 1988, p 4). Consultants played a greater role in policy formulation, while public (academic) intellectuals, community groups and others lost some of their traditional role in influencing broadcast policy development through ABT hearings and the like. This led to a definable inner and outer circle of consultants and industry figures recruited, fellow politicians enlisted, and journalists favoured by politicians. It left, as Armstrong contends, 'limited opportunity for those affected to have their say' before major policy statements were published. Their only redress was 'through the parliamentary process which attempts to translate policy into law' (1988, p 5).

With this approach to policy development, ministers, cabinet and departmental apparatchiks gained greater control over policy agenda setting. The department's close connection with government ensured that broader political programs were translated into broadcasting policy development in more direct ways than was possible with the independent-minded ABT staff of the early 1980s. Consultants and departmental staff also enabled comparable frameworks—managerial and economic—to develop across different industries. This suited the overall governmental policy agenda of the 1980s and 1990s of savings, economic efficiency, cost-effectiveness, and microeconomic reform across business and governmental practice. Policy development was politicised as policy making became firmly anchored within ministerial and cabinet control; and it was simultaneously made more abstract and consonant with other governmental agendas through the use of a stabilising argot—economistic knowledges. Thus increasing competition and removing barriers to it and leaving the make-up and shape of the broadcasting sector to market forces rather than government, became increasingly central to policy development (Dwyer 1991, pp 162–70) and drove the development of Pay TV policy making and the enactment of the Broadcasting Services Act in 1992 which replaced the old act (Cunningham 1992, pp 104–36; Davies and Spurgeon 1992, pp 85–92).

With the ascendance of an economic framing to policy and with social policy rhetorics and positions in retreat, the different players—industry and community groups—felt constrained to translate their agendas into economistic rhetoric. The ABT took an increasingly hands-off approach to broadcast regulation in the late 1980s as evidenced in its 1987 decision to lift restrictions on the amount of advertising shown on commercial television as a trial of industry self-regulation (which it had trouble reimposing in 1992). Such light regulation became adopted as a plank for the 1992 Broadcasting Services Act and the ABA. These developments represented a significant shift in regulatory philosophy, with longstanding social policy considerations being increasingly seen to stem from the adoption of a framework of economic regulation. In the 1970s and 1980s, the ABT had assumed that social policy considerations were potentially separate from, rather than a natural consequence of, economic and market development (Dwyer 1990, pp 157–62).

With the cross-ownership rules and larger broadcasters' market power, the economic regulatory body—the Trade Practices Commission (TPC)—became increasingly important in determining ownership and control questions in broadcasting. The TPC's regulation of corporate practice was different from the sector-specific regulation of the ABT and its predecessor, the Australian Broadcasting Control Board. As a general business regulation agency, the TPC does not take on board social policy considerations as such. Any concern for the social good on its part flows from its monitoring of the business system for restrictive practices. Its involvement in the media industry in, for example, the Herald and Weekly Times break-up in late 1986 and during 1987 confirms the partial move away from the broadcast regulator as the sole agency responsible for broadcast regulation.

In this context the development and extension of an Australian version of anti-trust through the TPC has become an issue for broadcast lobby groups and critics. With this comes a different set of arguments and concerns about Australian media industries. A competitive framework is assumed to be the best means to secure the policy goals of fairness, balance, and provision for the social good.

Understandings of television are taking new forms to accommodate changes in what is possible to contest politically. With media monopolies now more a reality than ever in the past, the criticism of them has shifted terrain. Where once attacking media monopolies was associated with calls for less cross-ownership, a 'less concentrated' media sector and more regionally based, single-medium ownership, it is now associated with additional television channels—including Pay TV services which would be run by large national or international groups—and support for a form of public or community television.

HIGH COMMUNICATIONS POLICY

So, too, ideas about networking, which once saw it as positive within the ABC and negative within the commercial sector (because it involved increased corporate power through a concentration of media ownership), have been superceded by a concern for the number, variety and type of national networks. Now it is a matter of either increasing the number of networks to ensure diversity, or regulating network practices such as relations between networks and affiliates.

CONCLUSION

The 'high communication policy' Carey speaks of in the US, with its emphasis upon national transmission, integrating the local and regional better into the national and the international, is now an Australian reality. The practices and policies of media players, the new federal broadcasting policy and business have seen the adoption of a policy of spreading messages further in space. The launch of the Australian domestic satellite AUSSAT was critical in allowing these networking and integrating processes to develop speedily as government, regulators, and commercial operators adopted a mind-set which removed the regional checks and balances of the old television system. Out of this moment something new had became possible: entrepreneurial television. But without the old television culture's checks and balances, it was to have a chequered history.

3 The rise and fall of entrepreneurial television, 1986–92

In the 1988–89 financial year, the Australian commercial television industry lost money for the first time since 1957. By September 1990, two of Australia's three commercial networks, Seven and Ten were in the hands of receivers. Seven had been that way all year; Ten was put into receivership that month—a little more than a year after former network owner, Frank Lowy, sold the network at a discounted price to Steve Cosser. Leading network Nine changed hands in 1990 for a fraction of its original purchase price; sold by Kerry Packer to Alan Bond's Bond Media group for $1.1 billion in 1987, it was repurchased by Packer in a deal which put the value of the network at between $410 and $485m.[1] The financial state of the Australian industry was represented by the Seven Network's earning of $4.83m *before* its interest and tax bills were taken into account in the 1988–89 financial year. A similar picture emerged for the other networks. The lowest rating Ten Network lost $114.3m in 1988–89, $7.3m in 1989–90 and $118.2m in 1990–91 (see Shoebridge 1990, p 23; ABT 1992, p 75). This crippled financial state led to dramatic job losses. Between mid-1989 and late 1991 an estimated 25 per cent of Ten Network staff lost their jobs. The medium-term outlook for network affiliates in regional Australia, servicing 34 per cent of the Australian television audience, looked increasingly bleak (Thomas 1990, pp 54–59).

As networks slashed production spending by as much as 40 per cent in this period, the independent program production industry, the major supplier of Australian commercial television programming, underwent a dramatic downturn. (There has been a 42 per cent decline in the number of 'consistent [film and television] producers' since 1988: Maddox quoted in Given 1993, p 23.) Established producers saw new productions cancelled or indefinitely shelved, and unemployment within the industry mounted. Not only did actors' rates decline but so too did work opportunities generally. Creative people sought overseas employment and production houses such as Grundy focused its efforts offshore in Spain, Belgium, Luxembourg and the Netherlands to service markets with greater production opportunities (*Screen Digest*, July 1990, p 150). Co-productions became more important with the 'purely Australian product' (which has been so successful on British screens with *Neighbours* and *Home and Away*) being seen by Terry Ohisson, chief of Crawford Productions, as too costly for 'an Australian network to shoulder' (*West Australian*, 30 June 1990). Finally, to meet US trade pressure, television station pressure and the Australian government's microeconomic reform agenda, regulations stipulating that all television advertisements should be Australian-made were overturned. This further diminished opportunities within the Australian film industry, deflated production costs, and saw some technological infrastructure leaving the country.

The recession of the early 1990s was not responsible for the disastrous results of 1988–91. But it helped prolong the industry's crisis into 1992–93, as advertising revenues fell 4.2 per cent in 1990–91 and the industry as a whole reported a $225.3m loss that financial year (ABT 1992, pp 71, 73). The period from 1986 to 1992, marked by boom conditions between 1986 and 1988 and bust conditions from 1989 to 1992, was one of the most extraordinary periods in Australian television's history.

By 1993 the television industry was on the way to a slow recovery (Given 1993, pp 23–24). But there was no going back to pre-1988 conditions. Additional competition from Pay TV was imminent, significant debts required servicing, low inflation altered acceptable gearing ratios and slow economic recovery meant smaller than expected increases in advertising revenues. But at least the industry was being regularised. The caretaker owners of the Ten Network sold it to a consortium including the Canadian communication company Can West;[2] and the Seven Network was floated in July 1993. While the mini-series and the telemovie never recovered their pre-1989 standing, the production industry was nevertheless becoming a more stable employment site with new programs being commissioned and greater levels of participation with international partners in co-productions.

What happened in this period? How did a previously profitable—and highly competitive—television industry with low levels of debt and expanding overseas export markets become a basket case which

41

would take years to rebuild, given its crippling debts, substantial production downturn, new media competition, and slow economic growth?

THE ENTREPRENEURIAL GAME PLAN

The Australian commercial television crisis of 1989–92 had its immediate origins in two unrelated governmental strategies: financial sector deregulation and the 1986 changes in broadcast policy. The deregulation of the Australian financial sector created long credit lines and fuelled an investment boom in which accepted price-to-earnings ratios became grossly inflated. The new television ownership rules and equalisation extended allowable market shares for television companies and the reach of the networks. More than this, the arrival of three commercial television services to the major regional television markets promised the integration of those markets with their metropolitan counterparts. The ownership changes and aggregation enabled companies to get bigger and exercise qualitatively greater control over the shape, profits, and definition of the television market than before. As noted in chapter 2, the launch of AUSSAT in 1986 promised a new television message delivery structure in which simultaneous networking of entire program schedules became routinely possible.

Networking, common ownership and a new delivery system seemed to offer additional advertising revenues, as the networks would control more national advertising. Ad space buyers would be able to do more or less one stop shopping in the larger markets, bringing added business and greater control over the television system. The networks, now national players at the pinnacle of the system, commanding up to 60 per cent of the national audience, would be in a position to dictate terms to the smaller regional and metropolitan market players which would have no alternative but to become their affiliates. The profits to be had from this, based on US experience, must have looked promising. Gomery (1984, p 63) notes that 'One [US] study...found that between 1964 and 1976 network income increased some 575 per cent...while payments to affiliates rose only 34 per cent (1984, p 63). Under the new conditions companies scrambled to control the key licences in the major metropolitan markets to reach the 60 per cent of total viewing audience permitted by the new laws. This legislation made it possible for a company to control four of the five largest television markets in the country and still come under the 60 per cent ownership limit. (The ABT's [1988, pp 46–51] calculations put SMBA and Perth at 65 per cent of the total Australian viewing audience.) Prior to the changes, networks were a loose grouping of stations operating in SMBA with the companies controlling Sydney and Melbourne licences dominating. But after 1987 some kind of branch office control was possible in two of the three markets of Brisbane, Adelaide and Perth in addition to Sydney and Melbourne, as companies with such holdings would remain within the 60 per cent limit. Control over a part of the same company was clearly preferable to dealing with another company concerned to protect the integrity of its position in the network.

The cross-ownership regulation in itself was bound to spark activity in media stock as companies readjusted themselves to the new environment. Similarly, the extension in market share was bound to create a speculative environment, as a premium price could be expected to be paid for effective control over the Australian television audience. This was particularly so in 1987–88, when it appeared that the 60 per cent audience share would be raised to 75 per cent. But the regulatory background and the logic of market opportunity cannot explain the resulting inflation of media asset values. Responsibility for that must be shared by financial deregulation and Australia's entrepreneurial business culture of the 1980s.

The prices paid for television stations were underwritten by domestic and foreign banks eager to lend in a newly deregulated environment. Local banks, fearing competition from each other and foreign banks, scrambled for market share, forgetting for a time all the rules about prudent lending and how to compete in an oligopolistic market (that is, 'compete' in an arranged sort of way so that risks are minimised and market shares become predictable—as had happened for most of the previous 30 years). They actively sought potential debtors, bidding against each other for the rights to service bigger and bigger debts of increasingly indebted clients.

The availability of easy credit fitted all too well the public company logic of the 1970s and 1980s which had been kept in check by financial regulation. That logic encouraged debt and discouraged equity and cash reserves as those made a company liable to takeover by another with long credit lines. In this climate, publicly listed companies had to go sufficiently into debt to stave off takeover bids from people seeking to convert equity and cash into tax-benefited debt.

Aiding this logic was the common practice of Australian corporate raiders to buy assets, revalue them upwards, and then borrow against them for additional purchases. Seven and Nine's new owners in this period, Christopher Skase and Alan Bond, were among the biggest culprits here. Revaluations upwards could even occur after asset-stripping. This revaluation was made possible by rising share values and market confidence in the players, particularly as they seemed to be so outward looking, and so keen to establish not simply national, but international profiles. These same corporate raiders also used the size of the interest payable on their debts to minimise tax payments. Only when interest rates reached the 20 per cent level, in the context of asset values which diminished rather than rose, did this logic unravel.

Of additional help were Australia's lax companies and securities laws, low accountancy standards, light regulation, and penal sanctions. Differing state business laws did not encourage transparency. Funds and the political will were lacking for corporate investigations. Creative accountancy practices could, for example, lead to public reporting of profits by companies such as Skase's Qintex group, in the 1987–88 financial year, projecting profit after tax to be higher than profit before tax (Donnelly 1990, p 19). The mid-to-late 1980s saw debt financing move into television in an *extensive* way. By early 1988, Alan Bond's companies accounted for 10 per cent of Australia's external debt and were among the companies which paid little or no tax.

Changes in the operating rules, combined with easy credit in a deregulated financial market and Australian corporate practice, did not simply inflate television station prices: it blew them out. The value of the Nine and Ten networks doubled overnight (*Sydney Morning Herald*, 27 April 1987). Max Walsh argued that Packer and Murdoch (who sold Ten) received a gift of $1 billion as the value of their assets rose from $800m to $1.8 billion (cited in Schultz 1989, pp 68–84). Speculation in television assets reached phenomenal proportions as the three networks acquired new owners for an estimated $2.5 billion price tag for all three. These new owners were prepared to pay a premium for such strategic positions in the Australian television market. The US broadcasting journal *Channels* put the prices graphically: Alan Bond's Bond Media paid US$88 per viewer for Nine; Frank Lowy's Westfield group paid US$80 for Ten; Christopher Skase's Qintex group paid US$49 for Seven (Ben Bock 1988, p 46). These prices per viewer made metropolitan Australian television stations among the most expensive in the world.

Corporate debt creation in television was further assisted because the new proprietors were taking their initial decisions in the midst of a share market and property boom. The share market boom ended in October 1987, so it cannot account for the profligacy of 1988 and early 1989, although it can help to account for the initial prices paid. The property market was levelling off by mid-1989, but until then it had seemed that no matter how much was paid for a property, it could be sold at a profit just down the line.

The companies who bought into television were not simply after media industry cash flows to service interest payments to finance further corporate expansion. They were also acquiring assets which could be integrated into their other diverse activities in complementary or 'synergistic' ways. Bond, for instance, was putting a package together that saw Bond University as a user for his satellite space (in the provision of distance education) alongside Sky Channel (a pub and club direct broadcast by satellite service) and the Nine Network. The journalism students at Bond University would benefit from the link with Channel 9 (thereby giving its journalism school a competitive edge over rival ones). Bond University was also part of a real estate development whose property values would increase by siting a university in the neighbourhood. Bond's brewing and other national companies would benefit from the Nine Network being within the same company stable: there was scope for integrated national marketing packages, including television program sponsorship. Finally, television network ownership conferred a certain prestige value which could be traded in the dealings of the company in the marketplace and with government.

Both the new network owners and the banks promoted the 'media' as a growth industry in the business of providing 'information services' and 'software' (as 1980s nomenclature came to describe the humble television program). Information was power. Information was a (tradeable) asset. Knowledge was power, and therefore control over knowledge was the route to greater power and wealth. The information sector was identified as the development sector. So our property developers (Skase, Bond and Lowy) moved in on knowledge and entertainment, bringing with them practices, accountancy techniques, and methods of asset development finetuned over years in the property trade. Underlying their moves appeared to be the notion that information asset values could be just as unrelated to cash flow and profit levels but, nonetheless, just as capable of enormous capital gains as real estate values. It seemed that a new and immensely profitable market was developing, where these property developers could occupy strategic places. In an emerging information economy, assets were now those previously intangible things that were only profitable in circulation: the fickle audiences and consumers of entertainment and information. Getting into television meant becoming part of the information revolution; in fact it was a pivotal institution in this process. And it was made more important by the convergence of telecommunications and mass communications.

Also, it was commonly assumed that, by the turn of the century, there would be (in the words of a Time Warner executive) only five or six large global communications companies. Skase and Bond, at least, wanted to have a shot at becoming two of them. They attempted to control as much of the circulation of intellectual property as they could. Bond extended his interests into Hong Kong television and British satellite television. Skase extended his interests to US production companies (inculding film and television 'colorisation' companies) and he even attempted to buy up a Hollywood major, United Artists. These companies were reacting to a trend towards international oligopoly in cinema, VCR markets, publishing, and Pay TV markets in the 1980s. This trend redrew established connections within and between language markets, pushing the international book, the international television program (including now information and sporting programming), and, of course, that old familiar chestnut, the international film.

COMING UNSTUCK

It is clear now just how misguided was this game plan. The television industry was not complacent in SMBA. There simply was not room for rapid increases in advertising revenues there. Australia, according to 1984 rankings, was second only to the US in terms of advertising expenditure as a proportion of gross domestic product. Additionally, television's total market share of advertising revenues compared favourably with equivalent market environments, Canada and the US, where 'networking' was often held to be more advanced.

The expected benefits of national integration was also based on some questionable assumptions. Take advertising. The national integration of advertising preceded the national integration of programming by many years. Sophisticated national advertising placement strategies evolved in ad agencies to get around the then relatively disconnected Australian television system. Just because the networks were not doing the coordinating of national advertising did not mean that efficient and effective coordination was not being done by the ad agencies.

The national integration of programming and the move to simultaneous programming produced mixed results. The previous system, wherein connection and disconnection existed side by side, permitted a degree of audience community knowledge about appropriate program scheduling. The disconnected system accommodated the different climatic and cultural conditions in the different capitals. Subtropical Brisbane, for example, goes to sleep half an hour to an hour earlier than Sydney. Such programming flexibility and tailoring to local knowledges were now out. The national programming which evolved was, perforce, most critically centred on fitting somewhere between Sydney and Melbourne. Under these conditions, some of the benefits of a nationally integrated system were cancelled by the losses associated with locally unresponsive scheduling. Accompanying this loss of flexibility was a loss of local program production capacity and identity. Together, these may well have cancelled out any benefits from having simultaneous programming and national programming.

The extension of additional television services to regional Australia proved something less than a licence to print money. Regional television companies were faced with the huge capital costs involved in building and maintaining television transmitters and signal translation facilities. Problems of signal reach also accompanied their move onto the UHF band, not as suitable for signal transmission over distance as VHF. The regional stations were just not able to be milked of profits as the US literature suggested they should have been. In many cases, programs were already supplied at minimal cost to regionals to permit them to develop the infrastructure for the network of regional stations required by aggregation.

The attempt to establish asset values unrelated to cash flows in the information sector overlooked the difference between property values and information market values. The stability and profitability of the Australian commercial television industry was itself a product of cost monitoring and managed competition. It was not a given. Nor was it achieved by licence scarcity. By 1965 Australia had four networks reaching nearly 60 per cent of the viewing audience; with the advent of SBS-TV in metropolitan centre in the mid-1980s this had increased to five well-established networks covering 65 per cent of the viewing audience.

Each of the new commercial network proprietors had limited broadcasting experience. And this showed in their incapacity to manage costs and competition. Each used debt, not equity, to finance their takeovers. This exposed them in the contexts of high interest rates after 1988 and downturns in advertising revenues in 1990–91. Each, when faced with considerable interest bills in late 1988, engaged in cut-throat competition in an attempt to increase market share at the others' expense. Expenditure on local and imported programs dramatically escalated in the 1988–89 financial year: the cost of overseas programming doubled, local program costs rose by nearly a third, and general expenditure increased by a third (Wright 1989). Australia, with 17 million people, was paying more for the broadcasting rights of *all* kinds of US television than countries many times its population size such as the UK, Germany, Italy and Japan. Australian competition for 'scarce' US program resources led commercial networks to enter into unprecedented output contracts with US production houses and the Seven Network signed an affiliation agreement with the US NBC network in early 1989. Australian television was now carrying part of the cost of developing programs which US audiences, let alone Australian ones, would never see. And this was at a time of record domestic interest rates. Additionally, for at least the Nine and Seven networks, management fees paid to the management team and parent company more than doubled in the same period.

The result: television revenues, despite rising 15 per cent in 1989 (and 18 per cent in the financial year 1988–89), could barely meet the increased programming and managerial costs. This left virtually no money to pay rising interest bills on debt. Costs had to be brought under control; and this would mean a severe contraction in the television industry not seen since the oil crisis of the mid-1970s. But it was equally clear that getting costs under control would not be enough to save the entrepreneurial firms. They needed cashed-up partners to bail them out.

THE SHAKE-OUT

What was left for the entrepreneurial companies? With their ambition to be global media corporations coming unstuck and corporate survival looking increasingly shaky, they attempted to connect with global corporations. In September 1989, Lowy sold Ten to a consortium of local and overseas groups, suffering a $280m loss in the process (*Sun-Herald* 3 September 1989, p 6). The Ten Network's new owners exploited loopholes in the Broadcasting Act prohibiting foreign ownership above 20 per cent, leading to 44 per cent of Ten in control of foreign companies—including Thames television (10 per cent), Daily Mail & General Trust (14.6 per cent), BT Australia (11.5 per cent), and Murdoch's News Corporation (4.9 per cent). But even this was not enough to stave off receivers, who were called in by the network's bankers in September 1990 with the collapse of its owner, Northern Star Holdings, with debts of $455 m. Seven, too, went into the most spectacular receivership (the Qintex group of companies owed $1.4 billion).

In mid-1990, Bond Media executives dutifully plied the offices of US media companies seeking companies interested in an Australian junior partner. They reportedly had a consortium lined up which included CBS, Paramount, a Paramount executive, Television New Zealand, and Banker's Trust to take up a 30 per cent stake in Bond Media and provide a much needed capital injection into the company of some $232m (*Variety* 30 May 1990, p 48). International company integration, with Australia as an offshoot on the parent's terms, seemed set to occur.

This integration was supported by the banks. The Australian clients, to whom they had so assiduously extended generous credit lines and encouragement, were retrospectively labelled corporate cowboys. They supported television network moves to have the existing loophole permitting up to 49 per cent foreign ownership regularised. A lift of the foreign ownership level to 40–49 per cent was mooted by Labor officials before the 1990 federal election. Prime Minister Bob Hawke, was even alleged to have promised it to Nine's then Chief, Sam Chisholm. Creditors saw overseas investors, like the US networks and program production suppliers, adding a premium of somewhere between 30 and 40 per cent to network asking prices (Burchill 1990). It was assumed that US media groups would want to keep in place the unparalleled arrangements the entrepreneurs had entered into with them, that international media groups would want to buy into the Australian market to keep alive their hopes of developing global perspective, and that such groups would have the added incentive of the cheaper price of money in the US and UK markets compared to Australia. Of course this is not how the networks and banks represented the situation. These individuals were prepared to bail Australia out; they did not want to interfere in Australian programs; after all the regulatory authority, then the ABT, looked after that area effectively.

The federal government, and more particularly its communications minister, Kim Beazley, faced a stark choice. The loophole could be maintained or regularised. In the latter case all Australian networks would quickly become 40–49 per cent foreign controlled and probably affiliated to the three major US television networks, with consequences for the kind and nature of Australian commercial programming ([Melbourne] *Sunday Age* 13 May 1990). Alternatively, there could have been a return to 20 per cent foreign ownership which would leave each of the networks open to cheap takeover bids from Australian investors and leave the banks with substantial debts to write off (an estimated $2 billion of debt was estimated to be carried by the television industry in 1990 (*Sunday Herald* (Melbourne) 29 March 1990). The Labor government, facing a Labor caucus largely opposed to lifting the ownership ceiling as a means of bailing out the banks and the entrepreneurs for their bad investment decisions, supported Beazley in a return to the 20 per cent ownership level.

The effect of this ruling was immediate. Bond Media had trouble meeting its $367m debt and this drove the network's resale to Bond's major creditor, Kerry Packer. The limitation on foreign ownership made it more difficult for the liquidators of the Seven Network to get the $635m price-tag they demanded in January 1990. The liquidator, operating at the behest of the banks, was reluctant to see the price-to-earning ratio come down from the estimated 13:1 tag to the 5:1 ratio implicit in Packer's bid for Nine. The major bank creditors of Seven (State Bank of NSW, ANZ, Chase, Bank of America, Societe Generale and Hong Kong Bank), were faced with the prospect of selling immediately and facing a $235m write-down, or holding on for twelve to eighteen months in the hope of obtaining a better price (this stretched out to two to three years as the Australian economy entered recession). The receivers of Seven and Ten chose to hold onto the assets and in 1991 the major creditors—the banks—formalised their involvement as part-owners of Seven and Ten. Having caretakers in charge of two of the three commercial networks was not in the interests of industry stability, or long-term planning within the networks, and did not augur well for equalisation.

The real issue by 1990 was who was going to suffer the most for the corporate and lending madness of the late 1980s: the television industry or the banks. If it were to be the television stations, they would either be taken over or continue to be in hock throughout the 1990s (in such a scenario, ongoing local production difficulties and increased US television content could be expected). If it were to be the banks, they would have to accept losses and to write down media values to which they contributed so much, but this would lead to some recovery in program capacity should the economy move out of recession. In the event both paid a heavy price.

In 1990, Australian television managements was being hit on at least three fronts: continuing high levels of debt, high interest rates, and a dramatic slowdown in the rate of increase of advertising revenues (down to 6 per cent after a 15 per cent increase in 1989). The resulting cost-cutting threatened the standard and quality of television. The ABT, responding to television station submissions, made concessions on Australian content requirements. Australian programs, since the late 1960s, have been the key to prime-time ratings success. Their diminution, perceptions of falling quality, and a virtual moratorium on new programs on the part of the commercials left a gap in commercial network offerings to the public that the ABC, to some extent, filled through its partnerships with independent producers. It introduced new programs such as *Police Rescue* (1990) and *Sylvania Waters* (1992), and it screened 1991's highest rating local mini-series, *Brides of Christ* (1991), followed up the next year with *The Leaving of Liverpool*. (The former achieved ratings of 32–33 and the latter 23–25 in Sydney and Melbourne: see Given 1993, p 23.)

Commercial network cost-cutting did not just impact upon television's standing with its audiences; it also impacted upon advertisers. Ten's ratings suffered from public perception of corporate failure and cost-cutting, perceptions from which it was still recovering in 1993. Unlike previous downturns in the television industry there was no cross-ownership to limit adverse comment about television in newspapers (as Fairfax, Packer, Murdoch and the Herald and Weekly Times were alleged to have done in the past).

The television industry faced the 1990s feeling the chill winds that swept over their film, documentary and television mini-series cousins after 1987. A new austerity arrived. Gone were the $1m parties to celebrate *Neighbours*'s 1000th episode, the helicopter pub-crawls, the flash, imported grog on the premises. Staff were laid off, salaries were cut, productions were shelved and the marble decorated head offices were sold off. And there was no immediate end in sight as a deepening recession pushed television advertising revenues down delaying further any recovery in the balance sheets of highly geared companies.

In this context, Australian government funding initiatives through the ABC, the Film Finance Corporation, SBS and the Australian Film Commission became more important to Australian production capacity in mini-series, one-off drama, documentaries and documentary series (and, therefore, a greater proportion of the international export profile). New/old proprietors like Kerry Packer sought a return to a stable oligopolistic environment which would see them doing just enough to maintain an edge over competitors. Packer's record, like his father Frank's, was never one of destroying the competition; he simply wanted to maintain an edge.

THE LOST POSSIBILITIES OF AUSTRALIAN TELEVISION

So an industry which had not lost money since 1957 finally did so in 1989–90 and 1991–92. The first of these losses was a remarkable achievement, the second an outcome of the recession and the high costs involved in delivering equalisation. In 1989 television networks were operating at a loss in an environment where advertising revenues did not decrease; indeed, they actually increased well above inflation. Revenues had been mostly increasing since 1980. This was not an industry hit by falling sales, a recession, or diminishing returns. It was an industry 'hit' by rising sales, an overheated economy and increasing returns.

Many possibilities have been lost to the Australian film and television industry. Australian television had so much going for it. It already had a competitive television market dedicated to producing relatively low-cost television drama and informational programming. It was used to producing popular product. It was well placed to take advantage of the emerging export markets for popular television opening up in Europe and the UK with the introduction of commercial television, cable, and direct broadcasting by satellite. As the restricted and paternalistic services in the European system were being broken down, there had probably never been (apart from the beginning of the First World War[3]) a more propitious time for Australia to secure a larger international market niche. Furthermore, Australia had a comparatively debt-free television system. Apart from the capital requirements to enable equalisation and the third Perth licence, a television system was already in place with five-channel competition in the major capital city markets. Each of the commercial licensees were either longstanding companies whose investment had been recouped many times over or people who had not paid huge entry prices to get into the market. The existing Australian television networks were thus well poised to take advantage of the changing profile of international television and the development of demand for popular television programs.

Australia's comparative advantages did not stop there. As of the mid-1980s, the structural impediments to an effective nationally coordinated market in television programs, as distinct from a nationally coordinated market in advertising (which was there from inception), were removed. Perth joined the SMBA networks with its third commercial station. Equalisation permitted the greater integration of regional markets into the national system. For the first time it appeared that the whole television system, not just SMBA, would pay equally for Australian programming. Changes in the basic technological infrastructure, with AUSSAT sending messages over distance, led to a reduction of the networking cost. Australian television had the money and the technological infrastructure for an expanded and higher budget production capacity in drama and informational programming. Australia was, in short, lucky. The trauma and investment costs of establishing and managing a competitive environment were behind it. (France, Germany, Italy, Spain—even the UK—were only now moving into this era.) And the final pieces, conferring additional economies of scale in the national market courtesy of equalisation, were now in place.

The Australian television system was so well poised in the international market, well able to produce a commodity capable of export into English language and European markets, capable of producing not simply more, but better quality television. It was well placed to manage on its own terms the popular audience-oriented internationalisation taking place in the more profitable parts of the international television system and well able to develop a market niche as a medium-sized production centre.

But internationalisation was not to happen on quite so favourable terms. The Australian commercial television system managed to erode its comparative advantage of a debt-free television service and acquire debts in excess of television establishment costs. It increased production costs with no accompanying increase in standards and later stripped down production values with a loss in standards. Producers had to compete in the national and international markets without the benefit of a secure domestic television system contributing in generous measure to production. Yet for all these difficulties Australian producers continued to be relatively successful as medium-level international program producers. In a way, they had to be. Program export, co-productions and offshore developments were necessary after 1989 to ensure continuity of production and lock in desperately needed non-Australian sources of production finance.

While Europe was struggling because there were now more television stations reducing advertising revenues and new television stations eating into the audience shares of existing broadcasters, Australia was struggling with the same number of television stations and relatively static audience shares. Australian commercial television operators awash with talk of the need for an international orientation, turned inward instead of outward. Instead of managing a competitive market environment—as had Packer, Fairfax, the Herald and Weekly Times and Murdoch—the entrepreneurs engaged in a critically destructive competition which squeezed margins, lifted production costs and the price of imported programming and led to international integration on less favourable terms to Australian television.

PICKING UP THE PIECES

Creditors, the industry and politicians found the pieces difficult to put together. Adjustments were made more difficult by the deep recession the Australian economy entered into in 1991 and from which, by mid-1993, the economy was barely recovering. The recession affected advertising income and corporate expectations of growth; it fuelled bankruptcy and bad debt, and led to falls in interest rates and the low inflationary expectations and growth that had been a feature of the 1950s and 1960s. The governmental climate changed with instability in the governing party leading to a change of Prime Minister in late 1991 as Paul Keating replaced Bob Hawke, and the emerging possibility of a Liberal–National Party government dedicated to fundamental reconstructions of governmental taxation, investment and employment policies. All gave a sense of a continuing holding pattern of crisis.

With unemployment at 11 per cent nationally and contracting advertising revenues, large advertisers restricted their budgets and their spread to core metropolitan markets, and looked to overseas markets with better prospects for investment and returns on advertising expenditure. In these circumstances the networks faced limited growth opportunities or even contraction. But the recession's impact was worse in regional television markets. It came as the technological infrastructure, offices and production facilities in regional centres needed to be developed and paid for to permit successful broadcasting in the newly expanded service areas in New South Wales, Queensland and Victoria. With the national advertisers' partial withdrawal from regional markets to core metropolitan markets, the expectation that the regionals could expect a growth of their share of national television advertising revenues up to their proportion of the Australian market proved illusory in the short term. Additionally, large sections of the regional economy were disproportionately affected by the recession with sustained crises in wool, wheat and other commodities. Many regional television markets were in crisis. The federal government found it necessary to waive the collection of licence fees as a means of reducing the cost burden to the regionals at a time when they needed to meet the additional burden of establishment costs (this amounted to a $14.1m rebate in 1991–92: see Given 1993, p 24). Regional operators were forced to have a greater reliance upon local service area advertising, with many stations maintaining production facilities in regional centres to subsidise local advertising production. These operators increasingly dealt with the networks on the networks' own terms.

Meanwhile, Australia's wealthiest man, Kerry Packer, placed further pressure on Seven and Ten by writing down the value of Nine's program assets and moving to limit the debt burden of the network. This undercut the value of Seven and Ten and put pressure on their creditors to accept write-downs and losses. In late 1992 and early

1993 Westpac's own difficulties placed it under pressure to sell Ten to reduce its bad debts.

Packer was also at the forefront of moves against Australian content provisions, particularly in drama. In turn, the 'consensus' that had existed between the production industry and the television industry was overturned. The stations looked to additional revenue growth from multinational advertisers, for whom the high cost of developing a local television commercial had acted as a major disincentive to their market entry. They supported the lifting of the prohibition on the screening of 'foreign' ads (Australian audiences became habituated to ads for left-hand drive cars). Television network managements sought increasingly more favourable deals with local producers which forced those producers into deals with overseas broadcasters from product inception.

With a succession of different ministers (between December 1991 and May 1992 there were four different ministers—Kim Beazley, John Kerin, Graham Richardson and Bob Collins) and the prospect of a change in government in 1993, policy was destabilised. Further upsetting the mix was the problem of negotiating more television services (Pay TV, cable television, and additional free-to-air broadcasting), with these new television services being expected to reduce the audience and market shares of the existing television stations. Sections of business, particularly multinational corporations and some local groups, sought an opportunity to become involved in the new television technologies (while television proprietors sought to influence policy to minimise their impact upon themselves). With 'policy' in flux, different players sought different kinds of advantages with respect to television. At times the networks appeared to be accommodated on the grounds of local involvement, Australian content trade-offs, and playing political favourites in the context of a close 1993 election (ultimately won by the ALP). At other times policy appeared to favour the new television technologies by favouring 'new players' in the market, particularly the private telecommunications carrier, Optus, and local and multinational television and film interests. At the same time, decisions on Pay TV, once taken, were challenged in the Federal Court in 1993 and implemented badly (through faulty tendering processes). In such circumstances, the ground rules of television into the 1990s and beyond seemed in constant crisis which affected television's growth and investment prospects.

Television was now operating in the context of a new business environment resembling the three decades older, pre-entrepreneurial one, in that it was predicated on low inflation, conservative estimations of asset values, and low levels of debt. While asset values were expected to recover with share price recovery, television managements would have a different set of attitudes than the entrepreneurs: a conservative attitude to debt, a reliance upon equity, a careful management of costs, and an obligation to shareholders. Additionally, these businesses were operating in an environment in which regulatory, public and court attitudes to corporate behaviour enforced levels of probity and disclosure not required before.

In this context, television—particularly broadcast television—seemed to have entered a new phase of additional competition and limited advertising revenue growth. There was no fillip to the industry on the horizon to boost flagging fortunes and a down-at-heel broadcasting image like the introduction of colour television had in 1975. This time advances in television technology represented a problem for the economics, practices, and taken-for-granted norms in a way that recalls the adjustments in the wake of the third commercial station in SMBA in the last half of the 1960s.

In this context *Entertainment Business Review* declared that the broadcast television industry was entering a new phase: that of a mature (and possibly declining) industry (*EBR* 1991, pp 1–3). *EBR* identified the real issue facing television business in Australia as adapting to these new circumstances of limited growth and declining market shares for the foreseeable future. It argued that for the previous thirty years, television had been a 'growth industry' constantly requiring 'fresh capital' which tended to be 're-invested rather than distributed'; while a 'mature industry' does not 'justify the same levels of investment' and is 'managed to produce profits for its owners (and payments to their lenders).' (*EBR* 1991, pp 1–2). In such a stable and even declining market, profits can be obtained by 'cost-cutting and intense competition for market share' (*EBR* 1991, p 2). In these new circumstances, television managers simply could not continue as they had before. Spending too much would 'overcapitalise' the asset; cutting costs in the wrong places would endanger market share. Competition needed to be carefully managed, lest delicate cost ratios went out of kilter. *EBR* argued that in 'a mature industry' three strategies were possible: 'cost leadership' (cutting costs whilst maintaining market share); product differentiation (allowing for dominance of one or more segments of the market); and 'focus' (working hard to improve existing products and relationships with buyers'). Nine led in 'cost cutting'. It maintained market share in the context of an estimated across-the-board cut of 30 per cent in 1991–92 (*EBR* 1991, p 2) compared to Seven's aim of 10 per cent. Ten was best placed to pursue a strategy of product differentiation through the idea of a 'no frills' network seeking to dominate one or more market segments. Seven was working on 'focus', looking to translate its 'entertainment' lead over Nine into more advertising revenues and seeking to persuade advertisers to 'reconsider Nine's premium' (*EBR* 1991, p 3). *EBR* further argued that the transition to industry maturity required a rethink of the regulatory regime given that it was 'largely designed when the industry was still on a strong growth trajectory' (*EBR* 1991, p 3). Particularly targeted would be cost-sensitive aspects of industry regulation such as broadcast licence fees and Australian content requirements.

EBR's analysis must be qualified. The television industry is certainly in for the flat growth, cost-cutting and need for product innovation stage. But these were also a characteristic of the over-serviced SMBA television markets in the 1965–73 period in the wake of the advent of the third commercial licence introduced in SMBA between 1965 and 1966. Television advertising revenues in this period were also fairly static as television service hours were reduced, repeats increased and a renegotiation of programming costs was required. Low inflation, interest rates and conservative business management with regard to debt and asset valuation were also in place.

In the wake of the fall of entrepreneurial television, Australian television returned to familiar alignments and rhetorical figures from its past. For the stations, the production industry were their employees seeking favourable treatment at the expense of employers. Managers had a right to manage. Entertainment was set against Australian content. Australian content was pitted against flexibility of scheduling and the diversity of audience taste, as Australian content was asserted to be liable to cycles of public support. International competitiveness required an outward-looking industry. The project of 'Australian content' appeared to be the policy preserve of subsidising institutions such as the Australian Film Commission and the Film Finance Corporation. And these worked from the basis of government assistance rather than industry content legislation. The industry attacks on Australian content gained support from significant economic advisory bodies such as the Industry Commission (formerly the Industries Assistance Commission, 1989) and the Bureau of Transport and Communications Economics (1991), which pushed for an end to 'protectionist' measures such as Australian content regulations including those covering advertising.

Advertising was affected first. Big international advertising agencies representing multinational advertisers had long railed against having to remake their 'international' (mostly US) ads for Australian consumption (sometimes as a frame-by-frame remake) pointing to its added cost in the delivery of product and the disincentive it provided to their use of television as an advertising medium. In the new environment of economic efficiency their complaints were heeded, and new television advertising regulations took effect from 1 January 1992 (Mayrhofer 1992, p 124). These new regulations represented a partial deregulation of television advertising: they stipulated that 80 per cent of all ads on a television station over the course of a year must be Australasian-made (this replaced the former regulation requiring 80 per cent of each ad screened to be locally made). Advertising had played an important role in building up and maintaining a production infrastructure and in employing numerous people. The departure of this regulation led to some loss of plant and equipment and of ongoing reinvestment, thereby diminishing the competitive capacity of Australian ad agencies and producers in a newly competitive environment.

Further compounding the difficulties facing producers of advertising and scheduled programs is that they did not find it easy to speak out against this 'rationalisation' because they were either employees of the stations or heavily reliant on work from the stations and multinational advertisers. In this context, an increasingly embattled production industry called upon a rhetoric of social obligation. It sought to mobilise support from the ACTU and Labor politicians, and was caught up in positions which sought to eliminate the power of the media monopolies, the networks. The relationship between imports and local content so fundamental to the definition and politics of the Australian television service was once again being politicised—just as it had been in the 1960s and early 1970s.

4 Television's double face: Of imported and local programming

Television is local in the US and Japan. With local programs making up 96–100 per cent of the schedule, their television faces one way. Australian television faces two ways. Its medium size makes it more outward looking. It is a local window and a window to the world, with local programs making up only half the schedule. Audience allegiances attach in equal measure to local and imported programming. Schedulers attempt to combine the two into a successful complementary mix. Managers balance programming costs of each to competitive advantage. Australian programming negotiates a local presence in the context of imported programming; imported programming needs to be 'naturalised'. Without the cross-subsidisation made possible from cheaper imported programs, there would be only limited local production. But without local production, television would simply not have the mixed profile critical to the successful screening of imports. Imported programming is competition for local production *and* complementary to it. The mix of imported and local content forms the basic contours of television services for viewers, producers, programmers and regulators. For example, the locally produced variety and quiz shows of television's first ten years in Australia ensured that the Hollywood series and serials had a good platform from which to work. Without higher cost local programs on the schedule, those cheaper Hollywood series, serials and movies would not have been as successful. Imported and local programming often fit synergistically within the same program: *Nine's Wide World of Sports* incorporates regular international sporting segments in a locally framed sporting format; and news and current affairs programs (like *Four Corners, Dateline,* and *Sixty Minutes*) routinely incorporate international news feeds and segments.

Australian programming is significantly underwritten by profit margins from the screening of cheap imports. (Lower budget local programs also assist in cross-subsidising higher cost local productions). In the case of the publicly funded broadcasters, the ABC and the SBS, cheap imports fill programming time and free up funds for higher-budgeted local production. Such import cross-subsidisation is critical in all television systems except those of the largest countries. It enables the concentration of program production resources into particular areas and program formats (Cantor & Cantor 1985, p 516).

There are good reasons for cross-subsidisation. Staple forms of television require localisation to be successful. Quiz shows, 'today' shows and 'good morning' shows some variety and sports shows, news and current affairs programs, do not work as exports unless it is to a geographically and culturally proximate market (such as the Canadian one for US producers or the New Zealand one for Australian programs such as *60 Minutes* and *4 Corners*). Working against their export as programs, but not as program concepts, are time differences, accent differences, generic characteristics of the format, the commercial market required by advertisers, and the kind of service expected of national broadcasters by regulators and the charters of public service broadcasters. Such programming is essential to the overall profile of television and the expectations of television regulators of a comprehensive level of service and local employment benefits.

Imports have been critical to Australian service development. They are cheap, prove acceptable to audiences, and they permit Australia—with its substantially smaller population and commercial base—to develop and sustain television services with lengthy operating hours, five national networks, a developed production infrastructure, and an advertising base. Imports enabled Australian television companies to cut the time from initial set up to eventual profitability, permitted a range and variety of programs that would not otherwise be possible in the service because of cost, and underwrote a television-rich environment commensurate with the most developed television markets (US, the UK, Japan). In 1970, for example, Australian television's operation hours were considerably in excess of those obtaining in the UK and western Europe (FACTS 1970, p 9).

But equally, imports led to service underdevelopment. Costly imports (20–55 per cent of program costs for the metropolitan commercial stations over television history)[1] inhibit domestic production by limiting funds available to local producers. By occupying and defining a particular program category there will not be the same need to develop local product. In the early 1970s, Australian content lobbyists claimed that US suppliers dumped low-priced product onto the Australian market, diminishing the market for like Australian programs. Television stations countered by pointing out that they were paying above the international price for such programming. In turn, content lobbyists argued that the high cost of imported programming overall diminished the amounts of money available for local production. More local programming would come from lower prices for imports. Surveying the television industry in 1973, the Tariff Board characterised Australian television as a market suffering under too much competition for imported programming, which had inflated the cost of imports. It even recommended a government program-buying agency to set a ceiling on the costs of imports to commercial stations (Tariff Board 1973, p 30). Imports may be 'cheap' in that individually they are well below the cost of production of equivalent local programs, but they become 'expensive' cumulatively, particularly when there is no substantial local presence in a program category. This is how import prices get set at the limit—and sometimes over the limit—of what the Australian market can bear. In 1973, Australia was 'regarded as capable of returns disproportionately higher than those expected from other English-speaking countries' (Tariff Board 1973, p 30), and this pattern continues today. The total price of imports is critical to the shape and direction of local production. Too high a price limits the extent and depth of the cross-subsidising available to local producers.

There always will be cross-subsidisation. Program producers—whether Hollywood or Australian—expect to gain less from their export markets than from their local markets. Purchasers of imported programs expect a greater slice of profits from imports than they expect to get from equivalent local productions. Without that greater profit share there would be no incentive to import, and import substitution dynamics would emerge, leading to an overall reduction in the export market. Although disputes between Australian stations, program producers and Hollywood producers are not in any conscious way about the extent of the cross-subsidisation taking place but simply about minimising/maximising prices, cross-subsidising dynamics are a fundamental characteristic of the market. As Jock Given observes:

> It is the result of television stations paying as little as possible for *all* kinds of programs in a market where Australian programs, which Australian

broadcasters desperately want, will only be made if substantial licence fees are paid by Australian stations. (Given, correspondence 5 May 1993).

Like the television stations, the local program production sector benefits when as little as possible is paid for imports. This enables local producers to maximise the opportunities for cross-subsidisation; commercial television stations to maximise audiences for and profits from the screening of those imports, and publicly funded broadcasters to get more value for the public money expended. Foreign program exporters, for their parts would like to see greater prices paid in Australia which means keeping cross-subsidisation to a minimum. (The struggle for commercial advantage between television stations and local program producers is over their respective shares of the cross-subsidies available from imports.) Stations and producers enlist Australian government support to ensure that the allocation of resources benefits them more than foreign television exporters, while such exporters (usually) enlist the US government.

Australian regulation, from inception, ensured local ownership of television services. Since 1960 it has mandated various levels of Australian content (Appleton 1987, p 212). Content was first regulated in advertising and regulation was extended over the 1960s to a proportion of scheduled programs and then to specific, high-cost programming formats in drama series and variety. This regulation had important commercial consequences. Content and ownership provisions helped Australian television companies to negotiate with Hollywood suppliers, they ensured that domestic market advantage through vertical integration with US production companies and networks was not available as a form of domestic market leverage. The measures created a kind of floor price for US programs in the Australian market. Additionally, such regulation adjusted the relations between the stations and the local production sector. Content regulation afforded the production sector greater bargaining power in a commercial context which favoured importers and the distribution/exhibition structure of the local television station and network. Regulators saw themselves as arbitrating the relationship between stations, domestic producers and foreign exporters (usually to local production sector and network advantage).

There are clear limits to Australian content regulation. Australian regulators have encouraged a local 'supplement' in particular programming areas such as drama, documentary and variety but also respected the basic economics of the service (the structural importance of imports, the seller's market for US programming, and Australia's limited capacity for indigenisation). They took account of 'the financial viability of stations' in determining content regulations (Brown 1986, p 137). Brown points out that because content regulations extended to all stations, they were 'designed to maintain the solvency of those which are least profitable' (Brown 1986, pp 137–8) and they tended to be set at levels already achieved by stations (Harrison 1980, passim; Moran 1985, p 32). Consequently, content regulations were designed to have, at best, a marginal effect upon production. (During the 1989 Australian Content Inquiry, ABT head, Deirdre O'Connor, repeatedly stressed this as a safety net function of Australian content regulations.)

Generally, US (and British) exporters demand and hold out for higher prices from Australia and Canada than other markets as they regard them as their linguistic and cultural backyards. They always assume prices could rise, so they seek ways of altering market settings in their favour. In this they rely on the economic and structural place afforded them by a competitive television market in both countries. US exporters typically resist regulatory intervention. They make Australian regulation a bilateral trade issue between Australian and US governments, so as to exert more US pressure on Australia to greater effect. And this is a relatively effective strategy: under pressure the French *retaliate*, but the Australians have no option but to continue to negotiate. In the early 1970s and again in the late 1980s and early 1990s US producers enlisted their government's help to wind back state intervention in world cinema and television markets. As part of a push to liberalise trade in services, they particularly targeted, in the later period, production subsidies and content provisions in Australia and elsewhere. As in the early 1970s dispute, when the US producers had the support of local television stations, agricultural exporters would gladly trade regulations in the audiovisual and service sectors for improved access to US markets (Given 1991, p 3).

But pushing Australia too hard can—and did—backfire. Setting too high a price has encouraged import diversification, import substitution and managed competition for US product. In the mid-1960s, stations acquired Australian television drama series following *Homicide*'s extraordinary ratings. This Australian drama presence helped wind back prices for program imports. Program buying 'strikes' instituted in 1966–67 (Moran 1985, p 30) forced import prices down. In the early 1970s, the Seven stations looked to British product from ITV in addition to US product, putting additional pressure upon US prices. In 1970, the ABC became firmly positioned as a purchaser of British product, substantially withdrawing from the high-cost ends of US program purchase. Buying pools came and went, from television's inception in Sydney and Melbourne until the mid-1970s. By the late

1970s these were replaced with less formal agreements to work together on prices paid. The federal government, in its turn, considered intervention aimed at lowering the prices paid through the establishment of a government agency managing program purchase for the commercial sector (Tariff Board 1973, pp 29–30). The threat of intervention helped stations in their negotiations with Hollywood exporters, while receivership of the Ten and Seven Networks in the late 1980s and economic recession in the early 1990s led to a renegotiation of the onerous output agreements with US producers and US networks.[2]

Periods of intense competition for US programming have been followed by periods of sustained cooperation on reducing import program purchase costs. This appears to be a cyclical characteristic of the television market, a consequence of Australia's open commercial system and the important structural place imported programming has in it. Attempting to secure programming advantages through paying more for imported programming is usually undertaken by the lowest rating commercial stations and networks (and sometimes by the ABC, as it is prepared to bid higher prices to secure a particular program). This leads to matching prices and sustained competition, followed by a levelling out and, often, contraction.

The ABC and the SBS rely upon imports just as much as the commercial stations (The SBS even more so), but as national broadcasters they filter and manage program flows differently. The commercial stations' relationships with imported programming are regulated by content rules and commercial competition for audiences; the ABC's and SBS's relationships are determined by the availability of government funding and their respective charters. Driven by social and cultural policy, the ABC and the SBS are expected to complement the commercial stations and to pursue a broadly educational and informing mandate. Unlike the three commercial networks, which rely upon the output created for three—and since 1989 four—US commercial television networks, the ABC and SBS routinely select from a wider range of programming sources. Of the programming the ABC imported in 1984–85, for example 32 per cent was from the BBC, 22 per cent from other British sources, 36 per cent from the US, and the remaining 10 per cent from other countries (calculated from ABC 1985, p 75). Alongside its non-commercial mandate, this enables the ABC to pay less for imports than the commercials. Nonetheless, the ABC, with its greater funding, national reach and audience (on average four to six times the SBS's), pays a competitive import price: anywhere between 40 per cent of what the commercials generally pay to in excess of that amount for sought-after drama series.[3]

From 1970 the ABC dropped out of intense competition with the commercial networks for premium-priced US product—network-screened series and serial programming, and blockbuster movies—and focused upon lower priced programming in children's, movie and sporting areas.

The ABC is limited by its wedding to the BBC as the major source for its prime time programming imports. Its long term associations with the BBC tie it closely to that organisation, giving the BBC an advantageous bargaining position as the Anglophone world's producer of educational, informational programming and 'quality' television drama. These agreements have historically enabled the BBC to factor ABC sales into production budgets, leaving subsequent sales to the Australian commercial stations (after their two ABC screenings) as profit. By contrast, until the late 1980s output agreements, US producers might expect Australian sales, but they could never be sure.

The SBS is in a buyer's market as it is the only Australian network which picks up multilingual programming. It can set prices for imports and rigorously control their cost. Its English language broadcasts rely on sources traditionally ignored by the ABC, such as the US PBS, Canadian CBC and UK's Channel 4. The SBS also picks up product rejected by the ABC. The lower prices offered by the SBS, ensure that its competition with the ABC for programming is to the ABC's advantage. Thus the national broadcasters are more cost-effective in their import management than the commercials.

THE SHAPE OF THE DOUBLE FACE

Both English-speaking Canada and Australia figure disproportionately as markets for Hollywood. They pay more and they buy more series than others. In 1990, for example, both paid more than any other country for half-hour television series. When adjusted for population, Australia paid four times as much per half-hour Hollywood series as the UK. Table 1 compares the average prices for half-hour series and serials for Hollywood programming in 1990. It shows that Australia, with its then estimated 17m people, paid consistently more for Hollywood series and serial programming than the very much larger British (57.4m), West German (62.3m), French (57.6m) and Italian (58.1m) markets. This was also at a time of financially crippled networks and an economy moving into recession.

Canada and Australia represent the best that Hollywood can expect from television exports. Both are Anglophone, culturally proximate to the US, and medium-sized. As noted in Chapter 1, their size limits their import substitution dynamics, particularly at the costly

Table 4.1 Top ten markets for half-hour Hollywood series and serials in 1990

Ranking	Average Cost Country	Cost	Ranking	Average Cost Per Million Viewers Country	Cost
1	Canada (English)	25 000	1	Canada (English)	1 250
2	Australia	15 000	2	Australia	878
3	France		3	Canada (French)	727
4	UK	12 000	4	Hong Kong	608
5	Italy	7 250	5	Belgium	401
6	Germany	6 750	6	New Zealand	341
7	Japan	5 000	7	France	261
8	Canada (French)	4 750	8	Sweden	228
9	Belgium	4 000	9	UK	209
10	Hong Kong	3 500	10	Netherlands	199

Source *Variety*, 15 April 1991 'Global Programming Prices', p M-107. These calculations were made from *Variety's* annual list of global television programming prices. *Variety* lists a minimum and maximum price. The average of the price range has been taken.

end of production. Both rely on US program imports across the drama spectrum and pay a premium price for such programming. Additionally, both have had competitive commercial marketplaces over a long period. This market mix ensures keen competition for imports.

Competitive markets increase overall advertising expenditure and so create a greater pool of funds for program purchase. Australia and Canada occupy second and fourth position respectively behind the US in terms of advertising as a percentage of GNP (1986 figures, Dunnett 1990, p 25). With the US accounting for half of the world's advertising expenditure in 1986 (Dunnett 1990, p 25) locally produced, high-budget programming dominates at the expense of imports. Likewise Canadian and Australian television have a larger pool of funds available for program purchase than in comparable countries. But their smaller size ensures that competition for programming extends to imports and not just to local programming. This enables US program makers to secure high prices and to bargain from a position of strength. Thus Australian and Canadian commercial television dynamics blow out the price of imported programming and also inflate the price-tag for local programs which do not compete with imports—infotainment and sport—with large salaries for local news readers, quiz masters, premium sporting events, talk show hosts, and personalities. However, in the high-cost continuous drama series format—where the local product competes directly with imports, where there is not so much import-substitution as import-supplementation with the local product—there is a tendency towards cost-consciousness.

In Australia and Canada, US producers have been able to organise forms of block booking, whereby Australian and Canadian television buyers must acquire programs they do not want in order to secure programs they do. Such ongoing arrangements provided one of the means by which US producers have tied up the Australian commercial television market to exclude English-language producers from Britain, Canada and New Zealand. As noted in Chapter 3, this Australian purchasing situation became even more distorted in the late 1980s by Australian networks entering output agreements with Hollywood studios and affiliation agreements with US networks. (By early 1993 the Australian networks were seeking adjustments in their favour—they were hoping to get contracts written in Australian dollars, no increase in prices and less reliance on deals which required them to buy programs they did not want along with those they did. They made some progress on these issues.)

With the US being the world leader in commercial television, Australian and English-speaking Canadian television look to high-budget US programs and US styles for their program scheduling and innovation alongside their local innovations in program content and scheduling (the Australian and Canadian comedy 'booms' of the late 1980s and early 1990s). Both countries have, more than other countries, positioned themselves politically, socially and economically in relation to the US and the UK. Their US orientation leads to a greater reliance upon US imports as there is a greater capacity for Hollywood programming to be accepted on local television in Canada and Australia. Stabilising import sources allows for an element of predictability to enter the import component of the service. Their British orientation helps explain why import diversification for both primarily means British-created television. There is less import diversification in Canada and Australia than in European markets, despite the availability of other English-language product. This UK and US orientation goes some way towards explaining why both, apparently importing as much in prime time today as Spain, Germany and France, tend to pay more for programs. Even with the dramatic expansion of operating hours, new broadcast stations, and the beginnings of viable cable and direct broadcasting systems in Europe, the US share of transmission time in Europe is expected to average 25 per cent (Sepstrup 1990, p 95). This is below the 34 per cent US share of transmission time for Australian broadcasters (including the lower rating ABC and SBS) identified by *Television Business International* (1990, p 508). With US programs dominating high-rating commercial network schedules, their US import averages are around 40 per cent of transmission time.

The lack of import diversification by Australian commercial networks inflates imported programming costs (metropolitan commercial stations devoted 45.4 per cent of their overall program budget in 1970 to imports and 31.4 per cent in 1990). However since Canada and Australian rely upon a greater volume of US product, both set upper limits for costs per program. This means that France, the UK, and Germany sometimes pay more for sought after series, serials and movies than will their Australian and Canadian counterparts. But Australia and Canada import more (this parallels the situation in the cinema in the 1920s, when Australia imported more feature films for cinema screening than did Britain [Thompson 1985, p 137]). Although industry statistics on the television export trade do not provide cinema-style country-by-country box office breakdowns and rankings therein, Hollywood's overseas television sales representatives identify their principal export markets as Canada, Australia, the UK, France, Italy and Germany, (and these account for up to 75 per cent of sales (Lenti 1989, p 49). Australia and Canada are also important markets for British exporters. Australia is the next most important market for the British after North America (Lange & Renaud 1989, p 287).

On the up side, both have program export capacity beyond their market size. They operate in the English language (the language to dub and subtitle from in the international system). The need to compete directly against the US product in their domestic market leads to the routine creation of internationally competitive drama programming. Because of their historical positioning between Europe (UK) and the US, their programming circulates in European markets. However, because Australia and Canada buy more Hollywood programming, pay more for it and pay an inflated price on a per capita basis, the amount and nature of locally produced programming is limited by these factors diminishing the funds available for local program production.

THE CHANGING DOUBLE FACE

The relationships between imported and local programming have changed over Australian television history. Take television's developmental phase, 1956–65. Television was introduced in Brisbane, Adelaide and Perth two and three years after its Sydney and Melbourne opening in 1956, arriving in Canberra and the larger regional centres in 1962 and other regional centres from 1963. A third commercial station was added to SMBA between 1964 and 1965. Brian Davies encapsulates this period by describing it as 'radio days, cinema nights' (Davies 1981, p 11). The 'radio' was Australian, the 'cinema' Hollywood. Although only sketchy information is available, it points to stations spending roughly half their program budgets on imports.

Stations in the major capital cities began as stand-alone entities with their own management structures, scheduling priorities and television personalities. In the absence of well-developed interconnections between them, television stations developed a marked local orientation. In SMBA and Perth, television studios were built and well utilised for local infotainment shows, (chat shows, variety shows, tonight shows and news programs) which attracted high ratings. Local production became concentrated within low cost, live television for the local service area and, after 1962, adjacent service areas. Although these locally produced programs were often shared around, they were mostly popular in the metropolitan television market in which they were produced (the local service area dynamics of each market worked against gaining a wide audience outside local areas). The exception here were the quiz shows (carried over from radio and already having a national audience) and some daytime shows.

The availability of imported programming underwrote station independence, the quick expansion of television opening hours and the extension of television services into daytime and the periods immediately before and after prime time. US and British television imports made up for the lack of market interconnection. These provided a source of relatively cheap, high-budget programs which subsidised the local programming infrastructure, provided a schedule for the marginal regional commercial operations, preserved jealously guarded station autonomy and materially assisted stations in moving into profit after their high establishment costs. The old Hollywood movies, contemporary series and serials, and documentary series (nature and adventure) of relatively certain appeal were made cheaply available to Australian television. These Hollywood programs were immediately accessible to audiences and there were not the expectations of Australian-made programs in these categories.

Australian television stations committed themselves to a reliance on US programs, which put them in a seller's market. A two-tiered price structure for their imports emerged, with a premium price being paid for new Hollywood series and serials and a cheaper price for 'old' movies. So high did the series and serial price become that Ken Hall secured the cooperation of competitor stations to institute a program buying pool for them in the late 1950s (Hall 1991, p 42).

There was no pressing need to develop national network markets for local programs. As imports were readily available, the Australian service could survive with a weakly developed 'national' service grid. Television thus took on a largely 'disconnected' character far removed from the kind of service then provided within the US and the UK. Imports ensured that the television stations were favoured at the expense of Australian program providers. This made the situation very unlike that in the US. There the networks (which own stations) were program providers of information and drama to the bulk of US television (and, in this period, retained significant subsequent control over the programs screened).

As cross-subsidies from imports benefited programs generated within local service areas, the common elements in the television services of this period were imports and ads created for national and multinational companies. In this way, imports held up industry rationalisation, efficient networking and cost-sharing of program production between stations. The availability of Hollywood imports encouraged some television proprietors—most notably Frank Packer—in the belief that little local production capacity apart from information programs were necessary for stations to be successful. Ken Hall describes going to TCN 9 in Sydney and finding a place 'not designed to be a television station' because 'they'd built it to run on American product' (Hall 1991, p 40).

Through the period 1956–65 the top ten rating programs were shared by locally produced infotainment and variety and Hollywood serials, series and movies. Local producers were excluded from the higher budgeted and more culturally valued ends of the industry, drama and documentary. In 1959, Hector Crawford estimated that 98 per cent of drama programs were imported (Crawford 1959, p 13). Calculations based on the 1963 Vincent Committee estimates put local drama in April 1961, April–June 1962 and June 1963 at 1.9 per cent, 2.1 per cent and 1.7 per cent of total drama programming, or 1.1 per cent, 1.2 per cent and 0.9 per cent of metropolitan stations' total transmission time (*Vincent Report* 1964, p 31).

With only a weak national market for Australian programs, it was difficult to develop Australian participation in higher budgeted programming areas. Such television relied on economies of scale, central organisation, and effective cost-sharing by stations, factors not then available. Furthermore, television was introduced without any Australian content rules other than the vague directive for stations to use, wherever possible, local talent. Without such rules in place, there was nothing to encourage the development and care of nationally provided programs, the organisation of scale economies, the formalising of networking agreements and cost-sharing for program production in them. As a consequence, television further disenfranchised an already disenfranchised Australian film industry at the nadir of its development. Neither drama producers nor documentary makers found a significant place within television until the mid-1960s. In these circumstances producers of drama and documentary had to look to US and British television for production work. Charles Chauvel made a documentary series for the BBC—*Walkabout* (Cunningham 1987, p 37)—and Lee Robinson worked on high-rating US documentary series productions (Moran 1987, pp 109–10).

This situation drew criticism. Station dominance over program production encouraged industry critics to identify stations with overseas program suppliers. Advertising agencies in the early 1960s railed against the absence of local drama vehicles for their multinational advertising clients. The 'cinema nights' saw the development of a cultural argument for Australian content—particularly drama content—with the existing import profile being seen to have 'undesirable sociological and cultural consequences' for Australia (*Vincent Report* 1964, p 32). This argument provided a purpose for Australian content regulations as a defensive cultural measure. These regulations were designed to address the undeveloped national service grid while ensuring the continued independence of regional and metropolitan stations from the Sydney and Melbourne groups. They were specifically designed to encourage a move towards higher budgeted television programming in documentary and drama.

The regulations—advertising and general Australian content quotas in 1960, drama quotas in 1967—contributed to the formation of a national market for high-cost, nationally circulated programs and so increased the production industry presence in television. The regulations had the bonus of regulating overseas prices by stabilising the proportion of advertising revenues to go to pay for local productions. Also, setting a regulatory floor under existing Australian content levels ensured that competition for audiences was on the basis of this level. Advertising regulations had the unexpected by-product of modernising Australian film production infrastructures, later critical to higher budgeted local production.

In television's middle period, 1965–86, imported and local content entered into a different relationship. The third commercial station and the extension of television to larger regional markets brought a second stage of industry rationalisation requiring formalised networking in SMBA. The third commercial licence in SMBA created a demand for programming that the existing international industry simply could not meet (Moran 1985, p 30). As a consequence, operating hours had to be cut back, the number of repeats went up, and the 'national service grid' became critical to local operators as a means of rationalising local production. More television in SMBA thus destabilised the existing local–international nexus and led to intense and crippling competition for US programming. These conditions ensured that overseas programs continued to make up a very significant cost component of the service from 1966 to 1972, despite the development of a national program market in this period. FACTS estimated that 45.4 per cent of Sydney and Melbourne budgets for local and imported programs were spent on imports in 1969–70 (FACTS 1972, p 41). This period saw the partial integration of regional and metropolitan television markets and desperate attempts by metropolitan stations to widen audience reach by attempting to reach adjacent population centres, with Sydney stations attempting to incorporate Wollongong and Newcastle. This resulted in a gradual decline in local service area programming over the period, replaced by the bicycling of videotapes and from the mid-1970s the increased use of microwave and coaxial facilities.

Political and cultural demands from 1966 to 1974 mostly revolved around Australian content and therefore the recognition by politicians, policy makers and regulators of a production industry separate from and necessarily having different interests in Australian culture than the stations. These demands underwrote moves to reduce import program prices so as to increase the cross-subsidies from the screening of imports to favour local producers and to a lesser extent television stations.

This goal had been partially achieved by 1975, when overseas program expenditure had contracted to 30 per cent of program costs (Brown 1986, p 134), at which point it stabilised for the next seventeen years. The ratings success with Australian television drama, and the limited development of an export market for it in UK, New Zealand, Ireland and sometimes the US, resulted in local drama programming becoming a pivotal component to a weekly schedule. In the late 1960s and early 1970s this led stations deliberately not to schedule high-cost Australian drama programs against each other (one of the positive features of Australian content regulations).

This started to change as Australian drama programming moved towards forms of stripped programming across the week in the wake of *Number 96*'s success (1972–78). These programs—*The Sullivans* (1976–82) in the late 1970s; *A Country Practice* and *Neighbours* in the 1980s—became pivotal to stations' rating profile. This drama format enabled Australian-produced drama's proportion of overall drama broadcasts to increase from 9.2 per cent in 1974 (combined ABC and commercials figure) to 13.1 per cent on the commercial stations in 1988, with the ABC remaining static on 9 per cent (AFC 1975, p 15; calculated from ABT 1988, pp 94, 100)—a far cry from the 1–2 per cent share that characterised Australian television in the late 1950s and early 1960s. However, Australian-produced drama still needed to acquire significant audience shares to keep its place on the schedule.

By the late 1970s this was changing. The regionals were routinely showing much more Australian content than the metropolitan television markets, picking up Australian product from the three networks at competitives prices. A more significant commercial television presence in sports, current affairs and news ensured that an even more integrated national market for infotainment was emerging. As a direct consequence of a more fully developed market for local programs local programs became more important and, the presence of imported programming in the ten top rating programs diminished (Jones 1991, p 28). Overseas programming increasingly occupied filler positions within prime time. This was reflected in the approach to Hollywood program purchase taken by the stations. In the words of a US television production company executive, 'the Aussie broadcasters would band together, screen the shows in Los Angeles in May, then leisurely wait until December to buy when the program had a track record. Also by sticking together they kept prices low and the Americans furious' (Coftus 1987, p 26). Further underwriting these developments was the extension of Australian production presence in the high-cost mini-series (after 1978) and theatrical feature film (by the late 1970s) components of television schedules due to state subsidies and, in the 1980s, tax concessions. In this way the feature revival ensured a presence of Australian movies on local television, inflating Australian drama's schedule presence.[4] These changes are shown in import expenditure as a proportion of local and imported program costs. Import expenditure declined from 42 per cent in 1973 to 32 per cent a year later, leading to an historic low of 22 per cent in 1982 (Brown 1986, p 134).

The contemporary period (since 1987) has seen yet another adjustment in the relation between imported and local programming. The change in ownership of the major metropolitan stations after November 1986 ensured that the pre-existing 'price collusion' for imported programming was replaced with a 'competitive market' as older broadcasting management practices went into eclipse. The new situation was described by a US seller: 'Once again it's a competitive market. The new owners and competition have changed everything' (Coftus 1987, p 26). This competition for US programs was supplemented by a rise in money spent on local program production as a new generation of television owners ignored the cost structures and previous thresholds of the service. Not only did an unprecedented competition for local talent in infotainment genres ensue, but so did the new owners overturn the arms-length thinking that had kept the local stations and US exporters apart for the previous thirty years. To secure domestic competitive advantage, the networks weakened their bargaining power by entering into output agreements with US producers and affiliations with US networks. The concurrent lifting of the two station ownership rule to a maximum population reach for commonly owned stations and the onset of equalisation in regional markets (which saw three commercial stations in regional markets after 1990–91) ensured that national market coordination reached a new level. For the first time, nationwide networking and simultaneous scheduling had reached the 95 per cent of television homes US television accessed from the mid-1950s. This encouraged the further ensconcement of nationwide sporting, variety and infotainment programming and ensured that the existing states-oriented production capacities in those areas were significantly reduced and integrated better into the national grid.

Australian content regulations were no longer required to coordinate the system. The system could now be coordinated on the basis of common station ownership and the equalisation process. Consequently, television station and the network's toleration of Australian content provisions was replaced with varying degrees of antagonism. The 'networks' had always been, of course, publicly against content regulations; but this did not stop them from enjoying the benefits of these regulations 'on the sly'. They became powerful lobbyists against Australian content provisions just as the FACTS membership had been in the 1960s. With the industry shake-out after the excesses of 1987–89, the networks bought fewer local programs, paid less for them and became more resistant to new programming ideas (*EBR* 1991, p 3). Without program innovation and program replacement, local programs—particularly the long-running serial dramas—could no longer sustain their near dominance of the top ten rating programs. Their places were taken by international, usually US, drama programs. Scaled down local production caused import programming costs to rise (because of the greater demand). Additionally, outside production finance contracted with the diminishing value of the tax concessions and the production fund ceilings created by the Film Finance Corporation. The cost of overseas programming increased as a proportion of local and overseas program costs, moving from 20 per cent in 1987–88 to 31.4 per cent in 1989–90 (ABT 1990, p 31); and pressures towards internationalisation through co-productions were felt not only in mini-series but in series and serial production, as industry and non-industry sources of finance contracted. Local production companies looked towards exports, this attention extending to documentaries such as the ABC's international co-production *Nature of Australia* and, for the first time, to infotainment programming, with Beyond International leading the way (Treffry 1991, p 20) with its diverse production slate including *Beyond 2000* (exported over 70 countries and dubbed into five language [Cash 1990, p 10]).

Gradually the cultural argument for Australian content shifted ground from its 1960s and 1970s role of guarding against the 'undesirable sociological and cultural consequences' of imports, to be replaced by the arts 'cultural sovereignty' argument of the 1980s and by the cultural expression, diversity and innovation argument of the 1990s (flagged in the 1993 ALP election platform, 'Distinctly Australian'). In these last two drama has a special role to play whether in developing a sense of national identity and culture or of utilising Australian potential, and they are used to justify film and television production subsidies. This shift reflected the relative confidence that an Australian presence in infotainment programming and sports was secure under networked arrangements but drama not.

GETTING IT WRONG

In the current television environment, additional adjustments are being made to regulatory and market settings with the Broadcasting Services Act and, in the medium term, with the provision of additional television services through Pay TV (Davies and Spurgeon 1992, pp 85–92). Against this backdrop a growing body of criticism of existing broadcasting arrangements has emerged. Critics see Australian television as another cosseted Australian industry that needs to be exposed to the discipline of the market (McGuinness 1990; Jones 1991; Industries Assistance Commission 1989a and 1989b; Bureau of Transport and Communications Economics 1991). Australian content regulations generally, drama and advertising regulations particularly, and foreign ownership regulations have been targeted. With Australian advertising content being deregulated, pressure is applied to program content regulations, which are seen as significant barriers to international trade and economic efficiency.

These critics allege that Australian content quotas and ownership provisions are inefficient market support mechanisms, provide indirect subsidies to the Australian film industry, 'discriminate in favour of dramatic actors against other performers' (Jones 1991, p 72), and constitute an unacceptable tariff 'designed to protect local dramatic actors from imported competition and should be abolished' (Jones 1991, p 72). They argue that existing arrangements needed changing so as to enable the television stations more flexibility to meet popular demand. As the Bureau of Transport and Communications Economics put it:

> [T]he main problem with the current regulatory arrangements for Australian adult drama is that these arrangements distort the broadcaster's decision-making process by limiting programming choice in response to audience preferences. Programmers have been required to meet a certain quota of Australian drama irrespective of cost or whether viewers may prefer to watch other programs. Consequently, the requirements also provide the domestic drama production industry with considerable protection by 'guaranteeing' a market for a certain amount of output. The output guarantee, of course, would also lead to upward pressures on production costs. Without the Australian drama quota... programmers would have an incentive to show low-priced, Australian produced, popular programs in preference to drama. (1991, p 148)

Yet Australian television has been, in western terms, one of the *least* protected and cosseted of international television industries. It operated a competitive television environment long before the UK and western Europe. Its television market has provided one of the most enduring and profitable markets for US and UK television suppliers. Its drama programming quota was created to provide greater program diversity.

Drama was not as significant a cost burden to the networks as was news and current affairs, which exceeded drama program expenditure by a factor of 2.5 over the three years 1989–91 (ABT 1991b, p 83). Drama programming costs were on the same level as sports programming and well below costs of infotainment. The disincentive to produce lower priced Australian programming was exaggerated. In terms of the pre-eminence of drama programming on the television schedule—representing 55.6 per cent of prime time on Australian metropolitan commercial stations and 34.7 per cent on the ABC in 1990 (ABT 1991b, p 24)—its Australian component was 16.3 per cent on the commercials and 6.9 per cent on the ABC (ABT 1991b, p 32). There was three and a half times more imported drama than Australian-produced drama on the metropolitan commercial stations in prime time despite content rules; and there was five times more imported drama than local drama on the ABC in prime time. Between 6 pm and midnight, Australian drama made up only 10.4 per cent of Australian programming on metropolitan commercial stations (on the ABC it was 3.3 per cent), 5.2 per cent of all programs and; 1.7 per cent on the ABC (ABT 1991b, pp 34, 36). Australian drama quotas were not designed to replace substantially either imported drama content or low-priced Australian programming. Rather, they were designed to underwrite, within the drama programming category, a limited Australian presence. Australian-produced drama as a programming category was not in a position to 'take over' from imports in prime time; nor was it a substantial inhibitor of alternative Australian programming. But it was no surprise that drama—without the natural advantages conferred on other program categories like sports, news, quizzes, and current affairs—was targeted. It is the high-budget local programming that is most dispensable, and the programming area in which the extent and direction of cross-subsidy are most politically contentious.

There is little evidence of Australian content quotas putting upward pressures upon drama production costs. Upward pressure is exerted in areas where a significant local advantage exists and where competitive pressure from imports are not felt. Industry featherbedding is rife in news, current affairs, light entertainment and sport, and not nearly to the same extent in long-running series and serial drama. The settings adopted first in the points system and then in its later incarnations ensured that such low levels of Australian dramatic content were stipulated that domestic drama producers would continue to operate in a competitive market. Consequently, cost-conscious television persisted in series and serial production right through the industry excesses of the 1980s. Of additional assistance in keeping costs under control was that series and serial producers were excluded from participation in the subsidised and tax concession feature film and mini-series cost explosions of the 1980s.

Measures like direct assistance and tax concessions (under section 10BA of the Income Tax Assessment Act) are to many economists more 'transparent' structures than quotas, and so should lead to greater efficiency in the allocation of resources. Under this analysis, long-running series and serial dramas have been disproportionately advantaged by the protectionist regime (McGuinness 1990, p 21). But this was not so. Nearly thirty years of content regulation never led to the cost break-outs under 10BA; instead it led to a cost-conscious and export-oriented programming (as producers needed to look to overseas sales as a way of increasing slender profit margins). This was something which drama's infotainment and light entertainment cousins never had to do. Australian television's regular—though minor—presence on Dutch, German, English, Irish and New Zealand television over the past two decades has been mainly through this series and serial output. This is why the Australian drama series industry is seen as one of the most efficient and cost-effective in the western world and proferred as a model in Europe of film series being put on a 'highly industrial footing' (Lange & Renaud 1989, p 119).

Regulation and production subsidies were not mounted in drama because of outrageously high-cultural demands for quality which discriminated against other forms of entertainment (contra Jones 1991, p 26; Docker 1991, passim). Australian policy makers—reacting like most western policy makers—tailored their program quotas and subsidies to 'problematic' program categories for which an indigenous programming presence could not be taken for granted. Content regulations have been successful in nurturing an internationally competitive television drama industry because they were specifically designed to have only a marginal effect. They ensured an Australian supplement in drama. They did not aim for an Australianisation of the drama component of the schedule, and they made some producers from Hector Crawford on to seek export markets. This economic rationale can be lost sight of because the purpose behind the regulations is cultural, not economic. Although this cultural logic is based on a non-economic calculus of cultural expression and national identity formation, it is nonetheless associated with an economic strategy for Australian television production which adjusts market settings to maximise the competitive edge of Australian programming.[5]

Changing the regulatory structures would readjust relations between imported and local content in television. US exporters could extract more money from the Australian market if its local content rules were abolished and replaced by a 'more transparent' strategy of direct production subsidy. This would remove the marginal advantages enjoyed by Australian drama producers, adjust upwards the 'ceiling' placed on imported program prices, and would translate into a greater proportion of US drama programs being screened on Australian television. Network cost-cutting also inflates import program prices and volumes as Australian programming is the first cut, being the most expensive per unit of time. Drops in local production reduce the diversity of local output, turning attention to and increasing competition for imports. Given the important place of drama on the schedule, less Australian television drama would increase the US bargaining position in the category. Without drama content regulations, there would be a further concentration of local production funding into infotainment programming as the help provided by regulations for drama content was removed.

New television services and television technology delivery systems require long lead times before moving into profitability (to cover high establishment and distribution costs and low initial audience shares). This limits their local production capacity and leads to extensive import slates and associations. New services also require adjustments on the part of existing broadcasters. They can be expected to put as severe a pressure upon the existing imported and local program production slate as did the introduction of a third commercial television station into the SMBA markets over 1964–65. New television services alter existing program purchasing arrangements and the settings in the imported and local programming relationship. In the short term (anywhere between five and ten years) they are likely to increase the import share of program-purchase budgets at the expense of local production.

New television services will also erode the position of the existing commercial networks and the national broadcasters. In the US, television network share has contracted to a 60 per cent share of the audience. Contracting audiences mean declines in the advertising dollar and impairing the capacity of the existing services to provide a comprehensive service. Such new services should become important competitors securing programming previously available on the networks such as sports and movie programming (the latter of which would be provided sooner after first release). This would affect Australian content in a number of ways: first, there would not be the same amount of money available for program expenditure by the networks; second, there would not be the same capacity or legitimacy to sustain Australian content rules because of the impact of the competitive market environment; and, third, the production infrastructure in new services would necessarily be limited to begin with, as the costs of providing the service would need to be met.

In television—even with new television technologies—it is never a matter of local production disappearing. Rather, it is a matter of the degree to which indigenising dynamics can be realised. As a medium-sized television market, Australian participation in some genres of television—the movie, the series, the serial, the mini-series—is necessarily going to be limited. Regulations can only ever be designed to have a marginal effect without prejudicing the viability of the service itself. The dynamic interplay between local and imported programming needs to be considered in any assessment of Australian television and its future. The competition and synergy provided by the local and the imported show the two faces of television in Australia (and in most countries of the world). But this double-face is not only central to the operation of the television system, it also critically shapes the national cultural formations carried by Australian television.

5 Television and national culture

There is no shortage of relations between television and national culture in Australia—identificatory, dramatic, critical, commercial and legislative. Australian content rules are legitimated on the basis that domestically produced television supports national culture. Production subsidies for mini-series and feature films are provided on the basis of maintaining and developing Australian culture. SBS-TV is the outcome of an official policy for Australian culture, multiculturalism. Critics (Moran 1985, pp 206–18; Appleton 1988, pp 204–6; Cunningham 1989, pp 39–51) often see Australian television mini-series as fostering a sense of identity in relation to other national identities as in *Bodyline, The Last Bastion, Cowra Breakout,* and as retelling events of national significance in *Eureka Stockade, ANZACS* and *The Dismissal.* Ads routinely draw upon national stereotypes and culturally significant landscapes to sell commodities as diverse as Toyotas, Coke, banking, and Australia Post (Cunningham 1992, pp 71–103). It is commonly assumed that Australian series dramatise a quotidian local reality, whether past (*The Sullivans*) or present (*Homicide, Neighbours, Bellbird, E Street*) (Moran 1989, pp 243–9). Sporting programs provide points of national identification in the international sports of cricket, netball and hockey and in the Olympics. As a pictorial, discursive and historical archive, national cultural and national political formations are drawn upon by advertisers, quiz masters, sports broadcasters and drama producers, not to mention critics.

So too there are the national readings of international events and news coverage, as public texts are created to discuss and frame programs, individuals and events: the 1992 Los Angeles Riots were used to frame discussions of Australia's difference from the US and Australia's black minority. Imports can be seen as assisting in the definition of a national culture through their difference. National culture is thus an important ongoing reference point for television.

Television is important to national cultural projects because—along with other mass media and education—it is an important agency of 'popular socialisation' (Smith 1991, p 11). It provides a common public or civic culture for a disparate population. Like other agencies of popular socialisation it is a vehicle for a 'common culture and a civic ideology, a set of common understandings and aspirations, sentiments and ideas, that binds the population together in their homeland' (Smith 1991, p 11). Television is then in the business of fostering a sense of citizenship, social identities and creating and representing a common cultural and political core. Following Smith (1986, pp 129–39) we can usefully distinguish between two interrelated aspects of this common national culture: the *national political*—the common political and civic culture involving citizenship and equality before the law—and the *national cultural*—the cultural core of memories, values, customs, myths, symbols, solidarities and significant landscapes shaping 'Australian' identity. Television sustains both kinds of national definitions. If Smith is right that no state can be workable without both a national political and national cultural sense of itself, television matters so much to public policy makers because it is an ongoing forum for national projects and ambitions.

While US and Japanese television provide a locally produced and defined common culture, Australian television is made up of local and imported components. Here only the locally produced part routinely provides for national cultural and national political ambitions.

Locally produced drama and documentary mobilise national cultural elements, news and current affairs mobilise national political elements, and infotainment and sporting programs combine both in varying measures. Cultural and broadcasting policy in Australia historically has tried to maximise the Australian component of this common public culture, to utilise it for public purposes and to guide its direction in socially and culturally desirable ways. Australian content drama regulations and production subsidies helped give television's common culture a national cultural shape. Other measures such as restricting the level of foreign ownership and the regulatory encouragement of local information programming (news, current affairs and documentary) helped provide common national orientations to the service. The public funding of the ABC and SBS created instruments with national cultural and political priorities as an intrinsic part of their remit. Multicultural and social equity policies urged the participation, accommodation and incorporation of ethnic, Aboriginal and disadvantaged groups into television for purposes of political, social and cultural cohesion. Such measures are thought to be required in a country like Australia because television is just as obviously *not* about national culture.

Broadcasting works on units that are below and above the level of the nation. Television's local and regional levels produce their own programming orientations and imagined communities of viewers (as Sydneysiders, Victorians, Westralians). These may be, at times, at odds with the national level. Aboriginal identities and non-white, Anglo–Saxon heterosexual male identities proffer alternative and sometimes antagonistic values to assumed national identities. Similarly, international programs and orientations within the service may be at some distance from national cultural and national political aspirations. Australian production is only partly made up of Australian originated program concepts. Ethnic and minoritarian programming is international in SBS's multilingual programming (SBS is sometimes thought to undermine national culture through its screening of such programming). And in a society in which so much of the population is first- or second-generation Australian, some audiences may identify with overseas-produced programming as much as with local programming: British immigrants may be closer to *Eastenders* than to *E Street*; Italian immigrants to SBS's Italian movies than to *Neighbours*; Asian immigrants to *Empress Wu* and Hong Kong video than to *Flying Doctors*. Such audience and program orientations are not straightforwardly supportive of nor intrinsically antagonistic to the national culture. Sometimes they are complementary, sometimes eccentric, sometimes antagonistic to it.

Television in these terms has a mixed relation to national cultural and national political formations. It supports them by acting as a vehicle for their transmission; and it undermines them through providing programming and orientations which can be antithetical or simply indifferent to such formations. In being transnational in programming and program concepts, Australian television is definitely international. As a consequence imports are often seen by those espousing and those condemning a national culture as bringing into question the notion of an homogeneous Australian culture. But, as we have seen, it is never that straightforward. Both audiences and producers customise those imported programs and concepts, tailoring them to the Australian market's language, customs and cultural traditions.

TELEVISION'S CULTURAL LEVELS

Such transnational and national orientations and cultures not only persist within television, but are true of the nation generally. As Schlesinger notes, the nation:

> ...is a site of contestation and inherently an object of transformative practices. In any case, to assert that national cultures might, indeed, do, exist does not by any means exclude the reality of there being a transnational or global culture as well. We need to think in terms of the simultaneous *interaction* and *parallelism* of different cultural levels within given social formations [my emphasis]. (1991, p 305)

Schlesinger's point is that national cultural levels interact with international, local and regional levels, and that international levels are not necessarily antagonistic to national cultural levels—in some cases they may actively *support* national levels. Television offers a multitude of orientations and practices in its programming. Just as programming may be local, regional, national, international and minoritarian, so too audience orientations to programming will persist across these levels. In television these distinct cultural levels are always co-present. These levels interact with each other across the sites of television, including television programming, distribution and technological organisation, broadcasting, policy making, politics, administration, business, viewing and television criticism.

Because television is an assemblage of projects and elements from textual to business strategies, from advertising to corporate plans, from criticism to audience behaviours, from communications policy making to cultural policy development, these plans and behaviours organise the interaction with and interrelationship between the different cultural levels. Television is thus shaped—as are other sectors—by the same business strategies and trends, the same international and national regulatory agendas in policy development, and by similar kinds of textual and critical strategies as for other national and international media.

The different cultural levels coexist in television, and audiences, the program schedule, and television institutions typically move between them. Television draws upon and negotiates these in the identities it proffers audiences, the programs it schedules, the politics it covers, and in its associated regulatory ambitions and policy formations. The relationships among these cultural levels can be *parallel* in that they simply may be co-present, without cohering—each pursuing its own ends typically organised through the television schedule and social space with a minimum of fuss. They may also be *dual*, inasmuch as they provide alternate identities formed in oscillating and potentially contradictory relationships with each other (Greek or English and Australian, Bananabender or Sandgroper and Australian).

They may be *convergent* or linked together as local, state and national programming and orientations may all inform an Australian identity. Additionally, international programming provides for an Australian reading by producers, presenters and audiences of Hollywood and British programs, and international news stories.

These levels may also be on a *collision course*, with cultural levels contradicting each other (state versus federal, Australian versus international orientation), or as identities become conflictual (Serbian versus Croatian, Anglophone versus non-English-speaking, settler versus immigrant, regional versus metropolitan; Aboriginal versus white).[1]

The co-presence of these identities in television ensures that television is a site in which the different levels and projects associated with them both compete against and complement each other. In this, television is just like politics and business. The adjustment between these levels is a matter of political and policy dispute within television. As chapters 2–4 demonstrated, different time periods have seen the relative ascendance of particular cultural levels, and preferences for particular relationships between them. Television's schedule and disposition thus organise these cultural levels differently depending upon the materials at hand, the historical circumstances (political, social and demographic), and the disposition of forces in the television industry and policy making.

Broadcasting policy moves between balancing out the different cultural levels and favouring certain levels over others (both justified with reference to the national interest). Television stations, for their part, respond by trying to manage the schedule in such a way as to create complementarities between the different levels while maximising profitability, audience share and minimising regulatory intervention. In this way, television's relationship to general Australian, international, ethnic or minoritarian cultures is a political matter tied up in the push of different parts of the service to secure advantages for themselves.

At any one time the overall configuration of the service is the outcome of the struggle between, the adjustments made to, and the relative complementarity of, the different parts of the service. This means that the relationship between television and national cultural formations, between television and international cultural formations, between television and minorities is a political question at the heart of debates about the direction, shape, content, and ownership of television. Should Australian content be reconfigured in ways which facilitate co-production and therefore an adjustment of the national to the international? Should television be more local to the service area in which it operates? Should it embrace policies which would permit a greater acknowledgement of people of NESB in local programming? Should transparent governmental subsidies replace the allegedly hidden subsidies provided by content rules? Should the networks as Australian companies be involved in Pay TV as a means of maintaining a national presence or would the participation of Home Box Office, NBC or Warner promote diversity in television ownership in Australia?

The conjunction of television and national culture in these contexts is always political. To argue for tighter or looser forms of connection between television and national culture is to argue for or against particular groups and vested interests. The convergence of polity and state, of culture and nation, presumed in the policy maker's injunction that television should have an Australian Look, is a symbolic currency mobilised to justify, give shape to and balance the relations between television stations, international producers, a local production infrastructure and social policy in ways which favour the local production industry and the television stations in their dealings with US suppliers. A new policy regime favouring 'free trade' would provide different reference points from which to manage the distribution of powers and priorities within the television industry and broadcast regulation. It would arbitrate the sectional interests differently. Australian cinema history suggests that freer trade regimes give more rights to importers than local producers, although it leads to stronger censorship of programming. Cultural nationalist policy outcomes give more rights to domestic producers and privilege locally oriented film production, managing the necessary connection with international production on the local industry's terms. The diverse interventions of politicians, regulators, producers, unions, stations, educators, sellers and buyers of programs, commercial and community lobbyists and marketers are negotiated in the program schedule, in the programs themselves, and in the public standing of television as a medium.

Such political adjustments between the players in the television industry and between the cultural levels within television provide in program schedules the materials that audiences themselves shape. Audiences in their turn negotiate these different cultural levels, adjusting their various identities in relation to them. They can try and eliminate the distance between programming and themselves, assert a distance between themselves and the programming, or set it up as other and not for them. Audiences fashion identities in relation to programming and the television service as a whole which can be inward or outward-looking, exclusive or inclusive. Programming, no matter whether produced at local, regional, national, minoritarian or international levels, does not simply fit audience identities formed at those levels. Thus audiences appropriate programming such that there are local readings of Hollywood programs just as there are internationally consistent readings of the same by virtue of syndicated gossip columns and the like.

By virtue of its local dimension, the Australian infotainment product is more readily drawn into the everyday lives of audiences than is imported product. The capacity of news, current affairs, quiz and variety shows to exploit local elements of the informational, political and cultural landscape is fundamental to their appeal and to their advantage over international news, current affairs and variety programming. Local drama programs typically centre the horizons of family, community and society, problems of living and working. These qualities, which are also seen in international drama programs, make local programming fit easily with local, regional and national identities and, to a lesser extent, with minoritarian and international identities. Local soaps help confer a positive sense of Australian identity and a comfortable sense of place. They are also internationalised as both Australian and international popular culture (as, for example, an Australian participation in the soap opera form of television). But, equally, these programs are sometimes constructed as 'not for us'. Those interested in the technical realisation of television find much Australian-produced television formally boring. Cultural elites decry these local programs for not being up to British quality. Ethnic lobbyists speak of a separate identity unrepresented in such programs. Local programs may also be used to organise religious and ethnic differences as when local programming is used by families to instruct children on differences between, for example, the general Australian behaviour and the appropriate behaviour of the group or community.

Equally, international programming can be localised in the sense of being easily drawn into the everyday world, particularly drama and music programs. Audiences may recognise such programming as a shared international or global audiovisual culture. International programs—particularly Hollywood programs—afford audiences a sense of distance enabling them, in John Caughie's words, to 'play at being American' (Caughie 1990, p 44). Consumption of US and UK imports variously encourage a sense of difference, as an Australian identity in comparison ('we are not like that'; 'we don't play football like that'; 'our politics is different from that'; 'we don't talk as obsessively about ourselves'; 'our programs are more realistic'); in antagonism, as exposure to UK and US imports fuels a ritualistic animosity to both cultures; and in envy, as both cultures become desirable ends and producers of forms of television unavailable to the Australian.

The appreciation of imports and the persistent and necessarily structural frustration with local television production destabilise and force changes upon locally produced programming and local identities. International symbolic culture is often 'good' in disrupting cosy and discriminatory local identities, in expanding the definitions of what is possible, and in providing a way out of the available—often conservative—Australian definitions. It is equally 'bad' in corrupting and forestalling local agendas and specificities, in arresting their development through time and space, and in stunting the development of national identities, political independence and cultural empowerment.

INTERNATIONAL CULTURE AND THE NATIONAL

Australian audiences routinely deal with local and imported products, and move easily between local, regional, national, international and minoritarian levels. The political and strategic differences within television and between audiences occur in an overall context of *continuity* between different cultural levels. International programming and the adoption of an international orientation are not fundamentally at odds with national cultural level(s) and diverse national identity ambitions, but are often complementary to them. This is clearest in the predominance of British and North American programs on Australian television screens. These programs attract the lion's share of the broadcast audience for imported programming and rival the ratings for local programs. This reliance upon products and concepts from the major Anglophone producers is due to a number of extra-televisual factors.

1 Given that language is a communication, trading, cultural and symbolic goods system in its own right, Anglophone program imports and concepts are that much more important in Australia than in non-English-speaking countries. US and UK dominance of the English language system (as the largest and wealthiest nations in that system) further explains their Australian programming presence. Television flows from the US and Britain to Australia are mirrored in educational institutions (with rival British and US centres for Australian university disciplines), in publishing, and in the exchange of governmental programs, systems and political campaign

ideas. UK and US screenings on Australian television are less programs of a global nature screened locally than they are the programming of a common cultural area based on the Anglophone information and cultural system.² In Australia, New Zealand, Canada and Ireland, this cultural area rivals the national culture as these national cultures adjust themselves in relation to the nodal points of the English language, the UK and the USA.

2 Australia shares much with the US. With the US it shares a common identity as an English-speaking *immigrant* country, a common foreign affairs outlook and close defence arrangements. The US provided Australia with a model for its federation, for federal upper house representation in the Senate, a decimal currency and a model of a workable poly-ethnic society based on immigration. It has also been a significant trading partner and investor of capital in Australia. In this sense Australian and US trade in drama programs and sporting and infotainment concepts is part of a wider system of exchange and similarity. US programming is in this case programming for an imagined 'American' (New World) identity. Thus, the USA has an importance to Australia which is over and above the fact that it 'bulks so large in most countries' lives' and 'cuts a figure that can nowhere be ignored' (JDB Miller 1988, p 237).

3 With the UK, Australia has colonial and blood ties. The largest and defining immigration has been from the British Isles. Charles Price notes that '48 per cent of the present population is pure Anglo-Celt, 22 per cent is non-Anglo-Celt while the remaining 30 per cent is a mixture of Anglo-Celt and non-Anglo-Celt' (1989, p 15). British programming can be interpreted as Anglo-Celtic programming in Australia for the 78 per cent with such ancestry. Current demographic changes support the continuing importance of the Anglo-Celtic but in a reshaped form, as the proportion of those with a mixture of Anglo-Celt and non-Anglo-Celt ancestry is expected to become the largest 'ethnic division' if current immigration patterns continue (Price 1989, p 15). But the relationship goes deeper than immigration. As JDB Miller recently put it:

> Australians live in a society characterized by the English language, the English legal system, a monarch shared with the British, table manners which come directly from Britain, television programmes which often do the same, vehicles which drive on the left, and churches, professional organisations, trade unions, universities and armed forces which derive from Britain. The cultural heritage is strong, and is reinforced

by the occasional political group ... which puts great weight upon the monarchy and the memories of united action in war. (1988, p 235)

Up until recently the UK was also a significant trading partner and foreign investor. (In the late 1940s the UK took 40 per cent of Australia's exports; by 1982–83 it took only 5 per cent.) The fact that Britain provides the national broadcasters with programming concepts, personnel and orientations is part of a wider system of historical, formal and informal social, political and economic exchange. If the US provides a model of a new world identity, the British connection helps shape a model of Australian identity fashioned in difference from and continuity with Britain (Kapferer 1988, p 167).

4 The ethnic composition of people of NESB in the Anglophone countries of the US, Canada, and Australia involves many peoples for whom the Anglophone cultural area is culturally proximate. Anglophone culture is a part of a larger European (for Europe) or American (for Latin America) cultural area and identity. Additionally, the New World English-speaking countries have had to produce programming which takes account of the NESB populations, principally European, in their midst. Hollywood's need to produce for a culturally disparate US audience enables it to make product suitable for circulation to the poly-ethnic Australian and Canadian markets. The requirement to reach a culturally diverse society provides the basis for Hollywood's circulation to non-English-speaking countries. Both these factors aid Hollywood's and Australian commercial television's importance for Australia's NESB audiences.

5 Television also works ceaselessly to cover over the gaps, reduce the dissonance between itself and its audiences, and make imported programs local to the audience. As a medium-sized television market, Australian television stations need to work hard at making imported programming local, through marketing, scheduling and purchasing strategies (which attempt to maintain consistency of focus and orientation). Anglophone product, because of the factors mentioned above, is relied upon as the programming most capable of covering the gaps. US programming, designed as it is for a diverse and culturally mixed domestic population divided on regional, racial and ethnic lines, is the imported product most capable of travelling successfully through Australia's poly-ethnic social and cultural space.

6 US and UK programs pressure Australian programming to conform to their models and standards in order to succeed locally.

Pressures are also experienced in documentary and drama to produce material capable of export to other Anglophone markets. Australian television, particularly drama, is increasingly designed to include those international audiences. Those Australian drama series which are held to confer upon Australians an easy sense of identity are, by virtue of their similarity to Hollywood and British product, programs able to gain a minor international market presence in Anglophone and northern European countries. In this they are assisted by their production in the English language and their shared concern with family relations, domestic situations, success (and failure) and love and death (Moran 1985, pp 196, 200). The need for Australian programs to make routine adjustments to British and US program and production models arises because Australian audiences are familar with US and British import presence and because of the need to export internationally to sustain high-cost drama and documentary programming. These import/export contours ensure that local production becomes further defined in relation to the British and US nodes of the English language and less in relation to other international nodes.

A number of consequences follow from this. US and British programming is *not just* Anglophone programming for Anglophones. Anglophone programming has a pre-eminent position in international audiovisual trade in programs and program concepts. Thus Australian programming's British and North American inflection is not simply an English language bias it is also an acknowledgment of the role both play in setting agenda for television production worldwide. North American and Australian programming has appeal beyond Anglophone and Anglo-Celtic Australia because of the longstanding negotiation of melting-pot identities in the English language throughout North America (and including its significant shaping by NESB peoples) and to a lesser extent in Australia. On balance, British and US programming supports a variety of identities and projects which underwrite national culture and identity more than they undermine it. Even the expanded range of program imports on SBS is based upon broader, though nonetheless specific, cultural area identities (European, Western, Asian—the first two of which Anglophone programming self-evidently forms a part).

There are no large cleavages between national and international levels. These are mostly complementary, and the Australian television service, audiences and the broader social and political formations work hard to make them so. Nonetheless disputes over the relative limits of, and connections between, these levels can affect broader social and cultural outcomes privileging larger cultural identities at the expense of national identities. For all their essential complementarity the boundaries between international and national cultural levels are being adjusted constantly, creating winners and losers in a variety of sites (whether in national cultural policy sites in film and television industry production support or in broadcasting authority rulings respectively; or in international trade relation sites in GATT with US pressure upon Australian television content rules and production subsidies).

Any assessment of television and national culture needs to consider diverse audience responses, different cultural levels and variations in these over time. It needs to see the self-conscious activity of 'knowing about our national culture' as one of the activities associated with television viewing. It needs to pose the synergistic as much as antagonistic relationship between international programming and orientations and national culture. (Australian and imported programming should be seen as persisting on the same horizon, rather than local content constructing an Australian identity while imported program 'Americanises' or 'Anglicises' the audience.) It needs to account for internationalising pressures, shared identities (as immigrant Anglophone societies), and the presence, popularity and value these terms provide for Anglophone imports. It needs to account for how television policy and television programming's own relation to national culture is a political problem requiring attention and adjustment: a national specificity can be registered in the style of the resolutions, the compromises and the conflicts over television's form and shape. It needs to assume a multilevelled set of cultural formations crisscrossed by social class, ethnicity, gender, religion, values and geography, within which categories of national culture emerge. It needs to examine how national culture is simultaneously a political, social and cultural program and also an identity formation and cultural level in its own right.

NATIONAL CULTURE

National culture is not one project, but a series of projects which can be contending, complementary or simply indifferent to each other. It is not simply a matter of feeling and sentiment but of mobilised feelings and sentiments. It is not a matter of representation but of intervention, not of tradition but invention from available materials (Hobsbawm & Ranger 1983). As AD Smith writes:

> It is, of course, possible to 'invent', even manufacture, traditions as commodities to serve particular class or ethnic interests. But they will only

survive and flourish as part of the repertoire of national culture, if they can be made continuous with a much longer past that members of that community presume to constitute their 'heritage'. In other words, 'grafting' extraneous elements must always be a delicate operation; the new traditions must evoke a popular response if they are to survive, and that means hewing close to vernacular motifs and styles. (1990, p 178)

The various contemporary national culture projects listed below work within and test these limits. They rest on a series of loosely connected logics where national culture is defined:

- as emergent and continuously negotiated;
- in terms of immigration, particular homeland heritages and values;
- in relation to place, significant landscapes, historical events, and aspects of settler and Aboriginal cultures;
- solely in relation to the settler cultures;
- in terms of a combinatory logic: variously based upon the Australian redisposition of European and North American experiences, policies, and logics and cultural hybridisation based upon the regional, local, indigenous and immigrant mix;
- in geopolitical terms, as an international logic fashioning national self-interest in an increasingly global context.

These logics are combined in national culture projects and policies. The vision of a multicultural national identity envisages an Australian unity in diversity while allotting less of a determining value, importance and significance to the settler culture. The anti-republican conservative movement associated with retaining the current flag, winding back the excesses of multiculturalism, and defending the constitutional monarchy conflates the historically dominant British Isles immigration with settler traditions and values, and asserts a predominantly one-way cultural hybridisation leading to immigrant assimilation into Australian and British values (see Blainey 1984). The drive towards republicanism in the early 1990s combined an equally selective emphasis upon national events and traditions. Thus Paul Keating as prime minister in 1992 invoked Kokoda rather than ANZAC Cove as the foundation of modern Australia because in that campaign Australians were defending their country. He was seen to drive a wedge between the Anglo (the British) and the Celtic (Irish and Scottish). In his espousal of anti-British sentiments, he utilised the multiculturalist imperatives of incorporating ethnic groups into the national symbols–myth complex, he argued for national cultural change on the basis of international competitiveness, he asserted national (economic) interests at the expense of cultural area ties and alignments (to the Anglophone countries of Europe and North

America), and he definitively turned to North American models for inspiration, prioritising a geopolitical Asian accommodation along the way. The debates over whether the flag was an appropriate one for a poly-ethnic society in the last decade of the twentieth century seemed to be whether the national was defined in relation to a British cultural heritage or more in relation to civic, republican, legal, territorial and geopolitical interests.

While these debates are contemporary, they conform to longstanding ideological formations. Part of the promise of Australian culture and identity from the beginning was that of opportunity, the promise of starting anew in a new land, of an inclusive collective contribution to the development of a nation and culture. This is well expressed in that definition of an Australian as someone who just got off the boat and wants to be Australian (Lawson 1983, p 130). Australian culture here is predicated upon a shedding of previous identities and a preparedness to take on new ones, and an assumption of existing native-born identities attenuating theselves sufficiently to accommodate this new presence. Australian culture is perpetually emergent, as are all 'new world' nations formed in the cusp of poly-ethnic migration. Following Lattas, though, this very provisionality can be seen as foundational to a version of national culture in modern Australia:

> [T]he production of Australian nationalism is mediated through the production of an identity crisis. The continual questioning of who we really are is the essence of Australian nationalism. It produces the reflective space of distance, of removal, creating the alienation which we ascribe to ourselves as the secret truth constitutive of our identity. (1990, p 54)

National culture is in a constant process of identity formation, continually being adjusted depending upon the materials brought to bear upon it. It is a self-conscious program of construction and creation. Tradition is capable of being created anew.

But, at the same time, this openness promises a national culture which would not offend, would not be too different, and could offer itself as *continuation* of the culture from which one migrated, or to which Australia historically compared itself (always the US and Britain, and sometimes Canada). This is the historic dual identity of the Australian and the Anglo-Australian. It is also the basis for many multicultural identities inasmuch as multiculturalism promises adjustments which would secure greater continuity between ethnic homelands and the Australian host culture, and would accommodate the contemporary (and longstanding) reality of poly-ethnic Australian ancestry. It poses the Australian in relation to an (absent) other from which the Australian is declared different and a continuation: the

Australian and (Australian) Italian, (Australian) Asian, and (Australian) Lebanese. This is also the project of de-dominionisation (Davidson 1979, pp 139–53) which defines an Australian identity and culture with reference to British and British structures (hierarchical and class-based England, egalitarian Australia [Kapferer 1988, p 167]) and shared participation in events (Gallipoli, the Boer war, the fall of Singapore etc). Each wave of immigration through its passage redefines Australia, bringing with it a family, a network, a culture of elsewhere. The definition of England as home by those who have never seen it has its contemporary equivalent in similar identifications by Australian Italians of Italy as home.

Next to this culture defined by immigration, there is a culture of place and identity. For the cosmopolitan, there is the figure of Australia as a new nation in an old, old land; it reconciles a sense of youth, new beginning with a landscape, a unique flora and fauna and, more lately, Aborigines and Aboriginal heritage. This variously positions the 'bush type' (Ward 1978) and Aborigines as early accommodations to landscape and negotiation of a particularly Australian heritage. As Lattas observes there is a tendency today to mix the bush with the first Australians, the Aborigines:

> [T]he primordial and primitive otherness of Aborigines is seen as capable of providing a form of spiritual unity for the nation, it can provide the necessary mythology capable of overcoming that fragmentation of the nation which immigration and multiculturalism have produced. (1990, p 66)

As in the US and Canada, wilderness, bush and significant landscapes like Uluru take on an emblematic identity and point of reference. These suggest an apparently open and continuous point of identification posed inclusively in terms of an ongoing accommodation to the environment.

But this apparent openness runs into an alternative parochial national identity: a local settler culture of two hundred years standing. After all, peoples and families cannot live continuously in a place for two hundred years and not evolve distinctive cultural, social forms and identities, and distinctive bureaucratic, industrial and political identities. After four or more generations the importance of the diasporic origin is displaced by an origin of settlement. This is further underscored by patterns of ethnic intermarriage, which are producing a typical pattern of an Australian with several ancestries (Price 1989, p 6). Roots means a convict heritage; a trace back to the First Fleet; to particular locations, landscapes, incidents (Kokoda, Gallipoli), industries (pastoral); to longstanding state identities as Tasmanian or South Australian. National culture can mean here a limited set of symbolic tropes, landscapes, and pictorial archives. Perhaps this is because it is also a particular genre of speech transmitted socially and organised for occasions such as ANZAC Day. These versions of a national settler culture and identity are often seen today as the basis for a culture of intolerance, parochialism, exclusion and even pseudo-ethnicity. They appear to mock the openness declared in other versions, refuse membership as Australian to those who would wish to call themselves such. Often these constitute a target of social policy: the Ugly Australian that needs to be reshaped. Populists mobilise this culture to varying degrees. Some intellectuals—such as Blainey—defend it. Others—such as Hodge and Mishra—berate it as a 'bastard complex' arguing for its reformation in Aboriginal and multicultural terms (Hodge & Mishra 1991, pp 204–19).

Perhaps the predominant version of national culture stitches these different strands together. Most commonly, the culture is seen to be fashioned from the pasts of immigrant peoples, of the Australian-born, and of the Aborigines, with the weighting given to each dependent upon the proportions of native-born and immigrants at the time. These different elements forge an always emerging cultural hybrid, with its reality firmly planted in the poly-ethnic backgrounds of most Australians. This version of national culture is projected as the cement which binds and reshapes ethnicities, minority values, subcultural affinities into the overarching identity.

Another version adds to this what is shared with international English-language and Western cultures. Here, national culture is constantly being adjusted in relation to Australia's participation in international communication corridors and in terms of its local traditions and immigration. National culture is formed here as part of the modernising process with parallel communities formed at a national level around the cultures of work, sport, school, cultural participation, subcultures and politics—all of which diminish traditional associations.

Finally, national culture and national identity can be defined in geopolitical and territorial terms. This is the national political conception of nation. The geopolitical nation has always been a component of official nationalism given the need to fashion an identity and culture in the national and commercial interest through managing international relations in trade and commerce, politics and defence to strategic advantage. The contemporary version of this eminently political project of nation building is that the geopolitical nodal points of the immediate past—first Britain and then the US—need to accommodate a third nodal point, 'Asia' (meaning East and South-East

Asia). Here Australian national identity is to be refashioned in a mix of independent and interdependent arrangements in the Asia–Pacific region.

With so many different national projects seeking recognition, the nation comes under constant interrogation. The versions of national culture and identity proffer different visions, personhoods, and national self-definitions. Under some conditions these can be in conflict and competition with each other, under others simply co-present, producing a sense of unity and consensus with the differences between the parts going unremarked. National culture is produced between an identity formed in relation to a country other than itself, an identity of place as itself, combinatory logics, melting pot and geopolitical interests. Today, these are mostly in public conflict. It is not uncommon for multiculturalist projects to get posed against Australianist projects; for cultural diversity to be posed against de-dominionisation (Rowse 1985, p 75). Books are written with titles such as *Mistaken Identity* (Castles et al 1988) and *All for Australia* (Blainey 1984). Blainey argues that a nation divided by cultural diversity needs to be made good by reasserting core cultural and national values (those of the Anglo-Celtic mainstream); Castles et al argue for community without nation as a means of managing ethnicity with toleration (1988, p 148). Numerous feminist writers (see eg, Schaffer 1989; Summers 1975) tease out the exclusions and marginalisation of women from national cultural definitions and social life taking a calculated distance from them; whilst a number of Aboriginal and non-Aboriginal writers (Hodge & Mishra 1991; Willmot 1987; Reynolds 1987; Sykes 1989) argue that the unresolved colonial legacy with respect to Aborigines compromises the settler culture's claims to legitimacy. For some of these, the national subject is in terminal crisis.

The various projects of national culture provide a rhetorical field drawn upon by program makers, politicians, cultural critics and policy makers in television. National culture is an open policy technology inasmuch as it can be so readily associated with a variety of political, social and industry strategies and programs. Australian national culture with respect to television is an amalgam of different cultures (business, political, policy making, informational and industry) and multiple identities (as ethnic, Australian, Tasmanian, Aboriginal etc) relying on shared traditions, histories, experiences and memories. These cultures and identities are not just static life-ways seeking expression with television programming as their vehicle. They are dynamic and interventional strategies impacting upon broadcasting and cultural policy and television industry practice.

All national cultural strategies are a matter of policy and politics inasmuch as they involve forms of self-regulation, discipline, incitement and control over the social body. This is why national culture as a project attracts criticism and attention. And this is why every analysis of national culture is caught in the logic of an academic descriptive practice which is capable of some policy uptake, and an industrial, commercial, social and political logic of markets, policy, and politics.

Television's disposition of matters of national culture refracts larger debates about national culture while simultaneously being a site for their articulation and working out. The much vaunted Australian crisis of the national subject is over *which* kinds of nationalism, national identity and national culture will be ascendant in relation to which social, political and economic strategies, *which* kinds of internationalism in relation to the limits of political and strategic independence, and what the shape of national interests and identities will be in a new world order. Television is, as ever, simultaneously a stout perpetrator and an active underminer of prevailing national cultural and national political formations.

6 National television in the new cultural order

The changes in the relationship between television and national culture over the 1990s will mostly be driven by a combination of globalisation, minority self-assertion, and geopolitical refashionings of nations and national arrangements in the new international order. It is contemporary fashion not only to see these as holding out different prospects for television and national culture, but to see them as fundamentally compromising the projects of national culture—national cultural policy, broadcasting regulation, national identity. While these developments are clearly undermining some nations and national cultures, I don't think they will do the same for Australia.

Australian television does, however, face the increased internationalisation of television services because of more television services, more open international symbolic goods markets, and a largely deregulated domestic policy environment. Multiculturalism and minority aspiration are increasingly important to television and cultural policy; and geopolitical realignments are refashioning national political and trading interests in the wake of the collapse of the bipolar world of the Cold War (US versus the Soviet Union; capitalism versus communism) and its replacement by a many-centred world system. These refashionings adversely affect some projects of national culture, while others are advantaged (see Cunningham 1992, pp 37–70).

GLOBALISATION AND NATIONAL CULTURE

Globalisation has many meanings. In business and cultural policy it refers to the growth of world trade, its increasing internationalisation and interdependence, a new international division of labour prioritising international competitiveness, the growing role of stateless corporations in shaping national policy formation, and the increase of transborder information, monetary, population and symbolic goods flows (all less capable of national interdiction than traditional trade products). Globalisation sees national policy adjust by adopting market solutions, deregulating and privatising markets, and harmonising business and taxation arrangements between countries.

In international politics, globalisation refers to changing relationships among states: the increasing role of international structures in the European Community, North American Free Trade Agreement (NAFTA) involving the US, Canada and Mexico, the association of South East Asian Nations (ASEAN) and Australasia's Closer Economic Relations (CER) agreements; and the increasing role of international bodies like the Organisation for Economic Cooperation and Devolopment (OECD), the International Monetary Fund (IMF) and the World Bank in securing changed national policies in developing and developed countries.

Globalisation also refers to the strategies of transnational companies not only to diminish international differences but to organise those differences to their advantage. Whereas once globalisation simply suggested a 'global culture' modelled on and headquartered in the US, built on consumption of US goods and motored by US capital, now it also refers to a mixed scenario of strategies and nodal centres (Japan, Germany, European Community, US etc). Companies localise themselves in the markets they enter through involving themselves in national life (whether by sponsoring regional football teams, national Olympic teams or television programs), enlisting domestic elites, and producing customised product which turns national and cultural differences to commercial advantage, as in Coca-Cola's Australian-produced advertising (although some recent coke ads refer overtly to globalised capitalism or youth culture).

The central issue is one of the interpretation of these processes. Some see these policy adjustments as indicating a 'global waning of faith in the role of the state and culture' and as requiring states 'to come to terms with limited or shared political sovereignty' (Collins 1991, p 13). These globalising processes are further seen to have loosened the grip of nation states as 'cultural organisers' and 'sovereign' entities (Schwarz 1992, p 205). They not only limit national sovereignty but strengthen diversity within the nation as 'new, local forms of sovereignty, based on evolving (and imagined) ethnic and cultural identities ... compete with the claims for centralised authority inscribed in the ... nation-state' (Schwarz 1992, p 205). Alongside this there is the 'continuing large scale movement of global populations' (Collins 1991, p 13) in the wake of new international arrangements, uneven economic and political development, and civil war.

Such developments are held to compromise cultural policy based upon securing national culture. There is a worry that national film and television industries are an 'anachronism' impossible under globalisation, and that the national increasingly persists either as a marketing device for international consumption or as a reservoir of images and traditions to be exploited by multinational advertisers and national elites for domestic and international advantage (Jacka 1988, pp 122, 125). Under this logic, the contemporary transformations in Australian television, and society more generally, are interdicting the national in favour of the global and the multicultural. In television, globalisation is therefore usually used to describe:

- the move to embrace deregulation and markets in national communication policies at the expense of social and cultural logics. This move is seeing control over broadcasting shift significantly towards economic policy elites and away from national cultural elites. This changing of the guard is justified on the basis of 'consumer sovereignty' (popular audience preferences and identities finding expression through the operation of the market);
- the growth of world television trade with new television technologies, additional television services and deregulated television markets (an estimated '20 per cent of world trade is now in the information and communication sector' (Collins 1991, p 13)); and
- the existence of multinational communications organisations functioning as 'powerful transnationalising forces . . . in the cultural spheres'. These organisations take advantage of these new political and market arrangements by consolidating their influence within a number of markets, organising the transnational symbolic goods, mobilising existing cultural patterns extending beyond the nation state (Collins 1991, p 13). These developments are restratifying audiences, transforming domestic television industries, and eclipsing national organisers (Collins 1990, p 214).

These either/or scenarios of national culture or globalisation—cultural sovereignty or consumer preference, national culture or multiculturalism—are wrong-headed (Cunningham 1992, pp 43–8). They mask a situation in which national and international tendencies are co-present and are variously competitive with and complementary to each other. As noted earlier, internationalism as much underwrites as denigrates national political and cultural structures in Australia. Globalising processes do not in themselves compromise a cultural policy with national identity and national culture as goals. But these do readjust the relationship between international and national cultural levels and so reshape the character of domestic production industry support and content provisions. In this process, however, there are clear winners and losers. The television networks and especially the international television suppliers benefit more from a deregulated market than the domestic television drama and documentary production industry. But even here the results could be uneven. The move towards 'transparent' subsidies rather than 'content' regulations might be expected to advantage the 'quality'—high-budget limited episode—productions, particularly co-productions, over the more locally destined long-running series. Similarly, different national interests in broadcast policy making and the adoption of a different technology of regulation would remove neither national interests nor the state from the picture.

Yes, world trade has increased, there is a contemporary refugee and illegal immigrant problem and there is a marked increase in international audiovisual trade. But none of these are new to Australia (or Canada, or the US). Australasia, the Americas and Western Europe have always been participants in world trade. By virtue of the important place that agricultural commodities and mining have historically played in world trade, Australia has been a significant player well beyond its population size. Limited and shared sovereignty is nothing new to a former colony, member of the British Empire and country with a 'special relationship' with the US. Large-scale global movements of people are not new. The Americas and Australasia have been involved with migration from European settlement, whilst Canada and Australia have taken in refugees continuously from the late 1930s, and the US from the time of its settlement by Europeans. The big difference now is that Europe is a host site for refugee and 'economic' migration. Given these conditions it should not be surprising then that much of the globalisation literature comes out of a Eurocentric optic!

The international trade in audiovisual industries appears to have increased dramatically only because trade by European and developing countries started at such low levels. Their television systems placed inhibitions on audiovisual trade, Australia's did not. Because Australia had a mature commercial broadcasting market (as did Canada) with a developed and competitive trade from the 1950s, it did not experience significant increases in symbolic goods trade in the 1980s. What is comparatively new for Australia and Canada is their greater participation in the international film, video and publishing industries as producers, and the emergence of cultural sovereignty and national identity issues in those countries as matters for governmental consideration.

For Australia, international trade, internationalisation, limited sovereignty and audiovisual trade have been stable for most of this century. The British Empire was more than the largely symbolic forum provided by the Commonwealth Games and annual international meetings. US–Australian trade was significant from the teens of this century. National frameworks facilitate international trade through their administrative, bureaucratic and political structures (including international organisations) which enable such trade to develop and be sustained, including the repatriation of profits. When the US argued for decolonisation and the creation of nation-states after World War 2, it was not simply offering its political culture as the model for the rest of the world, but saw this as a means of gaining greater access to world markets and diminishing supra-national imperial relationships.

The deregulationist and private sector agendas in national broadcasting policy are part of an international change in the technology of regulation. National governments still pursue national interests, particularly national economic interests, as regulation shifts, as Dyson and Humphreys put it, 'from being essentially a domestic political process of realising enduring principles of (public service) broadcasting policy to becoming a process of [economic] statecraft'. By this, Dyson and Humphreys mean that 'broadcasting has become part of the calculus of national power and national economic welfare' involving 'intergovernmental relations and international developments'. So, broadcasting regulation and new media 'serve as a new form of (national) bargaining behaviour at the international level' (1988, pp 149, 151, 153). Deregulation and private sector agendas are then tied up with domestic political and economic strategies, international intellectual fashion, and pressure from international bodies such as the IMF, the World Bank and the OECD. The political push for change in Australian broadcast content regulation does not come only from the US. It also comes from an agenda which sees benefits in Australian industry becoming internationalised and competitive. Broadcasting policy thus becomes industry policy, not just cultural policy. Deregulatory changes refashion—not diminish—national interests in broadcasting. With national interests differing across nations, it is unlikely that the exercise of economic statecraft will lead to uniform international developments.

Similarly, the activities of multinational, global corporations do not completely erode national sovereignty and cultures. There has been a 'reversal of roles between government and the corporation' in that 'stateless corporations have increasingly learned to shape national climates by offering technology, jobs and capital', while governments 'find themselves engaged in a furious effort to capture more of the estimated (US) \$150 billion per annum they invest across national borders' (*International Business*, 14 May 1990, p 59). In this context:

> governments and nations that fail to create the right climate will find their living standards and well-being shortchanged. But those that can extract the benefits that stateless corporations can offer will emerge clear winners. (*International Business*, 14 May 1990, p 59)

But this is not new. Australian states and the federal government have over many years competed for US, British and more lately Japanese investment with each other and with other countries. AD Smith notes that the more that national governments project the nation's need to create favourable domestic environments for investment by providing an educated workforce and an internationally competitive outlook, the more there develops 'a growing sense of national identity and purpose in the face of external pressures' and the more the nation is located 'in an international hierarchy of similar "political-communities-in-the-making" ' (1991, pp 156–7). This leads Smith to claim that 'transnational economic forces may end up reinforcing the nations and nationalisms they were expected to supercede' (1991, p 157). As *International Business* noted, world companies are not so much 'abandoning identification with a single nation as . . . trying to become local in many countries' (14 May 1990, p 56). The problem they face is one of 'maintaining a balance between functioning as a global organisation while customising products to local tastes'. Such transnationalisation may on balance support the extension of regional, local and national cultures as much as eclipse them. Further support for the continuing importance of nation-states is provided by 'a shifting, geopolitical configuration' created by the forsaking of the bipolar (communist and capitalist) configuration of 'client states and regions' for a 'polycentric' configuration 'in which the right of nation-states to choose their own destinies is once more apparent' (Smith 1991, p 154).

Problems also attend the construction of global identities and cultures. Smith argues that it will be difficult to construct these because of the 'vital role' that 'common historical experiences and memories play in shaping identity and culture' (1990, p 180). Given that 'images and cultural traditions do not derive from, or descend upon, mute and passive populations' (Smith 1990, p 179), a global culture and identity needs to be 'based on shared memories and a sense of continuity between generations' (Smith 1990, p 180). It has little material basis on which to do so. Additionally, audiences 'customise' shared symbolic resources. For all the ways in which transnational programs like the *Cosby Show* bring Australia closer to Pakistan, Mexico and France; (and *Neighbours* may bring Zambia and Malaysia closer to Australia), there will still be many more ways in which Australia is divided from these. Hollywood programming on commercial television, British programming on the ABC and European programming on SBS are not so much evidence of a global culture operating in the Australian market as they are evidence of common cultural area identities—Anglophone and European—staged well below the global level.

Television policy was captured in Australia, as elsewhere, by domestic elites. But in Australia these were also—as in the US—business elites. Australian policy did not inhibit imports, service development or the development of popular local programming (in sport, infotainment and drama) as did European policy. Although Australian policy was also legitimated by social and cultural rhetoric, the strategies these rhetorics were attached to were pro-television business and pro-audience, as a competitive market and media monopolies shaped the television and policy environment. The producers and politicians who developed Australian content legislation were populist and in contact with their publics (Bobby Limb and Hector Crawford were involved in two of most successful programs of the 1960s, *The Sound of Music* and *Homicide*, while Senator Doug McLelland and Prime Minister John 'I love westerns' Gorton were associated with drama content regulation and subvention). Over its history, ABC-TV has been most attacked for failing its public service duty to be elitist (with, for example, *Countdown*, *GTK*, ABC sports, *This Day Tonight*, *Bellbird*, *Alvin*, *Certain Women*, *GP* and *Embassy*). Both the ABC and the SBS have also been forces for innovation and modernisation in Australian television, pioneering some programming concepts and formats later utilised by the commercials. As commercial and national stations have been operating in a competitive market from inception, the 1980s commercialisation and deregulation of television was not particularly new.

Television's import mix is becoming more important as additional television services develop, advertising growth becomes limited, and new services erode the audience shares of existing licensees. These developments will further tie Australian audiences into available international cultural area identities and constituencies. But Australian independence will be maintained. The cultural relationship between the US and Australia is close but not as close as that obtaining between Canada and the US. There is no common North American identity, rather an identity as an Anglophone country formed commonly by immigration and by program concept, intellect, social policy exchange of instruments, example and policy. If Australia is a kind of America, it can never be North America(n) as can Canada. Furthermore, there is not the same congruency between the dominant Anglo-American symbolic goods consumption and Australian interests in trade and commerce as there is in Canada. Quite the opposite, the contemporary trend is towards the declining importance of the trading relationship with the US.

As noted in chapter 2, the trend in Australian television, as in Australian society more generally, is towards national institutions, national networking and a reconfiguring of the local and regional. These reshapings are taking place alongside a partial internationalising of the economy and symbolic goods markets. The self-same internationalising pressures which have seen the weakening of central governments in favour of international agencies and greater regional autonomy in Europe have been experienced in Australia as a strengthening of the national government and a weakening of the autonomy of the states. They have enforced a sense of national independence (as neither the US nor Britain can be as relied upon as in the past). Increasing nationalising of issues, politics and instruments is in Australia the functional precondition for *international* exposure and integration. Internationalising movements shift cultural projects towards a geopolitical construction of the Australian nation/culture which is also supported by multiculturalism.

THE MULTICULTURAL NATION

In Australia, the question of ethnicity and minorities has a specific recognition in multiculturalism. Policy, cultural criticism, and the broadcast industry organise an Australian version of multiculturalism with its own particular identities and with separate institutions such as the SBS. This leads to a differently organised construction of minorities from that in the US and Europe. The minority challenge in Australia centrally involves federal policy. Minorities are mostly registered in terms of ethnic nationality and immigration (the exception being Aboriginal Australia), less in terms of religious beliefs, social values, cultural diversity, or because of longstanding second class citizenship status of non-white minorities (as in the US), or a separate cultural and territorial identity (as for the Quebecois in Canada). Like the US and Canada, though, Australian multiculturalism undergirds immigration, equal opportunity, affirmative action and anti-racism.

Multiculturalism is informed by cultural critique, emotional and cultural identifications, and a cultural and social project of nation building. Multicultural critique provides public criticism of Australian practices, mores and the like, draws out the exclusions of the nation, and supports, as a matter of political and ethical principle, the oppositional, the marginal, and the different in their relation to the social and cultural mainstream. Multicultural policy assists the public expression of continuity in tradition, emotion and affect between the various homelands and their Australian diaspora. It also imagines a culturally hybridised national culture defined as an accommodation of ESB and NESB peoples, of the (Anglo) Australian and the ethnic. Multiculturalism targets ethnic and mainstream cultures alike for change. It is a label which can variously mean separate sociocultural spaces, integration, new myths and symbols for Australian culture and identity, and forms of ethnic self-regulation. Though divergent and sometimes in conflict, these multicultural projects complement each other. Criticism—necessarily eccentric to policy—locates the gaps, absences and discrimination to be made good by policy. Emotional investment in a multicultural identity sustains popular and intellectual support for policy development, enabling 'intellectual work to be the expression and medium of identity' (Chicago Cultural Studies Group 1992, p 541). Policy prescriptions sustain criticism's social and political purchase on the public agenda by generating reports, research projects and grants infrastructure.

Multiculturalism is thus a family of related projects:

- a social and interventionist program aimed at generating tolerance, minimising racism and promoting understanding that is particularly targeted at transforming the Anglophone cultural core's perceptions and attitudes (and also those of potentially antogonistic ethnic groups);
- an equal opportunity and equal representation strategy mobilised on the basis of egalitarianism and giving people a 'fair go';
- a program promising greater cultural cohesion and fealty to the state, political parties, and nation among ethnic groups;
- a state policy whose adoption can be promoted at international forums as an antidote to the all-too evident recent past of the White Australia Policy (which excluded Asians and blacks), and racial discrimination directed against its indigenous people, who were not afforded citizenship rights until 1967;
- a state-sponsored cultural hybridisation program promising a new culture in which the Anglo-Celtic (and Northern European cultural core) would become decentred and attenuated so that Australian

culture could be more readily and easily defined through a mix of other cultural elements (first Southern and Central European and then Middle Eastern and Asian);
- a policy of ethno-specificity, cultural maintenance and limited sovereignty for ethnic minorities which recognises the need for separate institutions including broadcast institutions (the SBS) and career structures within minorities-based organisations; and
- a policy targeted at ethnic organisations and people requiring regulated forms of self-recognition and political mobilisation within an overarching national context.

Since its 1970s adoption, multicultural media policy has held out the promise of two related kinds of cultural rights to minorities: rights as an ethnic fragment, and cultural rights to full participation in social, economic and cultural life as Australian citizens. Multiculturalism is both an ethnic strategy promoting ethnicity in national and cultural terms and creating expectations of limited 'sovereignty', and a citizenship strategy defining ethnicity in terms of structural disadvantage, discrimination and lack of access to resources, these to be overcome through activist policy. Multiculturalism is a pluralist strategy which provides for the integrity and development of the particular minority and for the participation of that minority in mainstream institutions and social life.

These two strands sometimes conflict but are mostly complementary. The 'sovereignty' of the ethnic (or minority) group provides the disadvantaged group with a publicly sanctioned visibility, identity and integrity and so makes that mainstreaming all the more politically necessary. Combating racism, discrimination and promoting broader understanding is essential to the integrity and identity of ethnic fragments and other minorities. Sometimes these can be in conflict as, for example, when SBS-TV is torn between providing language programs for the ethnic fragment defined in homeland terms (often a first-generation immigrant ambition) and the project of mainstreaming ethnic identities on Australian terms (often a second-generation ambition). Equally, multicultural policy will stress one of these aspects more than the other depending on the context. For example, SBS at inception was called 'ethnic television' with this name suggesting a cultural sovereignty purpose; today, it is known as 'multicultural' television for 'special people, Australians', suggesting a citizenship purpose. With more local production it became necessary to stage the Australian experience of the ethnic groups and so present a poly-ethnic *Australian* reality. SBS-TV also has more pluralist ends inasmuch as minorities not defined through immigrant ethnicity, such as gays, Aborigines and the disabled, are accorded some recognition in the service.

Critical multiculturalism turns on this strategy's double identity: mainstreaming projects are held to limit the cultural sovereignty of ethnic and minority groups; cultural sovereignty and ethno-separate strategies are criticised for compromising participation in mainstream institutions and denying a poly-ethnic social reality. SBS gets routinely criticised either for not being ethnic enough or, in being too ethno-specific, not multicultural enough. Representations of ethnic identities where they exist are routinely criticised for being 'the wog the Anglos want to see' and for denying the on-the-ground cultural hybridisation that is the lived reality of most ethnic groups.

Multiculturalism is, I believe, becoming more important to Australian television. Once it simply referred to SBS-TV (dealt with in the next 2 chapters). Now it is increasingly affecting the core of Australian television in the ABC and commercials. This is partly a consequence of federal government policy to mainstream multiculturalism across social institutions and organisations. But it is also a consequence of SBS-TV being around for a decade, creating the expectation for changes in ABC and commercial television practice. Mainstreaming multiculturalism in television means that multiculturalism becomes not only an issue for SBS-TV, but for all television stations. The ABC and the commercials can be expected to inflect multiculturalism further towards mainstreaming. They have much larger audiences and local production slates than SBS-TV. Their audiences are constituted in 'general', not 'special' terms. Their language of broadcast is English, which is also the lingua franca of general public communication including communication between ethnic groups.

Different things can be expected and demanded of SBS than of the ABC and the commercial networks. SBS-TV can readily accommodate ethnic fragments in relation to their languages, cultures and homelands, recognising them individually through non-English-language broadcasts. This is simply not an option for the ABC and the commercials, which cannot be expected to broadcast routinely in ethnic languages and still to maintain their general audience shares. The multiculturalism accommodated by them is the ethnic fragment's relation to Australian society and culture, mostly expressed in English. This is necessarily a cultural pluralist project in that ethnic and minority issues would be represented within Australian programming and 'ethnics' would participate in the making of Australian-*produced* symbolic goods. Such mainstreaming inevitably changes the shape of the public identity ascribed to the ethnic fragment: it shifts from an Australian diaspora (which ascribed to the ethnic the status of perpetual immigrant, defined and self-defined in relation to the homeland) to a 'here in Australia' orientation which turns the central issue into—as in the US—the minorities' relations to the mainstream. Critical multiculturalism provides evidence of ethnic and minorities' social disadvantage and of media misrepresentation and under-representation in mainstream television offerings (see University of Technology, Sydney 1990). This evidence in turn forms the basis for lobbying directed at policy interventions into the mainstream (see Communications Law Centre 1992).

Lobbying for more multiculturalism in television is encouraged by the more general acceptance of equal opportunity, affirmative action and anti-racism policies targeting pluralist outcomes, better life opportunities and social and economic integration, and fair dealing within Australia as a territorial nation. Here multicultural programs are being designed for instrumental rather than expressive purposes. They are to deliver social cohesion, economic integration, equality of social outcomes, racial and social tolerance (particularly in the context of the settlement difficulties attending the large refugee intakes of the 1970s and 1980s of Lebanese and Indo-Chinese, the seeming creation of a bottom tier of the labour market made up of the semi-skilled and unskilled Southern European migration of the 1950s and 1960s, and the evident public discrimination against particular non-Anglo-Celtic groups—Aborigines and some migrants [Asian and Lebanese particularly]). Translated to television, these policy emphases would be readily measured through employment and representational outcomes in terms of the background of, for example, Australian Film Television and Radio School students, ABC and commercials staffing, and content analysis of Australian television programs. Multiculturalism becomes for the ABC and commercials a media mainstreaming project predicated upon English as the lingua franca and attenuated versions of symbolic ethnicity defined within the wider Australian society. In this, multiculturalism not only targets the Australian, but also the ethnicities themselves to be more inclusive, transformed, and their existing definitions decentred.

The multiculturalist challenge for mainstream Australian television is multifaceted. At a policy level it argues for adequate representation in terms of:

- mainstream reporting of ethnic issues generally;
- well-defined news protocols alive to cultural difference and pluralism and guarding against furthering stereotypes and giving offence to particular communities;
- an ethnic presence in Australian television drama protocols in

terms of greater kinds of ethnic specific presence in storytelling, normalisation of ethnicity into non-ethnic specific roles and non-stereotyped representation of ethnic groups;
- an ethnic advertising presence in advertisements and non-stereotypical ways of covering ethnicity in advertising;
- legislative intervention and educational campaigns to implement these multicultural policies in television organisations and production practices (see Communications Law Centre 1992).

The notion of a large NESB population whose aspirations are not met by existing televisual arrangements allowed a new way of making ethnic diversity actionable. Individually, no ethnic group—apart from the so-called dominant Anglo-Celtic fragment (which does not, by and large, recognise itself as 'ethnic')—was considered significant in its own right. But as part of a NESB whole, there was a large enough mass of people to legitimate televisual accommodation. The NESB category also had another advantage; it recognised the poly-ethnic mix in Australia in a way ethno-separate strategies could not. One marker of this poly-ethnic reality is marriage patterns. These reveal significant inter-ethnic and NESB and ESB intermarriage (57 per cent of immigrant NES men and 42 per cent of women 'have married outside their ethnic community; while over 70 per cent of second generation men and women have done so' [Price 1989, p 14). The category also provided a point of shared identity in relation to the dominant culture. While not having the sentimental attachments or culture of affect of the homeland's culture, the NESB is a cosmopolitan Australian identity with roots in an Australian poly-ethnic mix.

These projects associated with mainstreaming multiculturalism are a consequence of minorities' aspirations to participate and benefit from the wider opportunities available in the (non-ethnically marked) local cultural industries. Aspirant directors, actors and writers in television and film could only go so far in SBS-TV, given its limited funding for local production and its existing cosmopolitan definitions. Minorities also participated in Anglophone audiovisual culture as audiences, and this encouraged ambitions to seek work in it, to reach a wider audience, and to gain access to the greater varieties of role, direction and scriptwriting available to that culture. But in doing so, this new group encountered bigotry, bias, and the representational limits of the Anglophone commercial and national broadcasting culture, as well as the industry's limits as a medium-sized television service.

These circumstances meant engaging with the local television industry and attempting to broaden its definitions, employment and scripting practices. (It also meant supporting the production industry's aim of Australian-based rather than imported production.) The move from consumer to producer entails a move on the host culture—a move predicated upon a television logic of the Australian as a *melting pot*. This means ethnicity and difference must be normalised through non-ethnic-specific roles being played by 'ethnic' (which would see a Chinese, Lebanese or a Vietnamese Jana Wendt, and actors of NESB background routinely appearing alongside Jason and Kylie); through ethnically appropriate actors playing their particular ethnic roles (which often does not happen as, for example, with the series *Boney* and its part-Aboriginal detective); and through storytelling affording a place to ethnic communities and an Australian poly-ethnic reality formed out of religious mixed marriages and longstanding exogamous marriage patterns (in the Anglo-Celtic and Non-Anglo-Celtic mix, the third-or fourth-generation Chinese Australians, the Aborigines, and mixed race peoples). The outcome here is going to be ethnicity defined less in terms of homeland nationality (associated with the first-generation migrant and ethnic associations) than in terms of multi-ethnic Australians and Australian cultural and ethnic hybrids often in the second and third generation.

But it is important to recognise the limits of the NESB strategy. It is decidedly, not about a divide between two nations in Australia seeking sovereign expression. Many NESB groups are closer to the Australian-born than to other NESB groups. McAllister and Moore's survey of Maltese, Lebanese and Vietnamese ethnic fragments on the basis of perceived cultural proximity suggests that on most indicators, ethnic fragments feel greater cultural proximity to the Australian host culture(s) than to other ethnic groups (1991, p 135). Such results should come as no surprise—they are based upon the need for people to understand, operate, influence and broker Australian host institutions to personal, familial and collective advantage.

Furthermore, the ties that unite the diverse NESB fragments are often less than the ties that unite particular fragments of that NESB category to the dominant Anglophone culture. Even where there is geographical and cultural proximity (as with Serbs and Croatians, Macedonians and Greeks, Vietnamese and Chinese), emotional ties, identity and sense of commonality of purpose and political closeness are most often greater with the dominant Anglophone fragment than with each other. Today, this is particularly so as ethnic revivals in a post-communist Europe are affecting the southern and central European immigration of the postwar period, fundamentally altering the relationship between culturally proximate groups. Such cleavages make it difficult for a generalised ethnic Australian experience to be registered on television, and create obstacles for ethno-specific stories to function in a socially inclusive way. Social class within ethnic groups is also an important matter given that the changed immigration profile is seeing more skilled (and English-literate) migration from southern Europe and Asia than in the past, and is further fragmenting ethnic communities.

Unlike the English-speaking category, which defines a broad cultural area inasmuch as language systems form internationally shared cultural and communication corridors, the NESB category does not refer to a cultural area. It is made up literally of the rest of the world's language cultures. There are broad cultural area ethnic identities within Australia, such as the southern European or Latin identities based on Portuguese, Italian, Croatian and Spanish intermarriage, and these rely upon a stronger sense of common culture than between Anglo-Celtic Australians and themselves; similarly broad cultural area identities are emerging around 'Asian (Chinese)' and Islamic identities. But these viable identities of culture and affect are still very much smaller in membership than the NESB category as a whole and are consequently less politically visible.

Caution also needs to be taken with the disadvantage argument. NESB disadvantage is, *on balance*, a set of disadvantages in the labour market, wealth, business, tertiary participation rates and public sector employment which accrue more routinely to particular NESB groups. It is not a general condition. On a number of indicators particular ethnic groups do better than the Australian-born. Germans, Japanese, Malaysians, Hong Kongers, Singaporeans, Dutch and south Asians had higher median income levels on the 1986 census than did the Australian born (Price 1989, p 18); first-generation immigrants from central, eastern and southern Europe, and Chinese are well represented among the richest individuals in Australia (Jupp 1989, p 37); Chinese and Greek backgrounds are over-represented compared to the national average among higher education students (Hoston & Salaguras 1989, p 101); while Lebanese, Greeks and Italians were over-represented in business compared to the national average (Holton 1989, p 115).

These considerations inform the shift in ground that mainstream television can be expected to make to the multicultural challenge. Those ethnic groups and cultural areas with the most significant proportional population and/or influence—or whose negotiations with the mainstream have been more fraught over a longer period of time—maintain a stronger position to be named in television fiction. Hence the Australian television interest in Greek and Italian Australian experience, and in Asian and Aboriginal fictional characterisation. It is these culture area identities, the larger ethnic groups with high levels of marriage within their own ethnic community and typically greater suburban concentrations of the ethnicity (Greeks and Italians), and problematic 'others' with or without special claims—like Aborigines and Asians—that are likely to be negotiated on television. Take the TV comedy, *Acropolis Now*, based on the stage success, *Wogs out of Work*. It is designed for a Greek and general Australian audience (not for an NESB audience and an ESB audience). Such a program is possible because of the longstanding nature and history of the negotiations between Greek Australians and other Australians which provides for an evident Greek Australian symbolic ethnicity. Apart from Aborigines, Greeks and Italians, Australian television finds it hard to deal popularly with other ethnic groups except in relation to foreign relations (the typical way of dealing with east and South-East Asian Australians).

In the short term, news and current affairs, information and documentary programs are likely to stage greater equality of representation because such programs have a relatively direct relationship to social life. Television drama fiction is less amenable to immediate change. Nonetheless, some fiction genres can handle ethnicity as part of their story better than others. Comedy since *They're a Weird Mob* (1966) has involved ethnicity in some form in *Home Sweet Home* (about an Italian cab driver and his relation with his Australian children), *Kingswood Country* (with its son-in-law—'the wog'—who is the normal person acting as a foil for the monstrous Ted Bullpit), *Acropolis Now* (set in a Greek cafe), *Aunty Jack* (with its Wollongong NESB characters) and *Comedy Company* (with Con, a Greek fruiterer). Being lower budgeted, working off dialogue and social knowledges, these are typically directed at the local television audience. *Mother and Son* is the exception here in that it works to the closely familial horizon of the title relationship rather than Australian social texts. (Interestingly, this most universal of Australian television comedies is criticised by the University of Technology Sydney report [1990, p 42] for not having regular NESB characters and hardly featuring them in guest spots.) Similarly detective or police stories centring on investigations and crimes ensured a tour through social fragments, values formations and so on. This made them better able to routinely reference ethnicity (this saw *Homicide* and the court room drama *Consider Your Verdict* routinely stage ethnicity more than twenty years ago). Ethnic diversity is more possible in programs which are required to be 'true to the actual' and to consider public behaviours than in those which are required to be 'true to the probable' and survey private and domestic behaviours.

Soaps are less socially inclusive in that they are centred around the private, the familial and the emotional. A stable family in representational terms facilitates broadly based identification and diminishes the staging of ethnicity and inter-ethnic accommodation and friction (this is the case for Australian, US and British soaps). However, the mini-series, with its short form and event-oriented structure, has permitted the staging of ethnicity and ethnic intermixing within an overarching public, sometimes national, context.

The staging of ethnicity is not without its critical and conceptual difficulties both for television producers and critics (assuming, of course, a willingness on the part of networks and production companies to be involved). Critical multiculturalism, for instance, will need to move from a criticism of the excluded margins which associates any presentation of ethnicity with offence to the group presented, tokenism and the 'wog' the 'Anglo' wants to see (Carmichael 1991) towards a criticism which recognises distinctions in presentation and dramaturgical necessity. A comedy based on a claustrophic mother–son relationship (*Mother and Son*) is clearly going to afford fewer opportunities to reference ethnicity and cultural diversity than a soap based in a clinic (*A Country Practice*) or an action series (*Police Rescue*). If critical multiculturalism does not recognise such distinctions, it will function to discourage, not encourage, poly-ethnic representation of, and participation in, television production by different ethnic groups.

Working in favour of a televisual multicultural accommodation is the changing demographic profile in which people with a mixed Anglo-Celtic and non-Anglo-Celtic background are becoming the fastest-growing ethnic division (30 per cent now, and likely to be the largest ethnic division within two decades). With this changing demographic profile, it is likely that television will more routinely and increasingly offer roles and story space for *ethnically mixed* Australians. Such demographic changes, when taken in conjunction with multicultural policy development, will foster changes within the national culture and within television program production.

Writing in 1962, Ronald Taft noted that:

> Australia is a country where the son of a small-time Polish-Jewish tailor could become Chief Justice and representative of the English King, and where a penniless immigrant hawker from Russia could become the largest retailer Australia has known and a member, by marriage, of one of the leading families. (pp 199–200)

Yet such 'rags to riches' stories, though 'commonplace', played 'little part in the heroic myths of the country' (Taft 1962, p 199). The multicultural challenge to national culture and television is that representations of the Australian and the quotidian routinely mobilise this ethnic and social diversity. In this way the position of the Australian, declared as Anglo-Celtic by multicultural critique, would remain the point of reference for the melting pot, but would become more open and even attenuated as ways are found of including and acknowledging social and cultural diversity. It is not simply the Australian that would change. The ethnic groups would themselves attenuate their own specific ethnic identities, reshaping their sense of themselves and their priorities towards different ends and becoming in the process more akin to the Mary Kalantzis's multi-ethnic formulation in the ABC documentary *One Australia?* (1990) 'I am Australian in my diversity'.

The enduring legacy of the ESB and NESB political divide will be the way it has provided policy technologies with a means of promoting such reshapings. Given that expressive exactness and representational efficacy is only a part of television and national cultural ambition, the multicultural challenge will not simply be a demand that the 'anthropological' culture be represented in the 'symbolic' culture (which would prescribe news, information and social realist techniques), but that the symbolic culture, fun and entertainment, adjust its symbolisations, its negotiation of the materials of its tradition, and its civic and national inventions. Such renegotiations will not be a simple recalculation based on population proportions, or represent new beginnings; rather, they will graft themselves onto what is *already there*, what is brought to them by the ethnic mix and the prevailing international and local mix of symbolic goods. Popular recent examples of this are the north Queensland Italian identity in the mini-series *Fields of Fire* (which combined regional and ethnic specificity in a drama of English, Australian and Italian relationships) and the Greek Australian identity of *Acropolis Now*.

A relation to national culture is central to multiculturalism: the cultural criticism which is antagonistic to the mainstream becomes the basis for a policy perspective which mainstreams the multicultural. The multicultural challenge to national culture once enlisted in public policy supports national culture. Multiculturalism in these terms is and will remain not so much a populist policy or even a populist identity but a state-oriented and rationally geared discourse within which cultural critics and lobbyists can project an imaginary identity and unity in diversity and stage their policy involvement.

Australian multiculturalists have a necessarily ambiguous relation to national culture, as befits multiculturalism's multiple existence as policy and critique, alternative sociocultural space, alternative ethnic identity and a new melting pot Australian identity. They are at once critical and selectively supportive of state policy, lending support to state multicultural initiatives whilst simultaneously remaining suspicious of the imagined community of the nation. Mary Kalantzis, as one of the authors of *Mistaken Identity*, criticised national identity and national culture for its exclusions, and in its stead proposed community without nation as an antidote to bicentennial nationalism (Castles et al 1988). Later, she appeared on the ABC documentary *One Australia?* (1991) asserting her Australianness as 'Australian in my diversity' and arguing that multiculturalism should be brought to the heart of the mythical–symbolic complex of Australian identity and national culture. Kalantzis acts as a consultant promoting multicultural organisational cultures in the public service and business. She has also appeared on talkback radio commenting on television programs like the ABC's *Sylvania Waters* (a documentary series about a family in Sydney), arguing that such programs should represent Australia's ethnic diversity rather than concentrate yet again on the Anglo-Australian experience.

Multicultural criticism and policy will develop further over the coming decade. This development will not only be driven from below by the changes in Australian demography, but also from above because of geopolitical changes in the wake of the new world order, the economic importance of the Asian Tigers and Japan, and the emergence of trading blocs. These will make mainstreaming multiculturalism even more socially and economically functional.

THE GEOPOLITICAL NATION

Under the geo-political nation the project is nation building, not national identity; the national political, not the national cultural. Because the health, economic, and security future of the nation is at stake, the priority is the national interest. So the territorial nation asserts itself over the nation of community and sentiment. Social priorities lie in finding a future in the broader international political economy rather than in adjusting points of continuity between homeland and Australia or maintaining local tradition. The imperative is to refashion civic outlook, identity and image instrumentally in the name of a political and economic future and to keep up with other nations (Morris 1992, p 40).

Australia's external interests dictate a logic of nation building which optimises domestic human, industrial, and natural resources. Social policies in areas like childcare and unemployment are seen to maximise the use of human resources and facilitate structural change. Environmental issues become framed in economic terms as 'sustainable development'. Multiculturalism has the economic role of turning an ethnically diverse population to economic advantage in an increasingly competitive and difficult international trading environment. It is no longer enough that the nation should express itself. Workplace, corporate and educational culture need to be made conducive to international competitiveness and innovation. State interests require that cultural goods contribute to the formation of identities and social priorities that will assist nation building.

Under such logics, attitudes to the 'others in our midst' change. Australia is no longer to be imagined as the world proclaiming its one-hundred-odd nationalities and languages. New ways of distinguishing between the homeland and the Australian are required when the homelands and the broader Anglophone and European cultural areas become economic competitors responsible for diminishing national wealth in circumstances where foreign policy centrally involves trade policy. As homeland affiliations become politically (but not sentimentally) attenuated, ethnicity becomes defined politically in relation to the Australian state. Multiculturalism as a question of Australian integration is mainstreamed in terms of equality of opportunity and access for better economic and national cohesion. Increasingly, the panoply of civil instruments (from police to local government; from arts institutions to the federal bureaucracy) carry multiculturalism. It is a vehicle for overcoming discrimination, for creating better access, for making ethnic businesses and social practices more transparent and more productive for the national economy as a whole (Stockley & Foster 1990, pp 307–28). Social policy intervention in symbolic goods aims at mainstreaming solutions with broader, less homeland-defined identities encouraged. With the new international orientations, with Australia's ethnic diversity resembling the US melting pot of the early years of the twentieth century, with the gap between the ethnic composition of Australia and the British Isles widening, with increased Asian immigration, and with the need for greater integration of Australia with Asian nations, Australian national claims are becoming less those of a British and European diaspora or partner in Pax Americana, and more its own claims of territorial and identity integrity. Australia becomes a nation dealing with many such other nations at a cultural distance from it, a 'European fragment in Asia'. This means taking a certain distance from Europe and North America.

Dealing with Asia and Asian immigration in the 1990s has become a national preoccupation (Garnaut 1989, pp 286–300). The significant cultural 'other' occupying policy becomes the 'others' in our part of the world. This Asian orientation tries to accommodate the Asian nations and Asians in the popular image of Australia. Asian Australian well-being becomes important as Asian immigrants become economically important in helping to adjust Australian to Asian business, commercial, cultural and educational opportunities (see Shaw 1992, pp 34–40). 'Asia' is now economic and cultural opportunity, not strategic threat. In the film industry, for instance, Asia has become the focus of AFC market development activities (*AFC News* 108, 1992, p 1) and producers are seeking closer working relationships with television broadcasters in Asian markets.

Asian immigration is now associated with the internationalisation of the economy. This immigration is expected to serve the economic and cultural purpose of Asian–Australian integration. In a society whose historical identity was formed on Asian exclusion, 'Asian' becomes a valued ethnicity. Like the northern European immigration, Asian ethnicity is a vehicle for securing Australian commercial advantage. The skilled Asian immigrant comes to Australia, passes the English language tests and expects and obtains the kind of advantages of social hierarchy and command positions in the economy and professions as did his or her British and northern and central European counterparts in the 1950s and 1960s. Like those people, skilled Asian immigrants will be more skilled than their Australian counterparts. The pressure of external adjustment and domestic policy can be expected to reduce the marked hostility towards 'Asians'. Continued patterns of intermarriage with the predominant Anglo-Celtic fragment and styles of ethnic community cultural hybridisation should further erode perceptions of their separateness.

Australian identity has the problem of reconciling geography and (European) culture in the context of Asian and Pacific cultures. The increasingly important 'Asian' nodal points—formed in addition to the US (that most open of nodal points) and a declining European nodal point—is nationally defined and less inclusive than the others were. It will not be as possible for Australians to journey to Asian centres and obtain important posts. There is unlikely to be the phenomenon of the 'professional' Australian (like Barry Humphries on Clive James) on any Asian television service. There will be no Rupert Murdochs becoming Japanese citizens. Japanese and Hong Kong symbolic culture may be becoming more valued in Australia, but neither is as inclusive for most Australians as are Hollywood's and Britain's symbolic cultures. Australian (non-Asian) cosmopolitans can only weakly participate in 'Asian' culture and can only attenuate their own traditions so far.

The contours of these changes are evident in programs such as *Embassy*, the *Asia Report* (including its later mainstreaming into *Dateline*), *Vietnam* (1987), *Cowra Breakout* (1985) and *Children of the Dragon* (1992). The drama in these programs is one of Australia's adjustments to Asia. Increasingly, storytelling is turning to staging an adjustment to its own Asian ethnicities as regular Asian characters were introduced into the story line of *Chances* (1992) and *GP* (1993). In drama the need to make overseas, principally European and North American, television sales is making it difficult for an Australian marked in non-European terms. But it does enable drama involving a non-European Asia and European Australia (with Australia providing the Asian actors to play Asian nationals, and Asian locations—as, for example, Melbourne became Beijing in *Children of the Dragon*). In information and current affairs, this involves more Asian coverage, voices and competences.

The old dualism between entertainment and education, between the US and Britain, the commercials and the ABC, is being put on a different footing. Television's educational orientations are becoming less British and more North American and Asian. Australian broadcasters look to programming about 'their part of the world'. There is not the same congruency as there was once between the dominant Anglo-American symbolic goods consumption and Australian interests in politics, trade and commerce. As the trade and political gap widens with trade friction between Australia and the US and Europe, and with the increasing importance of Australian–Asian trade, Anglo-American television imports and their Australian consumption take on some of the characteristics of Dutch, Irish, Scandinavian and Singaporean consumption. The national political is no longer as closely tied to the national cultural. British programming increasingly becomes Anglophone programming, as it is seen on US public television, rather than programming proferring a British identity to the Australian nation.

Entertainment and fun are not as easily available to tactical redeployment as the political and civic culture. Nor can they be easily shifted from their historic moorings in Anglophone culture. US control over symbolic product and influence in the market will not only continue but will be extended through additional television services. Trends in Australian content to become more internationalised will favour Australia–US–Canada and Australia–UK–Europe connections more than they will Australia–Asian connections. The opportunities to reconstruct Australian identities in the preferred geopolitical terms will be limited. Under geopolitical logics, national broadcasters ABC and SBS should have an important role, as commercial dynamics cannot be relied upon to develop the necessary social and cultural cement of an Australian-based international outlook.

Perhaps this resistance is no bad thing. The Anglophone culture has been a source of Australian strength in providing models of the melting pot: ethnic tolerance to embrace, and intolerance to avoid. It will continue to provide these. For all the ways in which the Australian is becoming slightly daggy, lacking in cosmopolitanism and the like with the admission of a nation in economic crisis, the commercial and national television stations cannot generally embrace the logic of geopolitics. For them, the Australian national culture in its diverse manifestations will be a continuing source of inspiration, indifference, and resistance to these civil, rational and technicist projects. Not for the first time the residue of previous projects of national culture—official and unofficial—provides an alternative vantage point to top-down state fashionings. The cosmopolitan multiculturalists and geopolitical nationalists face the same resistances to a universalisation of culture in their own image as did their previous Anglo-Australian and Europeanist incarnations.

7 SBS-TV: Symbolic politics and multicultural policy in television provision

with Dona Kolar-Panov

> When I first saw SBS television, in my 20s, I cried... SBS was like a thunderbolt that had struck The Box... we all tuned in to the first broadcast. I hoped that none of my flatmates saw how it was affecting me. I didn't expect to get so emotional... Maybe I cried because I felt some part of my story, the drama of my life, had finally been officially placed into the jigsaw puzzle that is society, Australian life. Maybe I cried because someone was speaking not only to me but to people all around the country in my accent, in the language of my parents. Maybe it was simply the sight of another wog reading the evening news—a news service that connected Australia with the rest of the world and not just a few murders in Sydney and Melbourne before turning over to sport—that impressed me... SBS is the best thing to have happened to Australian television.
>
> Anna Maria Dell'oso (1991, p 22)

SBS-TV has a special place in Australian and world television despite its low ratings—historically between 1 and 3 per cent of the overall viewing audience. When introduced in Sydney and Melbourne on 24 October 1980, it brought a new dimension to Australian television. SBS-TV changed the Australian television mix, expanded viewer horizons, and provided a schedule of alternative programming for ethnic, cosmopolitan, minority and marginal audiences.

SBS scheduled programs that the ABC and the commercials paid little or no attention to. It screened foreign-language (in SBS jargon,

---

The ethnographic research that forms a substantial portion of this chapter and chapter 8 is taken from Dona Kolar-Panov's PhD thesis in progress, School of Humanities, Murdoch University. This chapter discusses SBS-TV in terms of multicultural politics and policy. The next chapter considers SBS as a television service.

'multilingual') feature films, television series and documentaries. It expanded the coverage of international events in its news and current affairs service. It greatly increased the range of information, documentary, arts and education programming available on television, supplementing the ABC's existing mix. It included soccer—a majority sport with patchy television coverage—and minority sports such as cycling with little existing television coverage apart from the Olympics. It expanded the range of program genres in television with local and international animation for adults, short films, experimental film and video and music clips. It innovated programming formats in current affairs (*Vox Populi, Asia Report*) and in drama, with multilingual mini-series (*Women of the Sun*), one-offs (*Six Pack*) and series (*Girl from Steel City*). In doing so it opened out a whole new area of Australian life for representation and commentary. Such programming defined SBS's diverse audience constituency of ethnic fragments, cosmopolitans, minorities, and enthusiasts of various sports. As a national broadcaster, SBS promised the 'ethnic' and the 'minority' a public recognition of their cultural diversity and a vehicle for the expression of their needs (even if it could not always meet this promise).

Unlike any other English language service in the 1980s, SBS provided a publicly supported window onto television and film worldwide. (The US PBS does not buy much product outside of its British and, to a lesser extent, Canadian sources. BBC and Channel 4 are only just now discovering Europe and offering more subtitled film and television, but neither devote as much of their program schedules to broadcasts in languages other than English.) SBS programming was both international and national. This made it unlike other Australian broadcasters for whom international programming meant British or North American, and whose Australian component included national, regional and local elements. SBS-TV thus broadened the international component of Australia's audiovisual culture by adding to the existing Anglo-American moorings (Hall 1981, pp 85–6). SBS represented a new and better vantage point from which to see the world from Australia. This was particularly so in the context of the economic and cultural importance of the European Community, changing external outlooks emphasising the Asia–Pacific region, the decline of Britain and to a lesser extent the US in world affairs, and Britain's decline from its pre-eminent political, economic and cultural position in Australian life.

SBS bypassed the existing import distribution channels for Australian television. The ABC and the commercial stations, with long-standing agreements with British and US production organisations, closed the market not only to multilingual programming, but also to other English-language producers such as the US PBS, the Canadians and the New Zealanders. SBS, by contrast, bought programming much the same way as did many overseas broadcasters—through the international television and film markets—as well as through associations with particular broadcasters. SBS thus internationalised program sources, drawing on predominantly European, North American (Canadian and US) and, to a lesser extent, Asian program sources for both highbrow and popular products. With the advent of Channel 4 in the UK at the end of 1982, SBS became an Australian outlet for its alternative documentary and drama programming. SBS exposed the limits of the service orientations of the commercials and the ABC. On SBS, British highbrow culture simply became a component part of elite cultural forms which included European, Asian and North American forms; whilst popular programming no longer meant just US, British and Australian programs. SBS opened out highbrow definitions, neutralised existing identifications of the highbrow within a typically British framing, allowed Australian-produced highbrow culture to achieve a different exposure, and afforded a televisual presentation for previously excluded kinds of film activity. For cosmopolitans SBS represented a new way of being international and connected to the outside world, and gave an evident form to elite culture's claim to 'be cultures of and for humanity as a whole' (Routt 1991, p 223).

Deliberately international, SBS managed the local and the Australian in a new way. The slogan SBS used in the mid-to-late 1980s, 'Bringing the World Back Home', is an important expression of this. The 'world' ambiguously indicated the homelands and languages of ethnic immigrants and a purposefully international, cosmopolitan outlook not tied to any of these. But these were not in opposition to 'home' in Australia. Quite the contrary. The 'world is brought home', with 'home' being unequivocally here in Australia and with the 'world' fitting into it. The force of the word 'back' lies in its prioritising of passage, of movement, of a bringing back. In this slogan lies SBS's comfortable mix of localism and cosmopolitanism, its articulation of the elsewhere in the here.

In providing a mix of imported programming and by encouraging different kinds of local program initiatives, SBS expanded the models and content available to film and television producers. In this it modernised the Australian television service and innovated Australian program concepts. It developed program formats, such as international motorcycling, which were later taken over and turned into profit centres by the commercial networks or mainstreamed into ABC broadcasts. It functioned as an entry point and testing ground for local programming concepts which could be subsequently adopted by the larger television networks. Its *World News* made the other stations 'more conscientious about their overseas coverage' (Johns 1991, p 16), while the relations between domestic news organisations and ethnic communities it forged led to the development of a new set of local news sources for the ABC and commercial stations. It made subtitling more acceptable for documentary and fictional productions (Semmler 1985, p 74). In naturalising English language subtitling, it provided a means for more Australians to find ways into making subtitled programming their own—as the trials and tribulations of Oshin provided a Japanese alternative soap opera heroine to Kylie Minogue in *Neighbours* during the late 1980s. It permitted programming which used Aboriginal Australian English often too difficult to understand without subtitling, and it permitted various ethnic Australian accents.

Unlike the existing services, which are necessarily more 'tradition' bound—given their need to protect their audience base—SBS could afford to develop connections with audiences that the larger stations simply could not. SBS showed that, in an Australian context in which some 30 per cent of the population are of mixed Anglo-Celtic and non-Anglo-Celtic descent, there could be a demand for drama and information programming which staged ethnicity and cultural mixing. Its experimental locally produced multilingual drama programming, its documentaries involving different ethnicities, and its imported multilingual programs paved the way for information and drama programming on other stations dealing with various 'ethnic' experiences in Australia including interactions with the 'host' Anglo-Australian culture. The mini-series *Cowra Breakout* told of failed cultural understanding between Japanese prisoners of war and their Australian warders just as the ultimately successful accommodation of ethnic differences was staged for Jewish refugees in *The Dunera Boys* or Italian cane farmers in *Fields of Fire*. SBS-TV also played a role as an entry point and training ground for people of an ethnic background in television.

A MINORITARIAN SERVICE

> Virtually no other country recognises the minority groups within their communities the way we do.
> Ian Hamilton, SBS Head of Production, 1986
> ([WA] *Daily News*, December 1986)

As a television service, SBS was constituted on a different basis from the norm. It was the first Australian television service created with a minoritarian brief. In the policy jargon it was catering to 'specialist needs', hence its title, Special Broadcasting Service. The ABC and commercials were mostly catering to general needs. (Channel 10 did, however, screen *Let's Go Greek* and *Greek Variety* in 1984 and attracted the largest Australian Greek audience for any program, see Bednall 1988, p 45; while the ABC had always showed special programs, and acknowledged multicultural elements in its flagship programs of the 1960s and 1970s *Bellbird*, *The Big Country*, *Weekend Magazine* and *Four Corners*.)

Most evidently, SBS's minoritarianism centred on ethnic communities. But in its service over the 1980s and into the 1990s it catered for other minorities. These included regional concentrations of other groups, Aboriginal Australians, various political, sexual and at times religious minorities, people with disabilities (particularly the hearing-impaired) and arts–cultural constituencies. With social policy targeting disadvantaged sections of society through access and equity programs, SBS typically provided appropriate programming to supplement such policy initiatives (hence its *English at Work* series with each episode 'fully sponsored by a company, union, or government department' [Reid 1991, p 6]).

SBS-TV was shaped by multicultural policy. The SBS organisation (radio and television) represents 'the single largest area of expenditure by the government in the implementation of its multicultural policy' (Johns 1991, p 17). SBS interpreted its multicultural mission in 1991 as contributing to:

> ... a more cohesive, equitable and harmonious Australian society by providing an innovative and quality multilingual and multicultural radio and television service which depicts the diverse reality of Australia's multicultural society and meets the needs of Australians of all origins and backgrounds. (SBS 1991, p 6)

Multiculturalism is premised on the acceptance of the principle of minority cultural and social rights within an overarching national context. As such, SBS provides a vehicle for ideological lobbying aimed at securing recognition of such minority rights, and provides television programming which embodies them. Multicultural policy obligates SBS to provide a service for ethnic, indigenous and disadvantaged communities; to target the broader Australian population in terms of its attitudes and orientations to ethnic, racial and cultural diversity; and to represent the public acceptance of the principle of cultural and ethnic diversity in its programming.

Also as an instrument for multicultural policy, SBS is exposed to changes in the direction of that policy. The relationship between

SBS's multicultural policy objectives, its audiences, and its service provision to them is a continuing issue for SBS; it also drives its external assessment. SBS is, thus, more of a public initiative in a social policy and political forcefield than are the ABC and the commercials (though during its first thirty years the ABC was more social-policy-driven than it is today).

SBS-TV is not just a creature of multicultural policy and its anticipated—and unanticipated—outcomes. It is also a television service with its own internal dynamics. Cutting across its dual existence in policy and television, SBS's important, even defining, relation is to one of its audience constituencies, ethnic communities. While the character of SBS-TV is obviously not exhausted by this ethnic orientation and ethnic television use is not exhausted by SBS (ethnic video hiring, home taping and community tape exchanges are, for example, important), SBS is significantly shaped by the changing nature of its relations with ethnic audiences and ethnic organisations.

DEFINING ETHNIC COMMUNITIES

Because the service was created for and expected to be beholden to ethnic communities and their spokespersons, it is important to be clear about the meaning of 'ethnic community' in the Australian context.

The term 'ethnic communities' mostly refers to the non-English-Speaking Background (NESB) immigrants from southern and eastern Europe and Asia (including the Middle East) who came to Australia after the World War 2. This term is a self-identificatory category based upon a sense of cultural and social distance from official and informal Australian society and culture. These ethnic immigrant fragments are at a greater social and cultural distance from the Australian mainstream than that obtaining for British Isles and northern European immigrant fragments. These groups demonstrate this by mixing less with the Anglo-Celtic (past and recent British Isles migration) mainstream, through suburban and regional concentration, through greater levels of cultural and language maintenance, and through high levels of marriage within the ethnic group and to groups other than the Anglo-Celtic. This cultural and social distance leads to the cultural maintenance activities of these groups being perceived as forms of non-incorporation. (By contrast, the cultural maintenance activities of Anglo-Celtic and northern European immigrant fragments are barely noticeable means of being in Australia.)

These ethnic communities are then an outcome, in part, of the differences obtaining between them and the broader Australian community, the character of the forms of political representation available to them, and the senses of incorporation within the political, cultural and social project of Australia possible for them. The notion of an ethnic community, in terms of social policy, is also based on evident racial and sectarian discrimination, lack of equality and access to services, and more limited life opportunities available to some NESB communities (Jayasuriya 1983, pp 23–4) compared to Australians generally, and in particular to British and northern European immigrants. This 'disadvantage' understanding for social policy often sees Aboriginal, New Zealand Maoris, black Africans and other non-white races included within the ethnic and multicultural rubric (but this labelling as an ethnic minority is often refused by Aborigines). The designation of ethnic community has primarily, but not exclusively, existed for this mix of groups—groups which are socially constructed as *other* and sometimes construct themselves as '*other* to the (ethnically unmarked) Australian'.

There are difficulties in restricting ethnic communities to the NES peoples of southern Europe and Asia and to indigenous and racial others. The common culture shared by the Irish, British, Scottish, Welsh, New Zealand and North American immigrants with Anglo-Celtic Australians is more a series of resemblances than a system of identities. There is a cultural specificity to northern European immigrant cultures vis-a-vis the Australian although these cultures have always contributed to Australia's cultural mix and occupy a relatively valued place in it. There is no rigid division between ESB (English-speaking background) and NESB fragments in Australia. Rather there is a shifting set of divisions connected to, though not defined by, language. Additionally, much recent immigration from southern and eastern Europe and non-refugee Asian immigration is likely to be competent in English, skilled, and culturally sophisticated. These groups often bear less similarity to their existing ethnic fragment in Australia than to those fragments of Australian society their education and training enables them to associate with.

But ESB immigrants are closer to Australian society by sharing more information resources and political structures in common on arrival. Northern Europeans (German, Dutch, Scandinavian) with their similar customs, already significant knowledge of the English language and interaction with the British Isles, have always fitted in relatively easily, and have at times in Australian history been favoured by government policy and programs over other English-language ethnicities such as the Irish. Northern Europeans did not acquire a separate ethnic identity in the way southern Europeans and Asians did. Their levels of first-generation intermarriage with the Anglo-Celt were always much higher, they tended to be geographically dispersed

(Price 1968, pp 104, 109), their incomes closely matched and often exceeded their Anglo-Australian counterparts (Price 1989, p 18), they tended to be skilled rather than the largely unskilled or semi-skilled southern European immigrants (Price 1968, p 102), and their rates of language shift towards the English language were greater than for Greeks, Italians, and the groups in former Yugoslavia, all of whom exhibited higher degrees of language maintenance (Jayasuriya 1988, p 7). Some of the major figures associated with Australian cultural nationalism such as Henry Lawson [Larson] and PR Stephensen were drawn from this northern European group.

To be 'ethnic' in Australia in some circumstances can extend to other NESB immigrants, particularly northern European migration. Where multiculturalism is equated less with language and more with cultural diversity and the experience of immigration, ethnicity can also extend to English-language ethnicities. After more than a decade of multiculturalism as an official policy all immigrants are tending to be seen as ethnic nationals and increasingly to understand themselves in these terms. The inter-ethnic soccer violence between Greeks and Macedonians is replicated at a lower level in recent cricket crowd incidents between Australian and British supporters.

Ethnic immigrant communities constitute a particular problem for public policy makers. This is particularly so in the context of Australia's large postwar immigration program continuing to this day, which has been more significant in terms of a percentage of immigrants versus Australian-born than were the US proportions at their height in 1910 (Jayasuriya 1983, p 23). Accommodating immigration whilst ensuring a minimum of social disruption, disaffection and alienation on both the side of the broader host community and the immigrant has been an important social and public policy goal. Since the late 1940s, such a large immigration program necessarily turned citizenship, the national culture and national political definitions with respect to ethnic immigrants into public policy matters. Australia's large immigration program since World War 2 has been variously seen as central to policies of modernisation, economic development, defence, foreign relations, and labour supply.

Policy in this area is now represented by notions of multiculturalism and cultural diversity. From a public policy point of view, these terms presume that Australia is an emerging culture and society being formed from its constituent immigrant and host elements. Earlier formulations—like the assimilation and integration policies—saw the process as one in which ethnic communities either gradually became 'dinkum Australians' or were successfully integrated into broader social and cultural values and economic life. Multiculturalism by contrast proclaims the outcome of that cultural mixing as open, not preordained, 'a journey, not...a destination' (Johns 1991, p 14). This emergent Australian culture made from the mixing of many cultures, most particularly the mixing of many ethnic cultures with the host culture, is expected to complement rather than to be at odds with different ethnic cultures.

This emergent culture typically exceeds the character and definitions of it provided in official and semi-official representations. Official recognitions, formed as they are in policy and politics, may lag behind the cultural mixing of some ethnic immigrants with each other and Anglo-Celtic fragments but be in advance of the cultural mixing of some Anglo-Celtic fragments with other ethnic fragments. Indeed, the emergent culture—because of the time involved in policy formation—*may* always be constituted conservatively with reference to the unequal negotiations between Anglo-Australian and ethnic institutional and political structures.

By the same token, ethnic community leaders and their associations similarly lag behind a cultural reality for their members, given their tendencies to constitute ethnic self-identifications with reference to the national–political homeland (Price 1989, p 8). First-generation immigrant identification is often as much with particular villages and regions as it is with the homeland nation (this is particularly so for Italians and the different nationalities in former Yugoslavia). So too the experience for most ethnic immigrants is of a culturally hybridised multi-ethnic community formed through intermarriage and the adoption of host customs and values rather than the more culturally homogeneous ethnic fragment espoused by some ethnic organisations. This multi-ethnic dynamic is further underscored by the 'rapid break-up of ethnic communities as a result of second-generation migrants marrying outside their own communities' (Jayasuriya 1983, p 25). These dynamics help account for the surprising survey results of the Office for Multicultural Affairs in 1988 (cited in Betts 1991, pp 165–6) which found that only 7.4 per cent of the survey thought of themselves as belonging to an ethnic group other than Australian or British, while 84 per cent responded to the survey by disclaiming membership of *any* ethnic group, and claimed instead to be simply Australian.

The 'ethnic community' that SBS and multiculturalism recognises includes:

- relatively ethno-separate communities formed in relationship to the homeland with significant language and cultural maintenance beyond the first generation. Currently, an estimated 17 per cent of

the population uses a language other than English at home with these mainly being Greek, Italian, Croatian, Serbian and Macedonian with Arabic, the Chinese languages and Vietnamese becoming more important (Jayasuriya 1988, p 6);
- indigenous peoples (Aborigines and Torres Strait Islanders) and non-European racial groups (typically Asians and Arabs) defined through original occupation or immigration;
- first-generation immigrants generally—regardless of whether these are English-speaking or non-English-speaking—who are at some cultural distance from the Australian host community with public policy being concerned to meet their special settlement needs.
- and, more recently, multi-ethnic communities formed in Australia as a consequence of ethnic intermarriage and mixed ancestries from the first generation.

It is against this ethnic community dynamic that SBS-TV came into existence and subsequently flourished.

SBS AS SYMBOLIC POLITICS

> Ethnic television, in the long run for Australia, is one of the worst things I've ever heard of in my life. It is divisive to our society—and the last thing we want is a society divided on an ethnic basis. It is nonsense, but there is no way we can shake the Government on this one. I know of only one other country which has ethnic television, and that's Canada—where they have a separatist movement.
> Kerry Packer (quoted in Bostock 1981, p 189)

SBS-TV has always been politically controversial. Few public broadcasting organisations in the world could have continued through the kind of criticisms levelled at SBS from its inception. It has survived calls for it to close down, consistently low audience shares (1–3 per cent of the overall television audience over its history), a UHF reception ghetto after 1986 making it the only metropolitan television station on the technically inferior UHF band—which also imposed significant start-up expenses for consumers as new aerials and receivers were needed (discussed in chapter 8)—the tardy extension of the service to the 58 per cent of the population outside Sydney and Melbourne, many enquiries into it (1980, 1984, 1986, 1988), federal government moves to amalgamate it with the ABC (1986–87, see Foster & Stockley 1988, pp 176–9), and calls to improve it by changing it into an Australian Channel 4 (Evans 1987).

It initially had few friends in the television industry. Its creation was a slap in the face to the ABC, a possible threat to the commercials and, inasmuch as it was initially created as an import facility, a step backwards for the local film production industry. It embodied the nadir of relations between the then Fraser Liberal–National coalition government and the ABC (Ashbolt 1985, p 108). Its establishment reflected that government's perception—one shared with ethnic community organisations—that the ABC had been unresponsive in its programming to the multilingual and multicultural complexion of Australia's population (Ethnic Communities' Council of NSW 1984, p 3). SBS also reflected the Fraser government's commitment that new technology and new broadcasting stations would be set up through new structures, and not through existing instrumentalities. The ABC had wanted a second national station of its own from the mid-1960s—with a cultural and minority programming mandate (a BBC 2)—but when a second publicly funded broadcasting station was set up, the ABC was excluded. With SBS, the ABC acquired a competitor for federal funding allocation and audiences, and not simply the 'complementary' national broadcaster that the public faces of the two maintain.

Commercial station executives and owners rejected the idea of SBS. They argued against the move away from the general to various ethnically designated narrowcasted audiences (Leong 1983, p 9). Given the restrictions on the development of such audiences within broadcasting, the commercial stations worried—as did politicians and parts of government—about such a radical broadcasting departure, in which a government initiative undermined the prevailing forms, rules and national cultural identifications of the existing television service. Additionally, they objected to the initial proposals for SBS-TV to carry advertisements as it would erode the commercial television advertising dollar—at the time, they spoke of its government funding as giving SBS an unfair advantage in competition for the advertising dollar. For different reasons, advertising was not supported by many ethnic organisations, who argued that advertising would play down the communitarian and national broadcaster status of the service and prejudice the advertising base of the ethnic press.

For the Australian film industry, SBS seemed antagonistic to local content. Here was another television station begun on the basis of a telecine chain, a backlog of imported programming, and low levels of Australian content. In a service dedicated to ethnic needs defined in terms of multilingual programming from the ethnic homeland rather than Australia, the role for Australian-produced multicultural drama and information programming seemed slight. Additionally, SBS-TV was patently at odds with the existing direction and nature of television in Australia and the plans for its future. Developed largely outside existing broadcasting policy development, it had little precedent in existing policy—although it had large consequences for such policy.

SBS-TV was an unprecedented move by Australian television into uncharted territory. How was it possible? And how has it survived, given entrenched opposition from within broadcasting policy and from the television and program production industries? It could be because its origins do not lie in television or broadcasting policy (although the existence of ethnic radio certainly naturalised ethnic television).

SBS was generated by prime ministerial intervention. Its origins and its reasons for continuing are Politics with a capital P. It was promised during the 1977 federal election (Leong 1983, p 8). It owed its creation to the Fraser government's need to demonstrate a federal commitment to multiculturalism. With some of its ethnic credentials under fire, the Fraser government was committed to create new structures of multiculturalism which would be less politically contentious than the access radio experience of ethnic broadcasts on the ABC's 3ZZ (Ashbolt 1985, p 108). 'Ethnic television' as it was then called (Ethnic Television Review Panel 1979) was launched as a visible symbol of federal commitment to ethnic immigrant minorities.

SBS survived more for what it symbolised than for what it was. It was a currency exchanged at the highest governmental levels. It has variously been a symbol of Australian liberalism, tolerance and cosmopolitanism, and a flagship of multiculturalism; equally it represents ethnic and social division, and national disharmony inimical to one nation. In this sense SBS has always been more than a television station. It has been publicly defined rather more than have other stations by political strategies and expedience. As an item to be exchanged, argued over, and fashioned politically, the ways in which SBS invents television are often not as important as how it is politically promoted, exchanged and acted on in public debate. The public debate about SBS is tied up with debates about multiculturalism, the nature of Australian identity, Australia's trading and strategic position in a changing world environment, the relationship and rights of minorities to representation within the broader social structure, the politics of ethnicity, social integration and cultural mixing. Thus the public politics of ethnicity in SBS ensures its continuation: the importance of the ethnic vote for politicians, of promoting a caring face to immigrants, these dominate visible politics with respect to SBS.

But within the ethnic communities themselves, SBS is the site for another kind of politics. Here, position on SBS boards, in management, and on the screen become political matters. Political divisions between communities sometimes emerged over implied favouritism on SBS as particular ethnic groups were perceived to be over-or under-represented in the multilingual and multicultural programming and by on-screen personalities. This was expressed in arguments between ethnic communities over the program schedule in terms of times, days of the week and frequency of the multilingual programs provided for them. These were typically between those identified as the largest ethnic groups—Greek, Italian, Croatian and Serbian (formerly included as Yugoslav). These political divisions also emerged internally within the organisation, particularly with respect to the make-up of the SBS board, and over the way power was distributed among competing ethnic groups and fragments within particular ethnic groups. Additionally, there was some disquiet over the limits of what could be expressed politically by virtue of SBS's express policy to 'avoid political partisanship' with respect to intra-ethnic community and inter-ethnic community conflicts (Jakubowicz 1989, pp 105–27). So too there was resentment within the SBS organisation and outside of it over the way Anglo-Celtic domination of senior management and executive producer positions appeared to limit NESB personnel advancement within the organisation beyond a certain level (Seneviratne 1992, p 53).

Written large in SBS is the political force-field of ethnicity. As the most visible symbol of multiculturalism and the largest multicultural commitment, SBS was necessarily criticised by those who saw multiculturalism in negative terms, and by those who wanted to change the policy for the better. This means SBS is typically attacked and defended in terms of the life of the concept of multiculturalism and less in terms of its functioning as a television service.

SBS is criticised from the left and the right, depending on the circumstances and political values. It is attacked from the left for not being ethnic enough: for substituting television industry professional values for ethnic values, for serving yuppie Anglo professionals (Senator Button's oft-quoted remark about SBS), not the deserving and disadvantaged ethnic immigrant (Seneviratne 1992, pp 53–8), for providing quality entertainment and not the kind of demotic entertainment ethnic working class and petit-bourgeois audiences may prefer to watch. It is attacked from the right for being too ethnic: for having multilingual programs and news values which encourage ethnic people to identify themselves with their ethnic fragment and their homeland at the expense of their common Australian identity, society and social class fragment. From the left, SBS makes ethnic audiences available to better management and control through conservative ethnic community-based organisations (whose members are represented on

SBS advisory panels). From the right, SBS is accused of undermining the project of one Australia, leading to a lack of commitment to the nation and its peoples. It is also held to undermine English as the lingua franca. It is seen to be an example of the special pleading of a group of professional ethnics inventing a client base and furthering their own careers instead of representing an evident and legitimate constituency.

For their part, ethnic communities typically regarded SBS as 'our station'. These communities provided the political support which defeated the ABC/SBS amalgamation plans of the mid-1980s. Ethnic organisations and individuals regarded SBS as conferring political and cultural legitimacy upon 'ethnic Australia'. For them SBS was a separate political–cultural–social space within the mainstream. It came into existence in a context where traditional rights, social power and advantage accrued to settler Australians and to English-speaking and northern European migrants, and where the Anglophone culture threatened the cultural maintenance of ethno-separate cultures and powerfully entered into familial relations, often at an inter-generational level. SBS and multiculturalism downplayed the specificity of the invention of European Australia over nearly 200 years, all the better to focus on a present reality requiring negotiation on the part of that settler culture. In doing so, multiculturalism bypassed previous expectations of one-way ethnic assimilation into this Australian culture and political arrangements. In naming its ethnic separateness and in creating 'ethnic television' lay the basis for bringing ethnicity into the political and social mainstream. Multiculturalism's innovation in these terms was that the timetables, styles, and expectations of ethnic social, political and cultural integration should be determined mostly by the communities themselves. In this sense, multiculturalism is a policy that sets up a range of possibilities which cannot be known in advance, and which will provide many different styles and passages for realising policy outcomes.

Thus SBS's supposed disconnecting of ethnic audiences from the broader Australian community can equally be regarded the valuable work of better integrating ethnic Australia by making transparent the culture and information networks of the various communities. Its creation of a separate *ethnic* space is also a precondition for transforming previously informal cultural and commercial relationships into the mainstream. Its perceived erosion of English language dominance in broadcasting through multilingual screenings equally demonstrates the important role played by subtitling in English and foreign language learning, and the way such programming provides a basis for the better mixing of cultural elements.

As a state initiative, SBS is necessarily of a different character than commercial initiatives to tap the 'ethnic market'. Public funding forces publicly funded broadcasters to make social policy and political calculations, not just the calculations of the advertising market. Although SBS started to accept limited advertising and sponsorship in the 1990s, the station remains overwhelmingly dependent on its government funding base and community groupings (defined politically) in ways that commercial broadcasters are not.

The other side of the station's relation to policy is that SBS appears as something too important to be left to the control of the market, and as something requiring state assistance because of the failure of the market to deliver services in the area. Opening out a previously closed television system to foreign language broadcasts was a significant step. If this was left to the market or to public access broadcasting it would mean leaving a multiculturalist instrument out of direct governmental and policy supervision. Commercial dynamics mean that impoverished and smaller ethnic groups would be left out because they would not constitute a viable commercial audience, and public access broadcasting did not carry with it the same capacity to control political partisanship as would a national broadcaster (White & White 1983, p 155). SBS's public service charter meant that it could accommodate such social and structural disadvantage, and afford significance and some control, however symbolic, to existing ethnic community organisations and structures (through board membership, ethnic roundspeople and employment including on-camera positions). Thus much of SBS's behind the scenes marketing—such as that done when SBS services came to Perth in 1986—is concerned with mobilising ethnic communities and using their information networks to enlist support for the service.

Government could promote its SBS initiative as bringing such groups within the decision making structure, coopting them into the framework of a service which must be fundamentally liberal in outlook and committed to ethnic tolerance, understanding, and the Australian nation. This was as much directed at the latent prejudices *between* different ethnic groups as between the Australian mainstream and particular ethnic groups. So it is that Franca Arena in 1985 claimed that:

> Multicultural television has exposed people to a different cultural input and it has helped understanding, not only between the Anglo-Australian community and the ethnic communities, but between ethnic communities themselves. People forget that there is as much ignorance and prejudice amongst the ethnic communities towards each other as there is sometimes between older established communities and the new groups. (1985, p 99)

Market failure is an equally compelling argument for the formation of SBS. Here the federal government moved to set up a service in a marginal service area. In this sense a public institution serves as a loss leader for other desirable social, political and even commercial infrastructures. It is worth contrasting this with alternative scenarios such as that which developed in Canada. There an ethnic Pay TV services was founded on a 'commerce in ethnicity' principle. Subtitling in the lingua franca of ethnic groups, English, was out (it simply cost too much). This encouraged forms of programming inaccessible to both the dominant English language fragment and languages outside the ethnic group in question and meant more language programming for the larger ethnic groups. Unlike the SBS, such a Pay TV service could not stage an imaginary pan-ethnic unity, nor could it carry the symbolic power of state approval for ethnicity.

But SBS's close association with the multiculturalism policy, ethnic communities and political priorities does not wholly explain its longevity and success. It survived also because of what SBS did, its use to other broadcasting interests, its programming, its position as a national narrowcaster, and its complementarity to the existing television mix.

Television industry resistance to SBS was maintained through the 1980s, but progressively diminished as the chances of getting rid of it or changing it receded. SBS proved useful to existing broadcasting and film interests. It did not make the feared inroads into commercial station audiences, although as a competing national broadcaster it did, from time to time, erode the ABC's audience share. Ethnic audiences proved not to be just viewers of SBS-TV but also viewers of the commercial networks, the ABC, ethnic and mainstream video product. It proved useful to the commercial stations in that it provided a complementary rather than a competitive service, less of a threat to them than either the ABC or another commercial television service. Its presence made it possible for the commercials to argue against the extension of multiculturalism to their community service obligations. When advertising was finally formalised into a regular feature of SBS in 1991 the commercial stations raised few serious objections—the amount of advertising siphoned from commercial television would be small and the rules placed upon their screening set limits on it as a competitive advertising venue. The ABC, for its part, accommodated itself to SBS's presence, becoming more like it in the process.

SBS initiatives over time answered local film industry criticisms. Its development of television drama showed a commitment to Australian ethnic and indigenous specificity. It picked up and promoted local short films, documentaries and features which would never have been otherwise screened on television. It became another broadcasting venue for the product of the film industry tax concessions and subsidised film production sector with AFC and SBS partnerships. Although the film industry remained publicly critical of SBS in the mid-1980s for failing to 'represent the multicultural nature of Australian society to Australians' (Connor Report 1985, p 365), the industry became active in later campaigns for a better funded SBS so that more local multicultural programming could be developed. SBS also answered overseas non-Anglophone broadcasters' complaints that the Australian television market was closed to non-English programming, as it provided an Australian market for non-English programming at state expense.

SBS also met longstanding broadcast and social policy goals. It was cultural and educational television. It fulfilled cultural diversity aims by giving representation to minority viewpoints. Its subtitling provided hearing impaired people with a fuller experience of television. It was a valuable domestic and foreign policy instrument inasmuch as it showed evidence of Australia's liberal attitudes towards minorities, and canvassing of alternative viewpoints on world issues. It helped alter public opinion (particularly business and cultural elite Australian opinion) through encouraging greater understanding of Australia's near neighbours. Transcending the predominant Anglo-American cast of information sources about the rest of the world, SBS provided new ways of being cosmopolitan in Australia at a time when the old ways were becoming increasingly out of alignment with the transformation of the world in the last years of the twentieth century. SBS also fitted federal educational policy—particularly language policy—which sought to take into account the predominance of Australian trade outside English-speaking countries, its 'Asian future', and to utilise Australia's existing linguistic resources. SBS made language teaching easier at secondary and tertiary level, and it has stimulated the learning of language, and the appreciation of different cultures on the part of Australians.

It is now policy that SBS should be provided nationally. It was not always so. For the first few years SBS was localised to Sydney and Melbourne (and Canberra in 1983). It took five to six years to arrive in other major metropolitan and regional centres. This tardiness was not only due to a lack of money for expansion. It was also a question of policy. The smaller size of the ethnic audience outside Sydney and Melbourne appeared not to warrant extension. With SBS-TV initially called 'ethnic television', the 'ethnic audience' provided the policy basis for the service. Yet, as noted, SBS has always been more than an ethnic television service. The changing emphasis towards the multicultural part of this distinction provided important grounds for the expansion of SBS around Australia. It was helped in this by the development of a delivery mechanism in AUSSAT and the adoption, in the regional equalisation policy, of a principle of equality of television services. SBS became part of the broad equalisation package. So, in 1985 the service was extended to Brisbane, Adelaide, the Gold Coast, Newcastle and Wollongong; in 1986 to Perth and Hobart; with expansion to other regional centres continuing through the late 1980s and early 1990s. Once provided on a quasi-national basis, SBS's political existence and identity as a broadcaster was more assured.

Because SBS programming entered ethnic VCR patterns of use, its audience reach is larger than that suggested by the various ratings instruments. SBS programming circulates through off-air taping along community—family and friendship, and informal ethnic commercial structures—well outside its broadcast area. Before SBS began in Perth in 1986, video cassettes were regularly flown over from Sydney or Melbourne and circulated through newsagent and video outlets to Perth's Italian, Croatian, Greek, Serbian and Macedonian ethnic fragments. After its launch in Perth, video cassettes continued to circulate to ethnic fragments in areas not serviced by SBS. Croatians and Macedonians in Manjimup (south-west WA) and Carnarvon (central WA coast) gained regular access to SBS drama and variety programs and compilation information programs put together from ABC and SBS feeds. One of the authors has also found SBS programming in video stores in various parts of the former Yugoslavia. Inasmuch as what is taped is not only multilingual programming, but also news and information, the Australian view of homeland politics enter the political construction of events in the homeland and in Australia alike.

SBS'S MULTICULTURALISM

SBS-TV's 'multiculturalism' is tied up with a set of productive tensions which are definitional to multiculturalism generally. These are principally between an 'ethnic' position and a 'multicultural' position and between 'ethnic diversity' and 'cultural diversity'.

The 'ethnic' position holds that programming should be in the language of the ethnicity in question, that the service should provide content of specific interest to that particular ethnic group; and its programs should promote that 'ethnic' identity. By contrast, a 'multicultural' position espouses a liberal project of promoting understanding and the tolerance of diversity in the broader Australian community, whether defined in relation to ethnic diversity or in relation to 'minorities', religions and racial groups (Arena 1985, p 99; White & White 1983, pp 151–3).

Both are present in SBS's charter. At first this meant a rough division between multilingual programming, which was seen to meet ethnic needs, and English-language programming, which met multicultural requirements. But of late this neat division has become less clear cut. Its local and imported English-language programs also provide for specific ethnic needs, while imported multilingual programming also meets more general needs. SBS balances its general and special programming requirements by using forms of programming which could do both at once. This is why it relies so much on its news and current affairs service, documentaries and 'quality' film and television.

For SBS, the ethnic fragments are understood simultaneously as local to Australia and as a fragment of another homeland. As an Australian fragment the ethnic group is afforded a variety of minority representation in the service in its international and local news values, through on-screen reporters and through interviewees giving opinions and reports on events, and as documentary and drama subjects. SBS strategy is to encourage the local ethnic fragment to identify with other NESB fragments on the basis of their common Australian experience of a country at some distance linguistically and culturally from themselves. Local SBS programs are aired with announcers and reporters retaining to a varying extent their accents in spoken English. But they rarely speak in their native tongues, as this tends to be reserved for imported multilingual programming. Interviews, even though they could be conducted in the language of the interviewee to facilitate easier communication, are often in English. The broken English of the interviewee is sometimes subtitled in 'correct' English for communicability. Often—depending on deadlines and perceptions of the communicability of various ethnic English accents—there is no subtitling. There is a relative facility on the part of Australian audiences with particular accents (subtitling tends not to be required as much for Italian and Greek accents and is increasingly less of a problem for various Asian accents). SBS naturalises broken English even at the risk of diminishing the speaker. Where public and civic issues are stressed—in politics, information and news programming—ethnic self-identity is defined politically as an Australian ethnic identity in relation to the Australian political and social mainstream rather than culturally in terms of local life-ways and their relation to homeland cultures.

SBS's 'homeland'–'language' strategy works in a different direction. Here, SBS adopts the official recognition of ethnic cultures in relation to the homeland culture or language culture of which the local is a fragment. This is, in part, also an ethnic demand (itself a consequence of representing themselves as ethnic groups with cultural rights). If this leads *SBS World News* to cover as many as twenty countries in its nightly news service (George 1989, p 15; and see chapter 8 below), it also frames issues of cultural heritage and value in relation to homeland heritage and ethnicity. Recognition of local ethnic culture consequently takes on a quasi-international character. Thus respect for Italian culture is largely referenced in relation to Italy and its preferred cultural history, rather than in relation to the fragmented regional—usually southern Italian—communities in Australia. Thus the local fragment is either Italian or NESB ethnic with little space in between. Sponsored initiatives tend to be movies, drama and variety shows from Italy; or Australian Italian ethnics symbolically representing their ethnicity and the larger NESB ethnicity via their positions as SBS frontpersons or accessed opinions.

The particularity of the Australian 'solution' to ethnic diversity in symbolic goods is evident in these practices. In the US, cultural and ethnic diversity is staged in English-language, locally produced programs—thus registering ethnicity as US 'symbolic ethnicity' (such as the 'little Italy' of Scorcese's films, the *Rocky* movie cycle, and the African American of *The Cosby Show*). In Australia this is not possible to the same extent. Imported programs and limited local productions provide for the public presentation of that ethnicity in Australia. Local productions tend to be information programs rather than high-cost drama, due to the cost structures and comparatively small audiences involved. So, the ethnic tends to be staged in relation to the host Australian culture in local information programming, but in relation to the homeland culture through imported fictional programming. This conveniently separates the national–political from the national–(homeland)–cultural in programming, just as it is separated in many ethnic associations, to avoid too evident political partisanship. The diversity of Australia's NES ethnic make-up further means that locally produced information programs need to gain wide cross-ethnic and general appeal. The small size of individual ethnic groups ensures that they translate themselves and are in turn positioned as part of a larger NESB information space and political constituency.

The other major faultline within multiculturalism is between multiculturalism in relation to ethnic immigrant cultures, and in relation to a more broadly conceived cultural diversity within which ethnic diversity is simply one more component. The cultural diversity definition includes ethnic groups as one kind of minority cultural and social value system requiring cultural expression and maintenance through time, along with subcultural groups, indigenous peoples, religious groups, and forms of minority cultural practice, including high culture. That is, it includes both ways of life and aesthetic forms as part of its remit. Here distinctive cultural practices and ways of life are defined in racial, cultural, social values and political terms in addition to ethnic ones. This definition of multiculturalism provides a means by which existing and emerging social fragments drawing upon non-immigrant and immigrant elements can find articulation and recognition. SBS's acclaimed 'Women's' series of programs in 1989 incorporated different ethnic fragments into a common women's way of life (1992 saw a similar assemblage of programs with its 'About Men' series). So too highbrow culture becomes one more minority group requiring support on SBS, and finding it in *The Bookshow*, *Eat Carpet*, *Cinema Classics* and art programs such as the *Metropolitan Cats* (25 June 1992) on an exhibition from the Museum of Modern Art in New York about the artistic treatment of cats.

Multiculturalism as NESB, as an ethnic identity in relation to the homeland, and as a cultural diversity program ensuring minority cultural rights constitute distinct tendencies in SBS. If these elements are not always in tension with each other, often they are. SBS has variously been more of an ethnic service, more of a multicultural service and more of a minorities service (Patterson 1992, pp 43–52). The ascendance of ethno-separate understandings at SBS's inception (1980–84) saw it critically reliant upon multilingual programs and news imports. The ascendance of multiculturalism in the middle period (1985–89) had the service centrally negotiating its ethnic mandate in multilingual programs and multicultural programs through an expanded local program production emphasis. Contemporary demands (since 1990) for more English-language programming, the advent of extensive ethnic video networks, ethnic nationalisms in the homelands, and the logic of ethnic intermixing have tipped the balance of the service toward cosmopolitan and minoritarian emphases. The ethnic homeland was represented prominently in local news and current affairs, while the multilingual fictional and cultural templates as much underwrote cosmopolitan and minoritarian orientations as they did ethnic homeland orientations. This reflected the mainstreaming of multiculturalism, for all Australians, not simply first-generation ethnic immigrants or the more ethno-separate ethnic groups.

The different 'minorities' often sit uneasily together (see chapter 8). Ethnic fragments are often in conflict with each other and have different values to other recognised minorities (eg, religious, gender, and sexual preference 'minorities'). Yet these are lumped together and find themselves, as a consequence, not only competing for the same funds but also for space on SBS. The collocation of 'marginalised audiences'–'minority groups' can include gay and fundamentalist Islamic constituencies. But too much can be made of these differences. After all, it is possible for an audience member to be at different times in their SBS television viewing an ethnic person, a general audience member acquiring multicultural understanding about a culture or minority at some distance from them, and a member of a minority.

These different tensions in SBS should not be seen as so many contradictions to be resolved by SBS focusing its efforts on one at the expense of the others. A television service is always fragmented, providing diverse offerings to audiences. The tension between servicing different constituencies provides SBS with a source of internal conflict, enables it continually to transform itself, and permits it to develop a multipurpose character. Its failure wholly to meet ethno-separate, multicultural and minority aspirations is integral to its shape as a comprehensive television service. SBS's and multiculturalism's failure to establish a coherent, stable, comfortable and single multicultural identity is integral to its success in shaping an always changing multicultural identity.

Multiculturalism and SBS have always been in the business of managing ethnicity and social marginality in ways consonant with government policy. SBS is, after all, a public instrumentality driven by national social and cultural policy. But unlike previous initiatives, which were top-down, SBS actively enlists and significantly allows ethnic and marginal aspirations to shape it. This has meant conceding to ethnic immigrant fragments, Aborigines, gays, environmentalists and feminists both a televisual space and a public and structural acknowledgement of themselves. Consequently, SBS programming, participatory structures and multicultural philosophy provide a way of managing the social, cultural and political divide separating these groups from the broader Australian society and its dominant identities.

8 SBS-TV: A television service with Dona Kolar-Panov

> SBS is the lean, hungry, efficient, postmodern TV of tomorrow.
> John Hartley 1992, p 200

Too often the politics of multiculturalism overshadows an evaluation of the SBS as a television service provider. In this chapter we turn our attention to SBS as a television service with its own internal dynamic and consequences for the Australian television mix. SBS will be considered as a narrowcaster which has specialised audiences for its programs. We will show how its multilingual and news and informational programming provide ethnic, cosmopolitan and minoritarian audiences with a purchase on the service. We will consider SBS's largely productive responses to the low budgets available to it. Lastly, we will discuss its changing shape alongside contemporary social, political, and television industry developments inside and outside Australia.

A NARROWCASTING NATIONAL BROADCASTER

> If every Australian watches even one hour of multicultural television a year, I'll be happy.
> Bruce Gyngell, Special Consultant to SBS, 1982
> (Smolowe & Robinson 1982, p 18)

SBS is narrowcast television. It manages its programming mix in ways which seek not a general audience but, like a publisher, seeks a series of 'special audiences'. In this SBS works from a model of television as a publishing medium supplied by a diversity of 'authors' and releasing a range of titles from specialist minority material to popular bestsellers. It buys in material from other markets, and it commissions significant new work from local producers. (Hartley 1992, p 200).

SBS even employed a publisher, Brian Johns, who ran it from 1987 to 1992. The publishing model sees audiences dipping in and out of the schedule for particular programs (Hartley 1992, p 200) and attracts committed viewers for specific programs. As SBS Head of Television Andy Lloyd-James described the situation in 1991, 'We don't get huge audience flows, people come piling in for individual programs and they pile back out at the end of them and race off and do something else.' (Reid 1991, p 3).

SBS ensures this audience behaviour by quite self-consciously promoting 'audience share objectives... based upon building different audiences for different programs, rather than building and holding a single audience all the time' (SBS 1987, p 35). In doing so it admits the habitual fragmentation of television viewing, and promotes the notion of watching television for particular programs and discriminating between programs within the nightly schedule (Hartley 1992, p 200). This orientation also enables it to fulfil its 'special' mandate to 'complement and supplement the service provided by commercial television and the ABC' (SBS 1987, p 35). SBS sees its narrowcasting as reaching two broad audience groups: 'ethnic communities' and 'the general population'. The audience research of Frank Small and Associates commissioned by SBS (SBS 1987, p 61) identifies it reaching 'a group of people who wants and needs something different from the offerings of mainstream broadcasters' and ethnic communities for whom it 'provides an important role in the life of the ethnic groups surveyed, and provides an important part of their viewing'. These are determinedly special—not general—audiences.

The contrast with commercial networks could not be greater. They still target audiences, but these are audience profiles desired by advertisers advertising on a mass medium (rather than, say, in a special interest publication). Any targeting on their part supports this general audience orientation. With these demographics (age group, income etc) being neither ethno-specific nor minoritarian, this pursuit of increased market share in particular audience demographics still attracts other audience demographics rather than driving them away. Networks still have to manage the fact that audiences have always dipped in and out of television programming with little expectation of follow on viewing from the previous programs (Barwise & Ehrenberg 1988, pp 31–2). But they manage this audience behaviour through programming and counter-programming strategies which seek as large an audience as possible for individual programs throughout the schedule.

SBS's 'special' audiences are defined for it by the social policy mandate of multiculturalism and by the demands of and opportunities available in the television market. Its programs are expected to reach specific ethnic, minoritarian, and disadvantaged audiences as well as maintaining a part of the general audience. SBS is also expected to provide something for everyone at some time in its diverse schedule. As a television service it had to translate these objectives in the context of its funding base, the existing programming mix in Australian television, the domestic programming opportunities available to it, and the availability of programming in an international market place. It targeted ethnic and minoritarian audiences with tailored programming whilst simultaneously targeting the general audience in that audience's special interests, as, for example, news, sport, movie, or food program consumers. In this way SBS was able to reach a large viewing audience cumulatively by attracting different audiences for different programs. Its cumulative weekly audience reach in 1991 was about 3.2m individual viewers (Reid 1991, p 2).

Yet this is achieved at some cost. Its ratings are consistently small, with an average weekly audience share in Sydney and Melbourne of 3.4 per cent in 1991 (in 1982 it was 1.3–2 per cent in Sydney, see Grenard 1982, p 51). Narrowcasting means that individual programs do not claim to be for everyone, and so can be expected to drive viewers out just as they draw smaller committed audiences in. The 'special broadcasting service' orientation clearly limits SBS's capacity to develop flow-through audiences by pushing it to pursue 'special' audiences. Social policy obligations also place limits on the size of the narrowcast audiences available to SBS by mandating program selection for many small audience constituencies. For example, SBS cannot count on a single ethnic audience for its multilingual programs because ethnic groups are socially, physiognomically, and culturally quite diverse. Vietnamese refugees cannot be expected to watch an SBS program from Poland in preference to the Hollywood and Australian programming on the commercials, as English-language programs are closer to those Vietnamese by virtue of their Australian life experience. By the same token, English-language documentaries about the Vietnamese Australian experience are unlikely to attract as significant a Polish audience as a Vietnamese audience (although the similarity of immigrant experience will probably secure a greater Polish audience for this programming than for Vietnamese-language programming). SBS does, however, attract a general ethnic audience in its English-language broadcasts such as *World News* and *Vox Populi* than it does for its multilingual broadcasts.

This situation helps explain SBS-TV's mixed profile amongst ethnic audiences. In 1986, for example, 81 per cent of the ethnic audience would be watching the commercials while 15 per cent were watching SBS. This should not be interpreted—as it often is—as SBS failing its ethnic audiences; rather it is catering to them through narrowcasting. Programs in the ethnic languages and about the ethnic group do lead to high viewer satisfaction from within that ethnic group (Tulich 1986, p 28). While English-language programming of a more general nature and programs of major non-English-language film and television producers are more likely to attract larger ethnic and general audiences, such programming leads to lower viewer satisfaction with SBS among ethnic communities. Their first desire is for community-language programming from their homeland, or failing that for programming in their community language, or failing that in a culturally proximate language. This programming mix enables SBS to occupy the position of the national broadcaster for an ethnic audience with the 15 per cent ethnic viewing figure being close to that historically obtained by the ABC among the broader Australian community. To some extent, it is also the national broadcaster for immigrants—NESB and ESB alike. Forty to 50 per cent of its audience is born outside of Australia although only some 21 per cent of the population is (SBS 1989, p 23).

SBS-TV is continually caught up in the contradiction basic to being a narrowcast national broadcaster: the desire to maximise the size of its narrowcast audience, and to maximise its service to particular, highly-defined constituencies. The former drives program selection based on reaching larger special constituencies and securing the kind of general appeal necessary to justify continued governmental expenditure on a narrowcaster (Patterson 1986, p 55). The latter drives program selection based on smaller, special constituences which have little wider appeal. Both are an intrinsic part of its multicultural remit.

This is not simply a tension between the pull to be ethnic and the pull to be just another television service, between the pursuit of ethnic and of general audiences. The news and current affairs service, for example, is for a more widely defined and less ethno-specifically oriented ethnic audience made up of NESB peoples (Dell'oso's 'wog reading the news': see chapter 7) but it is also for a general audience. This enables it to combine its ethnic and multicultural remit attracting non-ethnically marked general audiences. Consequently *World News* has high ethnic viewer satisfaction and general appeal. In its prime time offerings, SBS-TV generally provides programs which can manage both ethnic and multicultural demands. Outside prime time, SBS-TV schedules more specifically to smaller—usually ethnic—audiences with multilingual programming.

SBS programming strategies vary along a spectrum from programs which are exclusively for a particular audience segment, to those which enable a number of different audience segments to organise themselves around the same program. In the middle are programs more for one or two particular audience segments, or programs mostly for one audience segment but which nonetheless pick up other audience segments. Its English-language news, current affairs, sport, and food programs attract ethnic and non-ethnically marked audiences alike. Soccer, an ethnically marked sport in Australia, was a logical candidate for SBS. It broadcast the 1990 World Cup in its entirety, it regularly telecasts matches from the European and South American leagues and it provides telecasts of the national league. Soccer telecasts also draw heavily on the British immigrant fragment (and on soccer enthusiasts generally), given soccer's role as the pre-eminent football in the UK. Another sport that attracts ethnic and non-ethnic cross-sections is bicycle races such as the *Tour de France*. Yet ethnicity need not enter into the calculation. The international motorcycling season was shown on SBS until taken up by a commercial network—a non-ethnically marked minoritarian sport with a biker following. This kind of mix of 'specialisms' provided SBS's minoritarianism with a populist and general dimension which has been critical to ensure its wide demographic spread. *Sports Report* (now *World Sports*) was also critically different from other forms of sport populism in that it foregrounded political and world contexts for sport making it able, for example, to carry segments on gay Olympians 'coming out' in the US; or its coverage of the Cerebral Palsy Games. Similarly, some of SBS's multilingual programs are able to mobilise both highbrow and ethnic audiences. As the Ethnic Communities' Council of NSW promoted it:

> The screening of Fellini's *Roma* with subtitles would be both an ethnic transmission (in subject matter and language broadcast) of specific interest to the Italian community, and a multicultural transmission because, being subtitled, it gives access to non-Italians to aspects of Italian culture which are also of general interest. (1984, p 2)

SBS-TV seeks audiences that treat its programs in the way in which serious or demanding programs are treated: as progamming for which the double jeopardy rule (the lower the rating, the lower is the audience's estimation of the value the program) does not apply

(Barwise & Ehrenberg 1988, pp 53–4). Lloyd-James claims success in this, arguing that SBS audience behaviour provides telling evidence that 'people switch their minds on when they switch SBS on' (Reid 1991, p 3). Traditionally associated with informational programming (non-tabloid-style television news and documentaries), SBS extends this exception to its multilingual programming (given the rarity value of popular programs in community's languages within television) to various minority programs which generate intense ethusiasms and identifications ('women's' and 'gay' programming), its sporting programs such as soccer, and its cooking programs. Thus, up till late 1992 SBS's highest rating program was an informational program—the first night of the documentary series *The Civil War*. It rated 12 in Sydney and 11 in Melbourne with subsequent ratings in the 8s, 9s, and 10s (Reid 1991, p 2). Its multiculturally inflected local drama *Six Pack* gained ratings in the 8s and 9s in 1992. The tremendous interest in SBS's 1990 World Cup soccer coverage is considered to have raised SBS's potential audience by 6 per cent. SBS food programs are among the most successful selling point of its merchandise division. Its ethnic and minoritarian programming report good ratings among target groups with some of its multilingual broadcasts attracting significant cross-ethnic and general viewing.

SBS's scheduling of multilingual, informational and cultural programs ensures it a mixed audience profile. It has an above average proportion of people with 'high disposable incomes and [a] tendency to hold white collar jobs' (Reid 1991, p 2). AGB McNair Anderson audience surveys in 1990 put SBS's reach among business proprietors, the self-employed, business managers, executives, professionals and senior government officials at 23 per cent compared to the 17 per cent such groups represented in the general population (SBS Annual Report 1992, p 56). The program mix ensures SBS has a slightly older viewing profile, attracting more people over 18, with large concentrations in the 55+ and the 40–54 age-group. Sports and information programs help it obtain a larger proportion of male viewers, 49 per cent of men over 18 compared to 41 per cent of women (their respective proportions of the total population are 36 per cent and 38 per cent). This pattern of television viewing is typical. Programming with an informational and serious bias gets slightly higher proportions of older people viewing it and sporting programs get more of a male viewership (as noted by Barwise & Ehrenberg 1988, p 29). The proportion of SBS's audience among manual, semi-skilled, technical, and clerical workers was the same as it was for their proportion of the total population (28 per cent on both counts) and nearly the same for the 25–39 year old age group (26 per cent SBS viewers compared to their 24 per cent of the total population). This shows that SBS's program mix routinely includes audiences which are occupationally lower middle class and working class. Possibly the most continuing and serious audience constituency not met by SBS since inception is the child and teenage audience (SBS 1992a, p 56; Connor Report 1985, pp 380-7). SBS reaches 29 per cent of those born in non-English speaking countries (who comprise 11 per cent of the total population) and 16 per cent of those born outside Australia in English speaking countries (who make up 11 per cent of the population).

This audience profile is evident in a Newspoll survey of perceptions of SBS (Johns 1991, p 19). The survey showed that 6 per cent agreed that SBS was 'for people with better education than me'; 22 per cent that 'SBS is mainly for people who like culture and the arts; and 30 per cent that it is 'mainly for people from other countries'.

Although there are problems with schematically rendering such a mixed audience and programming profile, SBS programming and viewing can be heuristically divided into the ethnic, the minoritarian, and the cosmopolitan. Although these three templates are more ideal types than an exact match with actual viewing and programming decisions, they are drawn out from multicultural policy statements and published SBS audience research. They are presented here better to get at the audience and program assemblage strategies found in SBS-TV. They are not sealed off from each other: one can be an ethnic audience for one program, a member of a minority for another, and a cosmopolitan for a third; programming can provide for one, two, or even all of these tendencies. These different audience constituencies overlap to varying degrees. It is almost SBS policy for them to do so.

The ethnic immigrant audience served by SBS's programming is not especially sophisticated, well educated, or homeland orientated. This audience relies upon family and communal networks in Australia and which stretch back to the village, the city or the region of origin. For this audience SBS provides a way of reconciling the 'Old World and the New' (Dell'oso 1991, pp 20-2) at a family and local community level. Here SBS forms a bridge between generations and also between the localised ethnic fragment and the broader Australian society. With children often possessing a greater English-language facility than their parents, this relative power of children undermined the authority of parents and, in turn, generated a reaction from the parent's part against the English-language context and society, and relations within it, in order to maintain their culture, their children, their authority, and their sense of worth. SBS's multilingual and multicultural programming provided a means of redressing the balance by publicly legitimating ethnic accents, the vernacular language of the home, and the ethnic Australian experience. It was designed to do these things (Ethnic Television Review Panel 1979, pp 2–4).

Sandwiched between this ethnic audience and the cosmopolitan audience is the cosmopolitan ethnic. Here the same informational and multilingual resources used by an ethnic audience enable a smaller, more articulate, and well educated ethnic audience to negotiate a cosmopolitan ethnic Australian identity. This also provides ethnic cosmopolitans with a pan-ethnic basis for identification (NESB peoples) within the context of an assured internationalism. The same informational, multilingual and high brow cultural programs also permit a cosmopolitan Australian audience to enlarge the scope and dimensions of its national and international horizons. This audience does not see itself as especially ethnically marked or as disadvantaged when it consumes the world's culture, keeps up with national and world events, and welcomes the cultural diversity and programming breadth embodied in SBS's multiculturalism. The sharing of programming resources enables the Australian and ethnic cosmopolitan to resemble each other inasmuch as both are provided through SBS with the same points of reference.

Finally, there is minority programming and audience orientations. (These are 'minority' in that they are formed outside ethnic immigrant dynamics.) The minorities' relationship to SBS and programming is one of finding a greater accommodation and recognition of their identity and social, political and cultural values. These are formed in terms of religious, subcultural, sexual preference and issues-based political values (eg, environmentalism, peace movements and feminism) which can often form minority cultures in their own right. Although the fit is problematic, this minority definition accorded Australia's indigenous peoples initial recognition within SBS. The Aboriginal 'homeland' is here, not elsewhere, Aboriginal languages are spoken nowhere else, this culture exists nowhere else. As such, Aborigines cannot be regarded as an 'ethnic' group; at the same time they also cannot be regarded as especially cognate with other minorities (see chapter 9).

MULTILINGUAL PROGRAMMING

SBS's multilingual programming strategy is based on the need to provide some programming in the languages of Australia's ethnic migrants, the availability of materials from the homelands, the suitability and quality of programming, and the need to select programming taking due regard to political sensitivities within and between ethnic communities (and homelands).

SBS shows a range of film and television programs for particular language fragments. In 1986 the station was transmitting programs in forty languages with regularity of broadcasts being in accordance with the size of the different ethnic groups (Tulich 1986, p 27). As its then Head of Programming, Peter Barrett, described the situation:

> We try to provide at least one program each year for every language group... For example we are looking at feature films from the Soviet Union in Ukranian, Lithuanian and Armenian languages. There aren't many of these people here, but we feel a responsibility to these groups so that every Australian has the opportunity to see the occasional program in their own language. (Tulich 1986, p 27)

Such a strategy was successful at targeting individual ethnic groups in that as much as 92 per cent of the group tuned into programs in their particular language (Tulich 1986, p 28). Together with its international and ethnic-oriented information programs, multilingual programs ensured that by 1982, 81per cent of all Melbourne families of NESB had viewed multicultural television at some time (Harrison & Mayer 1984, p 82).

Such ethno-specific programming requirements could never be totally met by the service. There are simply too many groups competing for the available slots on and off prime time (and for recognition in locally produced programs). Multilingual programming was more effective for the larger ethnic communities in that they obtained a greater proportion of multilingual programming. In the 1980s the dominance of Greek, Italian and Yugoslav state programming made other minority ethnic communities feel marginalised (Young 1986, p 51). For example, Turks, a small ethnic minority, felt inadequately represented on SBS in its early years. In recent years Turkish and Egyptian programming has become more centrally represented on SBS. This is partly because such programming forms an acceptable face of Islam in which issues of modernity, westernisation and urban living are presented (SBS will program a movie on women's rights in Turkey, or an Egyptian program dealing with adultery in Islam). The new emphasis on Middle Eastern programming is also evidence of SBS meeting the multicultural requirement to address disadvantage and discrimination, and so foster intercultural understanding.

The political limits of multilingual programming were evident in the troubles in former Yugoslavia in recent years. Here a whole archive of socialist programs became politicised and off-limits, leading to a noticeable absence on SBS schedules. By mid-1992, politically neutral Serbian programming—television soap operas—had made their return (but by then even that screening had become a political act for many Australian Croatian, Bosnian, and Macedonian audiences). While there was ample coverage on news and current affairs programming regarding the day to day situation in the former Yugoslavia, and voice was given to all the warring sides, SBS made no attempt to present any Serbian, Croatian, Bosnian or Macedonian documentaries on the historical background to the current situation. Instead SBS relied on English and French documentaries on the troubles as these were seen to be more neutral and authoritative. Research on these ethnic communities in Perth shows that propaganda videotapes of the same historical content freely circulated within the different communities.

Additionally, there is little program production in the homelands and language groups of many ethnic fragments. The smaller and less wealthy language markets have only limited television production infrastructures and this constrains SBS program purchase. The availability of programming was a problem in the early 1980s for Greek, Egyptian, Lebanese, Turkish, Chinese and Maltese programming (SBS 1981, p 20). Often what is available is deemed technically unsuitable for broadcast. Thus, the 1985-86 Annual Report reported that in the case of Greece, material had been 'identified by Acquisition for purchase, [but] suppliers have not been capable of supplying acceptable technical material' (SBS 1986, p 26). SBS problems with Greek programming did not end at this. There were also 'exasperating delays in the supply of material from the Greek national broadcaster, ERT' with diplomatic representations needing to be made about supplying this material to SBS. SBS was the one developing an international market for Greek programming, not Greek broadcasters and producers.

Suitability decisions see a lot of homeland informational and variety programs become off limits. Such programming is perceived to be either too inferior in technical standards (Australian standards of television imaging are higher than those in many television markets), too local in the sense of being too time- and space-bound, or too ethno-specific, given that such programming needs to serve a constituency made up of both the ethnic group in question and others. Television standards and context sensitivity questions favour selection of movies and television drama series (including mini-series) as SBS's premier form of multilingual programming. These preferences help explain why programming tends to be drawn not only from those homelands well represented in Australia's demography but also from those non-English-speaking countries with high imaging standards (Japan, Germany, France, Brazil, Italy, Spain and Hong Kong).

SBS program buyers' perceptions of television standards are sometimes criticised on the grounds that their professional viewpoints dominate to the detriment of the ethnic groups in question and push SBS-TV away from a community television orientation. Against this, SBS has a responsibility to program for an ethnic audience who may not be as up to date with the informational culture of the homeland as are more recent immigrants. And SBS needs to maintain a station image and equivalent standards to rival broadcasters as a means of being able to get its 'special' audiences. It is one thing to have different programs, quite another to put on imported variety and informational programming below Australian standards. This would only encourage the double jeopardy effect, as the station as a whole would acquire not simply an obscure ethnic image (which it has in television comedy on the commercial stations), but a potentially more damaging, substandard image.

The screening of multilingual homeland product often led to dissatisfaction on the part of the targeted audience. Some ethnic viewers were confronted with a contemporary 'culture of the homeland' with which they were unfamiliar (having left twenty or more years earlier), or with political viewpoints for which they lacked any sympathy. In such circumstances, SBS publicly defended its selection of 'homeland' programming on civil libertarian and quality programming grounds. This political issue was especially the case for Eastern bloc programming in the 1980s before the end of the Cold War (Tulich 1986, p 27) and for Vietnamese language programming to this day (Lan Tran 1992). Ethnic viewers watched this programming but did not especially value it.

This programming strategy can equally be seen to have brought a politically liberal dimension to television. As Allan Ashbolt argued before the collapse of Eastern and Central European state socialism:

> [I]t [SBS] has introduced Australian viewers to a modest measure of political pluralism... simply through pursuing comprehensive eclectic policies in overseas film purchasing. The screening of socially sensitive, non-propagandist films from countries like Hungary, Yugoslavia Romania, Poland, Czechoslovakia and the German Democratic Republic, along with films of social criticism from the capitalist democracies of Western Europe, has given an unusual cultural breadth and tolerance to SBS television. (1985, pp 109–10)

SBS defends its selection and scheduling of non-English films and television series on the grounds of quality and an apparently random selection process based upon getting the best possible multilingual programming from around the world. But this is not just a useful defence against would-be political censors or moral guardians of ethnic virtue. It also gives SBS greater flexibility in its multilingual purchases, ensuring that specific ethnic requirements only partly determine program purchase. The advantages of this were clearly evident in 1989–91 when, with the restructuring of Europe, previously censored or simply shelved films became available. This allowed SBS de facto Russian, Polish, German, Hungarian and Czech dissident seasons. Quality is also a selling point for the general and ethnic audiences in that it promotes the intrinsic value and standing of the product. This helps to create and sustain the impression that SBS's foreign language programming is of a higher standard than commercial television. This necessary fiction is critical to successful narrowcasting by a national broadcaster as it fits the 'special', 'serious viewer' logic of the service and helps find audiences for such programs.

This program selection policy is critical to SBS's attempts to secure both cross-ethnic and general (Australian and ESB) audiences for its multilingual programming. Without these add-on audiences, SBS ratings would be only in the one to two point range in prime time, as even the largest ethnic groups (Greeks and Italians) cannot be expected to ensure ratings points above that level. But there are limits to the additional audiences available. Cross-ethnic viewing is generally undertaken by the other, usually culturally proximate ethnic groups (such as the southern European, the Latin, and the central and eastern European cultures), while multilingual viewing from the general Australian and Anglophone audience tends to be from those with a cosmopolitan outlook (usually those with an upper secondary and tertiary education). Cross-ethnic viewing also has to rely on sufficient fluency in English to enable the comprehension of subtitles. But adequate English could not be readily assumed of many first-generation ethnic immigrants (van der Weel 1990, p 24).

SBS's attention to securing broader Anglophone and NESB cross-ethnic audiences sees it successfully use the product from the major European, east Asian, and Latin American film and television industries. Programming from these sources is readily available and of a higher standard and quality than that from other European and Asian sources. More importantly, France, Germany, Italy and Spain are major sources of imported programs in countries in Europe. German programming has a place on central and southern European television including in Turkey; French programming has such a place on 'Latin' screens. Thus the Australian screening of German programming could be expected to pick up some European ethnic audiences and French programming to pick up some Latin audiences (Italian, Spanish, Portuguese and Latin American). A 1987 survey shows the extent of this. Some 35 per cent of SBS's Italian viewers watched programs in French while 51 per cent of SBS's Greek viewers watched programming in German and Italian (SBS 1989, p 30). What these figures suggest is that cross-ethnic cultural area viewing is a kind of second-best option when homeland or language programs are not available. The same French, German, and to a lesser extent Italian, Spanish and, more recently, Japanese product could also be expected to gain an Anglophone audience because of the historic importance of these languages and countries to Anglophone cultures. French and German have been the foreign languages principally taught in schools and are part of a broader and common European cultural area. Japanese is a growth language in schools and universities, with a growing general interest in Japanese culture.

Within the context of 'elite culture', SBS's multilingual programming provides a window on quality film and television programming— particularly art-house cinema, award-winning television series and documentary programming and 'film classics'. David Stratton, who headed the Sydney Film Festival for many years, provides the most visible frontperson presence of this on SBS. Stratton introduces SBS screenings of contemporary foreign-language features in the festivals and art-house cinema circuits, the film classics, and co-hosts *The Movie Show* (which brings together European, Asian, Australian and Hollywood movies). With its film classics SBS effectively took over from where the (now defunct) National Film Theatre and film societies left off in the 1970s, with seasons of European and Japanese cinema. In the late 1980s it extended this to a wide range of television soap operas and mini-series. SBS thus worked to construct connections between high culture and particular ethnic formations on television.

These different considerations shape SBS's mixed multilingual profile. In 1988–89 SBS's major broadcast languages apart from English were: Italian (7.1 per cent of program time) German (5.3 per cent), Greek (4 per cent), French (3.3 per cent), Spanish (3 per cent), Japanese (2.1 per cent), Portuguese (1.6 per cent), Polish (1.5 per cent) (SBS 1989, p 114). This multilingual program purchase mix exhibits the different strategies behind the program scheduling of such programming and the availability of product.

The mix draws inevitable criticism. The National Forum for Equal Access to Public Broadcasting claimed in 1990 that SBS had been 'hijacked away from the ethnic communities it was set up to serve, in favour of English-speaking people' because its 'trendy French and German programs, which appeal to Anglo-Celtic yuppies, get highly favoured treatment' (*Sydney Morning Herald*, 9 March 1990). This kind of criticism has been consistently made over the life of SBS (see also Grenard 1982, p 54). It has its basis in the experience of ethnic viewers who would prefer broadcasts in their own ethnic languages rather than in other European or Asian languages. But such criticism needs to be set alongside the complexion of international image markets, the realities of SBS's cross-ethnic viewing, and the necessity to screen programs capable of attracting a sufficiently large narrowcast audience to justify continued government expenditure.

NEWS AND INFORMATION PROGRAMS

News and current affairs services have always been a high priority for SBS. The area represented 30 per cent of its overall program budget in 1986 (Tulich 1986, p 28), 12 per cent of its programming hours in 1988–89 (SBS 1989, p 115), and 48 per cent of its local program budget in 1990–91 (*Encore* 11–31 October 1991, p 3). By devoting roughly half its news telecast to overseas news, SBS was able to provide a limited homeland coverage and a genuinely international news service. In its first few years SBS news bulletins 'carried practically no Australian political and economic news, although local ethnic affairs got a run' (George 1989, p 15). Over the 1980s it expanded its domestic news gathering capacity, although outside Canberra, Sydney and Melbourne it tended to rely on stringers and footage from other stations (George 1989, p 15). In 1986 SBS introduced *Vox Populi*, promoting it as 'Australia's first multilingual current affairs program' (*Sydney Morning Herald*, 27 July 1986). This program provided a regular forum for ethnic voices to find televisual political representation. *Vox Populi* was one of SBS's highest rating programs in the late 1980s, alongside *World News*.

Christabel Young's research indicated a 'strong demand' by all the ethnic groups she studied 'for more Australian news' including 'general news, editorials and commentaries on Australian affairs, news of government services available, news of the ethnic groups in Australia' (1988, p 55). SBS's local news and current affairs was expanded in the late 1980s to meet this demand. This research also helps explain why SBS's then Executive Director, Brian Johns, claimed that news and current affairs programs were the best vehicle for 'social-justice issues of access and equity in multiculturalism' (Johns 1991, p 18). These locally produced programs provided an English-language forum for issues of concern to NESB Australians, previously only aired in the ethnic press. In this way SBS news and current affairs provided ethnic communities with visible public representation and knowledge that their stories and concerns were 'getting out'. This would always be a small audience but one which politicians and other media professionals monitored. SBS also had a larger audience among those with a greater facility in English (Young 1988, p 51). Because SBS's current affairs programs were in English, proficiency in English was necessary to appreciate multilingual programming outside the native tongue.

Those same news and information programs attracted a cosmopolitan interest from sections of the Australian and Anglophone population. Ironically, SBS's international orientation was as much a product of cost-consciousness as intent. With limited news gathering sources in Australia, SBS had a 'plentiful supply of overseas-made reports beamed to Australia by satellite':

> What the 0-28 planners [Network 0-28 was renamed SBS-TV in 1985] discovered was that out of twenty to twenty-five items arriving every day from the US and UK networks, not more than about three or four were being shown on any other television news programme, either ABC or commercial. By the simple expedient of inserting, say, seven to ten such items in a thirty minute session, 0-28 was able to appear more cosmopolitan, more expansive. (Ashbolt 1985, p 109)

SBS documentaries consistently pursued this same expansive and cosmopolitan orientation. They demonstrate SBS's typical assaying of current political and cultural issues within a progressive international politics (while remaining inside an Australian multicultural frame). Thus SBS screened, for example, a documentary series made for Japanese television on Asia and its effect upon Japanese social and economic life. *The Cutting Edge* series documentaries often relate to ethnic fragments and the politics of their homelands, but do so in the context of broader 'international' concerns. The series screened, for example, programs on 'Street Kids from Brazil' (16 April 1991), Carolina nuclear weapons facilities (6 August 1991), cigarette smoking (21 May 1991), the role of Sicilian women in the fight against the Mafia (14 May 1991), the 'slow progress' cleaning up 'the most polluted region in Europe, where Poland, Czechoslovakia and former East Germany meet' in 'The Black Triangle' (16 July 1991) (*Sunday Times*, 'TV Extra', 14 July 1991, p 32), and a special on 'Cambodia-Kampuchea' (13 November 1991). *The Cutting Edge* series also instances the way in which SBS routinely uses the alibi of a prestigious cultural form—that of the documentary—to deal with complex political issues and debates. Until the breakup of Eastern Europe and the disintegration of Yugoslavia after 1991, it seemed that no matter how controversial the issue in the political debates of the day or on the commercial channels and/or the ABC, SBS could move the political velocity of issues outside the frame of the strictly political and into a cultural framework.

This cultural pluralism was further underwritten by SBS's provision of a space for local and English-language independent and radical film and television work that would not have otherwise have had a television screening. Like its news service, this also was a function of cost and availability, as a decade of independent film production activity was available for local television screening. In this way SBS provided a forum for the expression of marginal and alternative values and viewpoints. Thus SBS runs seasons of feature films with homosexual themes: by 1992 it was screening its third season of *Out* (covering topical cultural, social and fashionable events of interest to gay people). But, like its ethnic programming, SBS looks here to programs which will attact a cross-over audience. So, for example, it screened *Double Trouble* in 1992, which SBS publicity described as offering 'a unique and compelling insight into the lives of gay Aboriginal men and women' (SBS 1992b, p 25).

SBS provided an additional public television forum for dealing with Aboriginal issues and politics, an ongoing venue for future work including its pioneering of Aboriginal language and perspective fiction in the mini-series *Women of the Sun* (1982—a full decade before *Dances with Wolves*), the first Aboriginal television current affairs program, *First in Line* (1989), with 'complete editorial responsibility placed in the hands of people of Aboriginal and Torres Strait Islander descent' (SBS 1989, p 39) and, in Rhoda Roberts, 'Australia's first Aboriginal presenter of a prime-time national current affairs program' (SBS 1992b, p 3). In presenting Aboriginal issues as cultural inside a cultural political framework, SBS was able to pose Aboriginal cultural rights and articulate an Aboriginal politics outside public relations and welfarist standpoints. It routinely included Aboriginal issues within the general framework of a culturally diverse Australia. Once program funds for local production became more available and the multicultural agenda less homeland-based, Aboriginal activists were able to push for SBS accommodation of Aboriginal issues, pointing to the sheer anomaly of the most disadvantaged and culturally and racially visible group in the country being substantially left out of the multicultural equation. SBS responded in the late 1980s by including an Aboriginal component as part of its documentary production slate concerning ethnic and cultural diversity. For example, in its 1991 *Connections* documentary series, it screened *Uluru: An Anangu Story* (which told the story of Ayers Rock as the local Anangu people tell it), alongside a documentary on Victor Chang (the Chinese-born heart surgeon murdered in Sydney in 1991), and the Dunera interns (Jewish refugees interned as enemy aliens in World War 2). Similarly, the Bicentennial-Authority-funded *Changing Australia* series included a documentary on the Aboriginal artist Albert Namatjira as one of its six episodes, thereby positioning an Aboriginal artist firmly within a multicultural frame.

LOW-COST TELEVISION

SBS is also low-cost television. It is low-budget television in terms of numbers of employees per output. Its facilities and technological base are limited. It offers producers in the international television market a discounted price with a set price-per-minute operating (in 1986 it was US$34 per minute) (Tulich 1986, p 27). It paid by far the lowest prices on offer in Australian television for independent Australian programming. Both international and national producers are often prepared to accept SBS's low prices because it is a means of getting their programs into the Australian television market. SBS operates a television monopoly on multilingual broadcasts. Although well below prices paid by the ABC and the commercials for English-language programming, French, German, Brazilian, Serbian, Dutch, Japanese and Greek producers at least gain an Australian television market sale. SBS developed a market within television for multilingual programming which had previously been confined to the foreign cinema market and later the ethnic video market. In doing so, SBS has diversified the Australian television market.

In terms of English-language programming, SBS is in unequal competition with the ABC for programming. The ABC, with its larger audience (on average some four to five times the audience size) and program budgets pays considerably more for programming. Consequently, SBS shows material in the English language unable or unwilling to be picked up by the ABC and the commercials (Tulich 1986, p 27), with such programs making up nearly 20 per cent of overall broadcasting hours in 1988-89 (SBS 1989, p 114). Sometimes SBS has to rely on good luck. John Darling and John Moyle's *Bali Hash* (1990) on the Hash House Harriers event in Bali, which turned the ethnographic camera upon the 'Western other' in Asia, was designed for sale to the ABC. It became available to SBS after the expected ABC sale fell through, and gained high ratings within *The Cutting Edge* documentary series. And SBS's highest rating program, US PBS's *The Civil War*, was first offered to the ABC.

SBS's multicultural mandate provided a *raison d'être* for its substantial development of food programming as a prime time concept. In doing so, it helped Australians to become more sophisticated about food and contributed significantly to the styles and range of cooking in Australia. Such programs, usually produced in Britain but about continental Europe and Asian cooking, formed an important part of SBS marketing and led to SBS developing locally produced food programs with Australian independent producers, such as *The Rich Tradition* (on the peasant cooking of Europe, produced by Camelo Musca).

Given that for SBS there would be no 'regional' programming for 'regional constituencies' BAPH program production expectations were met by SBS's relation to the independent program production sector. Such a relationship prioritised one-off productions within an overarching program series concept such as that provided by the Bicentennial, *Eat Carpet*, *Australian Shorts*, and the *Australian Mosaic* series of 1989–90. SBS looked to regionally produced programs which would be oriented to national multicultural issues and constituencies. Such programming slots offered a degree of creative freedom to filmmakers that is rare in Australian television. SBS, typically, sets general guidelines for programming, permitting filmmakers a great deal of latitude within productions, with executive producers and series producers not tending to have as significant a role in creative direction as is normal in ABC and commercial production. Such arrangements can be exploitative, with filmmakers often working long hours on minimal payments; by allowing creative latitude, SBS allows filmmakers to exploit themselves freely. Tight and rigidly set program budgets (by Australian standards) limit the scope and direction of projects, forcing creative solutions and careful planning. This combination of circumstances helps create a loyalty to and affection for SBS on the part of those involved. Moreover, such series provide opportunities for people to break into the film and television industry. Such people can be expected to work under these conditions on meagre budgets, with production for the SBS serving an industry apprenticeship function. In Western Australia, subsidised public facilities at the Film and Television Institute and in the university and TAFE sectors have been used to produce documentary programming for the *Australian Mosaic* and daytime youth television programming slots. SBS's low purchase prices have, however, caused considerable resentment among established filmmakers, as has its sometimes heavy-handed dealing with filmmakers' work.

Being low cost creates evident limitations. Apart from the core areas of news and current affairs, the lack of adequate programming budgets affects the local programming available to it. In particular, funding has limited SBS's capacity to create alternative comedy, drama and mini-series. Initially this did not seem to be a problem, as the station picked up local product from a decade of film industry subsidisation which had failed to find a release venue, given the ABC's 'in-house' production policy and the commercials' preference for more mainstream and continuing series product. Additionally, the film industry tax incentive scheme provided scope for limited partnerships between SBS and independent producers. But after 1987 the diminishing value of the tax concessions at a time of rising expectations of the service exposed the limitations of SBS's drama and documentary production formats. The high cost of drama and documentary production ate considerably into its local programming budget. Despite the success of the series *The Girl from Steel City* and *Always Afternoon*, continuous series and mini-series options were abandoned after the latter's 1987 production. These made their partial return in 1992 with the critically acclaimed *Six Pack* series.

Between 1987 and 1992 SBS looked to lower unit cost infotainment series, one-off documentaries and fictional productions. Programs in these areas tended to be 'specials', often put together through special purpose outside funding. In this way, SBS came to rely partly upon the priorities of other—usually non-film—funding sources (typically other government agencies) for its local program slate, aside from news, current affairs and sports programs. This reliance has been responsible for some of SBS's successes. Its breakthrough Aboriginal current affairs series *First in Line* (thirty-two episodes) was made possible by grants from the Department of Aboriginal Affairs and other federal departments; while its highly respected *Australian Mosaic* television series of one-off documentaries was substantially funded by the federal Office for Multicultural Affairs and the Australia Council (SBS 1989, p 39). But underfunding diminished SBS's control over its schedule in that it forced a reliance upon programming created from special purpose funding. This drove an inevitable tension between the broad policy objectives of the sponsor and the broadcast scheduling priorities of the network.

Underfunding to some extent made SBS uncompetitive, as it became a last resort for filmmakers with eccentric product or product the ABC was unwilling to take. Yet underfunding also pushed SBS innovation. Its Australian Film, Television and Radio School (AFTRS) collaboration for the 1992 *Six Pack* series is a typical SBS initiative, combining a multicultural mandate with an existing government training provision in the AFTRS and an independent production company. Shot in seven weeks at the AFTRS in Sydney during its vacation period and during the Sydney Film Festival, the series mostly used AFTRS-trained directors and scriptwriters (four of the six directors and three of the six scriptwriters were AFTRS-trained).

These series of programs—all one-off studio-based productions typically using only a handful of sets—gained ratings of 8 in Sydney and Melbourne (*Encore* 2–22 July 1992, p 2). Its less rigid schedules (than those on the ABC and commercials) could also be an advantage, creating opportunities for independent film and television producers to put together multinational programming deals with SBS as one television window (*Premiere* 22 February 1991). SBS also became a minor exporter of both its product and its subtitled programming, sometimes selling its subtitling back to the producer of the program.

When SBS spread outside Sydney and Melbourne it did so after the fashion of a Pay TV operation, with centrally originated programming broadcast around the country. SBS expanded through local retransmission of nationally generated signals or, in the case of Perth, a bank of computer-controlled VCRs recording and automatically rebroadcasting SBS after a time delay. As with Pay TV, the 'local' service area was redefined as communities stretching across the continent and across national boundaries.

No discussion of SBS-TV can ignore the problems created for SBS by federal policy to limit it as the only UHF metropolitan broadcaster from 1986. Up until that point SBS also broadcast on the technically superior VHF as Channel 0. The change to UHF only was taken as a means of clearing VHF frequency spectrum for FM radio exploitation, and opening up the UHF frequency for later television exploitation. The move initially disenfranchised many SBS viewers. Some of its ethnic audience, with few English-language skills, thought it had been taken off the air altogether, while some of the NESB audience lacked the financial resources to equip for the change—a new aerial and sometimes a new television set. Because of this, SBS's popularity, or lack of it, needs to be considered in terms of that part of the audience able to receive a UHF television signal (SBS 1991, pp 49, 51, 53). In 1986 less than half the audience in its principal markets could receive a UHF signal; by 1990 this had increased to two-thirds. Consequently, SBS's audience reach always needs to be set against the capacity to get an SBS signal and the quality of the SBS signal once it was received (in 1990 an estimated 700 000 homes in its nine principal markets received SBS pictures with some reception faults). Additionally, some cities were worse than others for receiving SBS. In 1990, 64 per cent of homes in Sydney and Brisbane, the largest and third largest of Australian cities, were capable of receiving SBS, with 71 per cent in Melbourne, 77 per cent in Adelaide and 90 per cent Canberra. Thus, if SBS's weekly reach of total homes was used rather than capacity to receive UHF signals, Sydney had a lower percentage audience reach than Melbourne (and Perth and

Canberra were higher than either); but when capacity to receive a UHF signal was taken into account Sydney had a higher weekly reach than Melbourne, Melbourne higher than Canberra and Perth. When UHF reception was taken into account, SBS's audience in SMBA was on average 9 per cent higher than indicated by its weekly reach of total homes.

SHAPING THE PRESENT AND THE FUTURE

By 1990–92, SBS television was being shaped by a conjunction of forces. Regular sponsorship rather than the case-by-case arrangements of the past created an additional funding basis. It was used to finance independent Australian production, with accords being made between SBS and the federal government film financing agency, the Film Finance Corporation. SBS moved to gain greater ratings points (the 1984 Connor Report [1985] recommended a 6 per cent audience share) to ensure its independent survival. Limited sponsorship saw SBS under pressure to go after a more generally constituted 'special audience'. Its increasingly national reach meant addressing less ethnically marked audiences than those in Sydney and Melbourne. In turn, this prioritised its multicultural, cosmopolitan and minoritarian dimensions at the expense of ethnic and ethno-separate elements. Increasing Asian and declining European immigrant intakes (which tended now to be more 'skilled' than their predecessors) led to different expectations of SBS. These were for a greater Asian orientation and for more locally produced programming. The 'backlash' against multiculturalism of the late 1980s—particularly with respect to its ethno-separate aspects—saw increasing demand for English-language programming, and this ensured that local production would be prioritised as the vehicle for multiculturalism (thereby diminishing the importance of multilingual programming, although its overall proportion of total programming hours remained intact). 'Nationalist' moves in public policy in the lead-up to the 1988 Bicentennial and subsequently between 1990 and 1992 saw multiculturalism defined as an issue for all Australians. This recast SBS as a service for everyone.

In the process, the logic of special needs met by a multicultural service shifted. The ethnic homeland and multilingual component of the service diminished in centrality in prime time while locally produced programs 'shaped by the experience of a pluralist Australia' (Johns 1991, p 16) became correspondingly more important. These different elements saw SBS reshape its program schedule and presentation. The logo 'bringing the world back home' which acknowledged the role played by quality overseas programs was replaced by 'Special Programming for Special People, Australians' with the music being retained to provide continuity. The most visible sign of this change was the move towards infotainment programs broadcast in English between 6.30 and 8.30 pm weekdays. Johns described this change as:

> a recognition of the idea that SBS is, as the Prime Minister declared recently, for all Australians, and a recognition of the need to put greater predictability for the viewer into what SBS is showing. (1991, p 18)

The profile of SBS's current affairs programming was lifted to sustain the momentum created by the news with the employment of eminent broadcaster Paul Murphy on a revamped *Dateline*. Locally produced programming became more important to the service. International elements still figured prominently in the news, *Dateline*, *World Sports* at 6 pm, the *Movie Show*, and *Face the Press*, but these were presented within an Australian context.

The changes met with resistance as ethnic groups which previously felt central to the service saw SBS partially turning away from the ethno-separate and southern European emphases of the immediate past. Franca Arena, previously a strong defender of the service, in August 1992 called for the dismissal of its then executive director Brian Johns and for control of the service to be given back to ethnic groups. As had been the case before, the future of SBS was integrally tied up with the direction, shape and nature of multiculturalism as a social policy and symbolic political instrument.

As a multicultural organisation, SBS is susceptible not only to social and cultural change within Australia but to adjustments within the homelands and Australia's relationship to these homelands. More than any other Australian television service, SBS has been affected by the end of the Cold War and the subsequent ethnic revivals.

The homelands of southern and eastern Europe have a particular importance to SBS given that the primary definition of multiculturalism in the 1970s and 1980s was in relation to these regions. The changes to *Vox Populi* is one marker of these contemporary changes to SBS. In pioneering this program in 1986, Vladimir Lusic served as a representative of all ethnic groups in Australia in terms of their common problems vis-a-vis the wider Australian society. He spoke on behalf of diverse ethnic groups reporting the ethnic press at the end of the program. But this became impossible with the severe pressure upon a common multicultural identity to fragment into homeland-defined national identities following the break-up of the Eastern bloc and the existing international order. As Yugoslavia and the Soviet Union moved towards disintegration and other eastern European countries experienced lesser but similar nationalist movements, the homelands looked towards political and economic support from their Australian diaspora. A new relationship between the diaspora and the homeland emerged as the older troubled relationships (often based on dissidence and anti-communist orientation in Australia—sometimes labelled 'terrorist' in the case of nationalist Croatians) were replaced by new relationships based on active enlistment of the diaspora on behalf of newly formed nationalist governments. This had severe impacts on particular ethnic communities, poisoning inter-ethnic association and widening the gap between groups as carefully constructed networks of trust and common multicultural identity were eroded. Lusic was too clearly identified as a Croatian. Given the nationalist aspirations of Croatia with respect to the Yugoslav state in disintegration, in 1991 he was replaced by Rhoda Roberts. Now it was an Aborigine, not a European 'NESBIAN', representing social and ethnic marginality.

SBS still looked the same, in that the survivors were the major ethnic groups: Italians and Greeks, who had significantly shaped the service anyway. These countries were not as affected by the new international order and had well established links both with their diaspora and the wider Australian community and its institutions. For these Australians, the relationships with their homelands in terms of programming provision and shared political outlook continued-especially as these were also the only European ethnic groups (apart from the northern Europeans) that could continue to provide an acceptable 'multicultural' identity.

However, Greek identity in Australia is not unproblematically culturally neutral. The shared political outlook of the Greek homeland and its Australian diaspora was clearly shown in early 1992, when the Greek government called upon its diaspora to influence Australian foreign policy against the recognition of the Macedonian Republic in former Yugoslavia. Research among Perth Macedonians and Croatians shows that during this period even newsreader Mary Kostakidis became problematic for some within both communities—as a representative of the political and cultural power of the Greek lobby. This perception was further underscored by the absence of material about Macedonia on SBS news, which was taken to prove its Greco-Serbian bias. The politics of Croatian independence saw an increasing identification of the Greek with the Serbian, in turn compromising the shared southern European identity which had been one basis for SBS viewer preference. The break-up of this common identity led to the foregrounding of previous informal perceptions of Greek and Italian dominance of SBS-TV as bitter public matters (within SBS radio such ethnic disputes are more common).

European ethnic revivals had decisively entered into community politics and ethnic self-perceptions. As homeland struggles and new political alignments reshaped those communities' relationship to culturally proximate groups, SBS found it increasingly hard to occupy a position as a multicultural voice providing a forum for the neutral presentation of ethnic viewpoints. For example, *Vox Populi*'s rundown of the ethnic press became increasingly problematic as that press was now too involved in homeland politics and furthering the political interests of the homeland. Ethnographic research in Perth showed *Vox Populi* losing popularity amongst the Croatians surveyed not simply because of the departure of Lusic, but also because of the program's changed agenda. That community looked to *Dateline* and to the ABC for 'unbiased information' with increased viewership of the *7:30 Report* and respect for the ABC's eastern and central European correspondent Pierre Vicary (Kolar-Panov & Miller 1991, pp 74–7).

SBS's multiculturalist agenda is adapting to these changes, maintaining an internationalist focus in its news and current affairs but foregrounding the Australian 'national interest' slant on these events. Alongside this is an increased orientation towards Australia and towards Australia as a multicultural site. Its Australian-produced programs become the desirable means to set the multicultural agenda. SBS may have had little choice in this. To pursue the homeland–Australian diaspora connections of the past would be to inflame an already delicate political situation. Although it continues to pursue a cosmopolitan internationalism, this is oriented towards less politically charged sites and more in alignment with overall governmental policies and external outlooks. In this context, North American and British programs become more important as a prime time program source reflecting the larger move toward programming and cultural diversity within English language production.

Additionally, the pressure of the contemporary immigration policy with its Asian migration focus and the identification of Australia's national interests as in the Asia–Pacific region saw SBS making a necessary Asian accommodation. This is expressed through an increased orientation towards Asian current affairs and events, towards Asian cultures and Asian Australian issues. *The Asia Report* was 'mainstreamed' into *Dateline*. Australian-produced programs such as *A Traveller's Guide to the Orient* were screened, introducing a tourist guidebook view of Asia in line with Asian countries' self-promotion of 'their history, their culture, their customs, their people plus their unique and fascinating attractions' (SBS Publicity July 1992). [This program can be particularly criticised for its orientalist outlook—

an outlook the overseas tourist organisations appear all too willing to promote as their preferred way for Australians to 'know' their countries.] In producing such programs, SBS is accommodating not only policy changes but also shifts in the demography of Austra-lian migration.

SBS is likely to undergo further changes over the 1990s. If present trends continue we might see it becoming more Asian in staffing and programming. Additionally there is some evidence from our audience research that demand for multilingual entertainment programming on SBS was reduced by the ethnic video explosion. In the context of widely available multichannel satellite services (eg AsiaSat and, possibly, southern European multilingual services) this demand may be further reduced. In that context, SBS would become even less an entertainment channel broadcasting in languages other than English (it still maintains a 50–50 split of English-language and non-English programming). It is, though, ideally placed to provide general current affairs and international news and analysis of the kind familiar from *Dateline* and *World News*. This should be of particular interest to the different ethnic fragments, enabling SBS to regain its position as a multicultural voice and of interest to internationally oriented Australians. However, the extent to which it can provide these will depend upon the availability of material, particularly with the possible development of alternative cable news services such as CNN International or the BBC in the Australian market. The ways in which television programming sources are being tied up by satellite and cable services internationally suggests that SBS programming imports will increasingly be dictated by emerging television service arrangements between itself and existing free-to-air broadcasters in the US (the Public Broadcasting System), Canada (Canadian public broadcasters), the UK (Channel 4) and in other European and Asian countries.

SBS's Australian programming orientation focuses on the Austra-lian experience of migration and marginalisation rather than towards the maintenance of the homeland cultural identity. It thereby lends the 'experience' a voice and expressive medium. Although Australian multiculturalism is now more locally oriented and less concerned with cultural identity expressed in terms of the homeland, there are financial and structural limits to its capacity to deliver locally produced multicultural programming in terms of its small audience shares and the medium size of the Australian television market. It will continue to rely on imports, with their supply increasingly dependent upon the general development of the media market in a post-Pay TV environment. It is likely that the service will continue to look much the same, although its operating environment may have changed dramatically.

Our study of SBS-TV has shown us an efficient narrowcasting national broadcaster in action which is tailored to an Australian broadcasting, demographic and political environment. Both its 'publishing model' and newness as an organisation have given it a flexibility and responsiveness which have made it a major force for programming innovation on television. John Hartley's 'post-modern television of tomorrow' (1992, p 200) is also a function of that specific social, political and cultural program centred on ethnic and cultural diversity, multiculturalism.

9 An Aboriginal television culture: Issues, strategies, politics

with Philip Batty

With Aboriginal television, we are dealing with a family of issues, sites and institutions.[1] There is an Aboriginal-controlled television station: from 1985 the Remote Commercial Television Service (RCTS) serving the Central Australian footprint of AUSSAT (remote South Australian audiences and Northern Territory audiences outside of Darwin) was in the control of an Aboriginal organisation, Imparja. Low-powered Aboriginal community television stations operate in Yuendumu and Ernabella. The Broadcasting in Remote Aboriginal Communities Scheme (BRACS) enables Aboriginal communities to intercept incoming satellite signals from the ABC and substitute locally produced programming (Venner 1988, pp 37–43). On mainstream television, Aboriginal windows provide limited episode current affairs programming for Aboriginal audiences. Nationally, there is the *Black Out* series (broadcast since 1989) on the ABC, and various initiatives beginning with the current affairs series *First in Line* (1989) on SBS-TV. Regionally, there is *Milbindi* on GWN (WA's regional broadcaster and RCTS provider), *Nganampa Anwernerkenhe* on Imparja, and the *National Aboriginal Video Magazine* series developed by the Aboriginal and Torres Strait Islander Commission (ATSIC) for tape distribution to communities and for broadcast on regional commercial television. There is Aboriginal programming for general (Aboriginal and non-Aboriginal) audiences on the ABC with its documentary series *The First Australians*, various one-off documentaries on SBS-TV and the commercial networks, and Aboriginal issue centred from time to time on arts programs. Television drama centres Aboriginal issues and lives in the mini-series *Rose against the*

Odds (1991) and *Women of the Sun* (1982); and feature films screened on television such as *Backlash* (1986) and *Tudawalli* (1988). Characteristically, this range of one-off film and television projects—usually documentary projects—involves Aboriginal subjects to the extent that those subjects influence the filming and production processes. There is also non-broadcast television, in the formal and informal video and film exchanges which create audiovisual networks at local community, regional and national levels, and in the video teleconferencing of the Tanami Network operating amongst the Warlpiri in central Australia. The Tanami Network permits community interchange, programming exchanges, and community news and information. It blurs the traditional separation between telecommunications and broadcasting (see Yuendumu Community Education Centre 1990a; 1990b).

This mix of initiatives is an impressive achievement. A decade ago, Aborigines had virtually no control over programming (see Michaels 1987c). Aboriginal filmmaking talent was not explicitly developed at Film Australia. Aboriginal programming produced in consultation with the Aboriginal community did not occupy a regular programming slot on the ABC. Aborigines had a limited capacity to affect and control the form of their representation in a way available to larger ethnic groups (Mickler 1992a, pp 43–4). They had to piggy-back on initiatives such as multiculturalism (designed for ethnic immigrants) or rely upon the feedback loop that sometimes developed with news and current affairs reporters, or with one-off ethnographic and documentary filmmakers who actively sought Aboriginal cooperation and acknowledged their duties and obligations to Aboriginal communities.

Now, film and television, together with their cultural counterparts in painting, ritual performance, radio, music and theatre, occupy a key place in indigenous self-affirmation and political development. Aborigines and their representatives are not only negotiating the form of their representation but are increasingly shaping the structures and practices through which Aboriginal representation is secured. As Michael Leigh observed, Aborigines are 'no longer aliens in an industry which for a century has used them for its own ends' (1988, p 88).

These Aboriginal initiatives are not only the consequence of Aboriginal activists battling and succeeding despite the system, but are also a consequence of their involvement in shaping governmental programs, policies and funding decisions. Each of the Aboriginal television initiatives has included significant non-Aboriginal involvements, from the facilitating role of Neil Turner at Ernabella and Eric Michaels at Yuendumu in the early 1980s to the non-Aboriginal crews producing 'Aboriginal' documentaries for the ABC. There is also a variety of Aboriginal purposes in their television involvements. Many Aboriginal community organisations want to intervene in existing forms of television, not so much to change things radically, but simply to get the matter of representation right. Imparja board members see having a piece of commercial television through television station ownership as important in the same way as any non-Aboriginal person would own shares in or run a commerical business. Both Francis Jupurrurla of the Warlpiri Media Association and those associated with EVtelevision at Ernabella want to control incoming television programming and to create appropriate forms of television that intertwine with their own traditional cultural forms (Michaels 1987b; Turner 1990). Wayne Wharton of the Townsville Aboriginal and Islander Media Association (TAIMA) wants to see the development of a regional or federal Aboriginal television network managed and staffed by Aborigines—a kind of Aboriginal SBS. The independent filmmaker, broadcaster and producer, Lester Bostock wants to see barriers removed to greater Aboriginal participation in and access to television and film production employment, funding, and scheduling (1983; personal communication 1992). Independent filmmaker and visual artist Tracey Moffat wants to expand the ways of 'being Aboriginal' by broadening the range of projects available to her as an Aboriginal filmmaker, wanting to be also known as 'Tracey Moffat, interesting filmmaker'.

MAKING DISTINCTIONS

> Ultimately, the only sure way to incorporate the Aboriginal view into broadcasting is to ensure that Aborigines produce programs. (Lester Bostock 1990, p v)

Television is a mix of interrelated activities including program scheduling, networking, production, technical operations, management, financial control, audience research, distribution, and policy development and implementation. The diversity of levels and practices in television creates different possibilities for the Aboriginalisation of functions. Characteristically, only one or other of these activities is Aboriginal-controlled, staffed, and directed. Rarely, for example, is there the range of Aboriginal involvement from station management, and licence-holding through to program content that is typical of Aboriginal radio operations in Central Australia through the Central Australian Aboriginal Media Association's (CAAMA) 8-KIN network. Although some Aboriginal groups involved in television seek that kind of control, others do not. It is therefore important to distinguish between these activities to get a clearer indication of Aboriginal purpose and aspirations with regard to television.

At the level of control we need to distinguish between:

- Aboriginal television which entails Aboriginal control in most television functions of production, distribution and financing in television (e.g. EVTelevision);
- Aboriginal programming on mainstream television which has significant Aboriginal participation and control in program production, but not in the overall television structure in which such programming is embedded (e.g. *Blackout* and *First in Line*);
- Aboriginal organisational control of a television licence or production company which entails varying degrees of control over programming, the Aboriginalising of positions in the organisation, and a particularly Aboriginal point of focus (e.g. CAAMA Productions and Imparja); and
- programming involving Aboriginals where there is some Aboriginal negotiation of the terms of representation and where overall control varies from being shared in collaborative documentaries such as Frank Rijavic's *Exile and the Kingdom* (1993, see Laurie 1993, pp 16–17) to lying mostly in the hands of non-Aboriginal film and television producers, as on most news, current affairs, drama and documentary programs.

Community-based television developments at the Ernabella community in SA and at Yuendumu in the Northern Territory are in the terms developed above 'Aboriginal television' as are some of the successful BRACS services in northern Queensland and the Northern Territory (Molnar 1990, pp 146–54). Eric Michaels (1987b), Philip Batty (1993) and Neil Turner (1990, pp 43–45) see the Yuendumu and Ernabella television developments forging a distinctive Aboriginal television culture fashioned out of Aboriginal control over the combination of these factors and distinctive forms of programming and use. Similar functions are served by Aboriginal video networks in both remote and urban contexts (Meadows 1992, p 6).

The ABC, SBS, and RCTS providers (and to a lesser extent regional operators) embed their limited Aboriginal programming—like any other element—in their regular services. Embedding and limited autonomy also characterise the situation for a growing number of Aboriginal filmmakers and Aboriginal organisations involved in producing drama and documentary programming for national and international television screening. Aboriginal programming is increasingly becoming Aboriginalised in the sense of being made by Aborigines, with those Aborigines shaping, selecting and controlling most aspects of production. Aboriginal units at the ABC and SBS are relatively autonomous with respect to both networks. Evidence of Aboriginal approval and involvement at all levels of production is increasingly sought and demanded by film and television funding bodies. Alongside these developments has come commitments to Aboriginal media training and employment on the parts of the ABC and SBS, and film and television training organisations such as the Australian Film, Television and Radio School. These, together with Aboriginal television and individual filmmaking initiatives, are helping to develop a set of professional Aboriginal competences in television reporting and production.

Imparja Television is an Aboriginal organisation operating and owning a regional commercial television licence and CAAMA Productions in Alice Springs is an Aboriginal-controlled television production company dealing with central Australian Aboriginal topics. Both are part of the CAAMA Group of Companies (see CAAMA 1989). Organisational control in Imparja's case has curtailed alcohol advertising on television, made the local news services accountable to Aboriginal concerns, and helped change non-Aboriginal perception of and relations with the local Aboriginal community. Nonetheless there is a fundamental tension in Imparja between expectations that it be an Aboriginal broadcaster and that it be what it had mostly become by 1991: 'a commercial station that takes account of Aboriginal views, rather than an outlet for Aboriginal broadcasting' (ATSIC & DOTAC 1991, p 51; see also Batty 1993). Imparja is limited by the fact that it is a marginal regional commerical television operation providing the same Australian and Hollywood diet of sport, information and television programming for a population the size of an AFL Grand Final spread over nearly a third of the Australian landmass (See DOTAC 1990, pp 63–4). Imparja has little if any control and influence over the programming it buys from Australian networks and overseas suppliers—its choice is between programs brought into the country by SMBA and Perth networks and those made locally at their behest. Consequently, it does not have a particularly pronounced Aboriginal focus—only some 2 per cent of its broadcasts are Aboriginal programming—and it has not been able to achieve the kind of Aboriginalising of positions within the organisation initially envisaged for it.

CAAMA Productions produces programming with substantial non-Aboriginal involvement but—like Imparja—is directly accountable to an Aboriginal board. Thus, its important *Satellite Dreaming* (1991) documentary on Aboriginal television for Australian and international release had a production crew which included only one Aborigine, the comeraperson. The director, script writer and producer were non-Aboriginal.

The emergence in the 1980s of Aboriginal television, Aboriginal programs on television and Aboriginal organisations controlling television services has put a great deal of pressure upon programming involving Aborigines and Aboriginal subject matter. Aborigines—communities, organisations and individuals—are demanding a say and some tangible benefit from the settler culture's interest in and appropriation of Aboriginal images and culture. This is affecting the conduct and budget of Australian television producers from news and current affairs to documentary and feature film producers to television advertisers (and causing considerable tension between Aboriginal groups and the film and television industry in the process). In response the ABC and SBS—and funding organisations such as the Australian Film Commission (AFC)—have developed Aboriginal consultative groups for programming made or funded by them and involving Aborigines. This is to ensure that programming does no offend Aboriginal cultural sensitivities and has Aboriginal co-operation. General journalist and filmmaking training programs are now required to take on board Aboriginal viewpoints. Aboriginal awareness sessions have become part of staff development in SBS-TV. Such initiatives are part of Aboriginal attempts to manage their own direction through separate though related television developments. They stress the need for relative autonomy within programming, separate funding agencies and television infrastructures, and changes in the style of interaction between Aborigines and non-Aboriginal media organisations.

Each of these initiatives has its limitations. Training does not always lead to employment. Producing Aboriginal programs for the ABC necessarily involves juggling the dictates of its 'house style' and the sensibilities of its non-Aboriginal audience. And as Lester Bostock observed, 'programs on Aboriginal issues are still predominantly made by non-Aborigines' (1990, p v). He went on to note that 'while most of these are made with the best of intention, they still run the risk of being inaccurate and paternalistic'. One culturally sensitive and community-approved Aboriginal program is not of itself going to affect the routine conduct of *Seven Nightly News*, *4 Corners* or *A Current Affair*. Programming involving Aborigines still gets broadcast without the kind of authorisation expected by the Aboriginal groups concerned. Eric Michaels' account of the ABC making a documentary in Yuendumu in 1986 which did not measure up to that community's expectations of consultation is as true in the 1990s as it was then (1987c). Probably the most intractable area in this regard continues to be news and current affairs at regional, state and national levels; and regular Aboriginal involvement in mainstream drama programming remains less them satisfactory.

The BRACS scheme is as much a failure as a success, due to inadequate resourcing (BRACS equipment consists of a receiver dish, a VHS camera, VHS video recorders, a microphone and audio recorders with re-broadcast units enabling the transmission of satellite-delivered signals and of local programming over a two kilometre radius; see Maher 1990, p 7) and a lack of training and consultation. Many units simply arrived without warning in remote communities which had no preparation for them (Office of Evaluation and Audit 1992, p 3; Meadows 1992, pp 36–8).

The Aboriginalisation of crewing, creative direction and management in Aboriginal television is limited by the lack of appropriately qualified people. Consequently Aboriginal organisational control cannot lead to the kind of Aboriginalising of positions and function expected by those organisations and Aborigines.

PARTICIPATION AND SELF-DETERMINATION

These different Aboriginal initiatives should be placed in the context of contemporary Aboriginal political and economic aspiration and stated federal government policy of Aboriginal participation *and* self-determination (or, in its strongest form, Aboriginal sovereignty). In practice there is a great deal of overlap between these aspirations. We can usefully distinguish here two broad communicative, political, and cultural strategies: inter-Aboriginal, and Aboriginal–non-Aboriginal strategies.

Inter-Aboriginal televisual communication is designed to facilitate self-determination. It involves the Aboriginal use of television variously to build local and regional Aboriginal communities, pan-Aboriginal political and social projects, and linkages between communities and political structures at a local, regional, national and international level. Such strategies are concerned with communication, culture, and political development within and across Aboriginal communities. Within this context, inter-Aboriginal programming turns on:

- A 'local' Aboriginal culture of Aboriginal law directed at cultural maintenance and the integrity or the community in terms of its local culture, its lands and its language group. This can be seen in the Ernabella and Yuendumu television developments which sit

uneasily within the context of other, usually broader, Aboriginal cultural concerns and the settler culture.
- A regional Aboriginal culture made up of a composite of groups where Aboriginal culture acquires a confederate shape. Programming such as *Milbindi*, *Nganampa Anwernerkenhe* and the BRACS tape exchange system operated by TAIMA (which circulates tapes among Aboriginal communities in the Queensland BRACS system) serve regional Western Australia, central Australian and north Queenland Aboriginal groups.
- A 'national' Aboriginal culture (sometimes called pan-Aboriginal) made up of a collection of communication systems and cultural and political elements. These can be seen in *Black Out*, *National Aboriginal Video Magazine*, and *The First Australians*.

These different elements are consonant with broader Aboriginal political, cultural and social conditions. Here the concern is for fostering communication within Aboriginal communities, between adjacent communities, within the state, within the nation and between indigenous peoples internationally. Aboriginal communication networks are being consciously reassembled and reinvented as television and video are deployed to facilitate Aboriginal political and cultural self-management.

Within this context, there is Aboriginal television for remote communities, the development of program exchanges within Aboriginal language communities, the bicycling of programming in informal Aboriginal video networks and in ongoing BRACS tape exchanges between remote communities, and the development of networking of Aboriginal programs for Aboriginal audiences, whether through the ABC *Black Out* series, the more informal video exchange and regional television's broadcasting of (ATSIC's) *National Aboriginal Video Magazine*, or Aboriginal programming on the RCTS services of GWN, Imparja and QQQ (Queensland). Regional and national interconnections within Aboriginal communication are becoming increasingly foregrounded partly as a consequence of this mixed experience. Some envisage the BRACS stations in remote communities and, to an extent, the regional media associations—such as CAAMA and TAIMA—forming a possible embryo Aboriginal television network (acting as a production resource facility and distribution point). This would be a networked cooperative of autonomous community stations. Others envisage a more centrally originated national Aboriginal television network set up on the national scale of the mooted network in New Zealand, and modelled in part on the ABC or SBS. Those espousing such a network look to programming not only of Aboriginal Australian origin from around the country but also indigenous English-language and dubbed programming from Canada and New Zealand.

There is broad agreement among Aboriginal broadcasters that there should be a coherent national policy framework which would separately fund and administer Aboriginal broadcasting (see Meadows 1992, pp 42–52). Their argument is that Aboriginal broadcasting should be administered as part of the existing broadcasting system, draw its funding from the *broadcast*-designated dollar rather than ATSIC, and run parallel to the existing national and commercial networks. What the existing projects and these plans for new projects have in common is that they aim to develop further inter-Aboriginal communication. In this they are self-consciously directed at serving and creating anew Aboriginal communication, cultural and social spaces.

On the other hand Aboriginal–non-Aboriginal communication and political strategies turn on participation in existing mainstream television. These strategies involve Aboriginal negotiations with settler institutions over equality of Aboriginal access and outcomes with respect to existing production resources, televison funding regimes, broadcasting infrastructures, and training institutions. They also involve discussions and confrontation over the form and shape of television representations of Aboriginal people. This is very much about mainstreaming Aboriginal issues, with Aborigines having a right to a say in the development of programming involving them and with ways being sought for Aborigines to ensure that their viewpoints are heard. Such Aboriginal–non-Aboriginal strategies within television are inevitably directed at the broader Australian social and political culture and, therefore, largely general audiences.

In terms of Aboriginal programming such mainstreaming entails four kinds of project:

- one which constitutes a general audience through the Aboriginal audience (ABC's *Black Out*). This is 'from us including them';
- one which targets the non-Aboriginal audience for education, combating racism, and for Aboriginal political lobbying. This is 'from us to them', based on Aboriginal control, limited autonomy within broadcasting organisations, and benefit from the non-Aboriginal interest in Aboriginal culture;
- one which targets Aboriginal and non-Aboriginal audiences as part of a general audience aiming for an evolving and mixed development. Programming is designed to manage, 'fuse' and 'respectfully dialogue' between both sites—Aboriginal and non-Aboriginal

—as in Yothu Yindi music video (See Muecke 1992, p 184). This is 'both of us together'.
- one which 'Aboriginalises' mainstream television positions in terms of television personnel, from presenters to production crews. This is 'us in the system', as with Stan Grant as anchorperson in the Seven Network's current affairs show *Real Life*.

These mainstreaming aspirations resemble multicultural claims for equality of television access and treatment and some ethnic minority management over the public information about the group. Thus, as public instrumentalities, the ABC and SBS responded to political pressure for the employment of Aborigines to the extent of their presence in the general population with employment targets of 2 per cent for the ABC and 1–2 per cent for SBS (ATSIC & DOTAC 1991, pp 45, 47). In terms of film and broadcast program funding organisations such as the AFC and the FFC, Aboriginal lobbyists argue both for greater individual Aboriginal filmmaker access to funds and for greater collective funding based upon the development, extension and support for the development of Aboriginal program production and skills. For its part the AFC continually monitors and changes its policy development in this area (see Langton 1993).

Mainstreaming inevitably politicised non-Aboriginal dealings with Aborigines in television. Most immediately, it raised the issue of positive versus negative stereotypes of Aborigines in television and witnessed Aboriginal demand that the mainstream media affirm rather than denigrate Aboriginal culture and initiative. Aborigines increasingly flexed the political muscle available to them for a say in the direction, imaging and development of programs. Aboriginal political priorities here included: concern for adequate Aboriginal depiction; the existence of appropriate mechanisms and financial benefits to Aborigines stemming from the production of programming using Aboriginal people, images, designs, stories and Aboriginal political viewpoints; and concern for greater Aboriginal involvement in film and television program production. The depiction issue is a concern for on-screen protocols to do with the representation of Aboriginal subjects, issues and designs. These constitute a political demand for an Aboriginal say in the character, dimension and structure of information about them, their society and its organisation. This also extends to demands for a greater variety of fictional roles and alternatives to the 'tradition of the victim' in fiction and documentary which endows Aborigines with a limited role and diminishes their recognition as politically capable agents. These contemporary political contestations see Aboriginal rights and priorities negotiated by Aborigines and television institutions to find ways of accommodating the Aboriginal presence.

Related to this representation demand is a demand for adequate protocols in the production process. This is seeing the evolution of continuously negotiated guidelines for treating Aboriginal subjects in the production process, the permission process, the appropriate stages and nature of negotiations (Mackinolty & Duffy 1987; Michaels 1987c). Central issues here concern the fit between the routine conduct and practices of non-Aboriginal television and those of Aboriginal Australia. The onus here is placed upon this routine conduct, in that it is being asked to reconstruct itself to take account of Aboriginal cultural practices and rights. The most sensitive issues in this regard are: journalism's handling of Aboriginal police relations, welfare issues, and the naming of dead Aboriginal people; the often routine inclusion of Aboriginal designs, performances and artworks in television programs; and the redisposition of archival material about Aborigines in new programs.

A final mainstreaming demand is the Aboriginalising of the shape and trajectory of Aboriginal initiatives. This means reshaping the extensive role and involvements of non-Aboriginal people in Aboriginal television and Aboriginal affairs. The general direction of political and organisational changes demanded are, on the one hand, towards non-Aborigines working *for* Aboriginal clients at Imparja, ATSIC, CAAMA Productions and the various Aboriginal Media Associations; and, on the other hand, towards Aborigines supplanting precisely that non-Aboriginal creative, crew, technical and managerial involvement. The character of this Aboriginalisation will depend on the community and its assessment of its needs. TAIMA and Lester Bostock see the development of a cadre of professional Aboriginal expertise as critical to the development of Aboriginal management of symbolic resources and of projects concerning them. They envisage the development of Aboriginal career paths in mainstream television *and* in Aboriginal media. For some remote communities the priority is rather one of managing their incorporation into and penetration by the wider non-Aboriginal (and sometimes urban Aboriginal) culture. In their case it makes sense for them to employ non-Aborigines to take care of 'whitefella business' and act as a buffer between them and the constant intrusions of film crews, photographers and the like.

In practice, inter-Aboriginal and Aboriginal–non-Aboriginal communication strategies are interconnected. For example, pan-Aboriginal strategies are directed both at Aboriginal and Aboriginal–non-Aboriginal communication; inter-Aboriginal communication is facilitated by mainstream institutions. The dynamics operating between and conflicts arising from these two distinct modes shape the contours of Aboriginal television.

ABORIGINAL CULTURES

This range of Aboriginal expectation and involvement, the diverse nature of Aboriginal-related programming, and the distinct political and cultural purposes associated with Aboriginal television turn on the fundamentally plural character of Aboriginal Australia. Owing to location, history and varieties of settler contact, communities are necessarily in different paths of development. These produce different requirements and the need to negotiate for different sort of conditions. Remote communities, for example, are not uniformly structured. This is mirrored in BRACS useage, where local programming has evolved for cultural maintenance in some locations, and in others is kept under the control of the local police officer or school teacher (Office of Evaluation and Audit 1992, pp 3, 24–5; Corker 1989, 43–4). The political, cultural and community development issues facing urban Aborigines in Perth, Moree and Alice Springs, where Aborigines are a minority, are different from those issues facing the Aboriginal majority in Yuendumu, Ernabella or Woorabinda. Aborigines in urban centres are themselves internally differentiated by social class, educational training and degrees of involvement—including intermarriage—with the settler culture. Different parts of Australia afford Aborigines a different political presence. In the Northern Territory, the Kimberleys in Western Australia and in far north Queensland, Aborigines make up a significant proportion of the population and so have developed a more effective political presence than is available in those parts of Australia where the Aboriginal population may be very much a minority (between 1 and 10 per cent of the population). In these—typically urban—settings, Aboriginal minority status requires a different kind of negotiation, enlisting different sorts of public support, and requiring more 'mainstreaming' solutions.

Aboriginal culture, like all other cultures is emergent, not static. It is the product of contestations, divisions and the mobilisation of resources by particular agents within the terms provided by cultural and social systems. To fail to accord it that much is to fail to recognise a culture's transformative capacity and therefore to regard any cultural transformation of Aboriginal communities as becoming less Aboriginal, more modernised, westernised. The contours of contemporary Aboriginal culture are also necessarily defined by what Aboriginal tradition and the set of practices associated with it permit to be transformed, what the settler culture permits Aborigines to do within and to appropriate as their own of the settler culture.

The national and international construction of Aboriginal Australia can also be both enabling and disabling. Aborigines are valued as a primordial ethnicity for conservationists (Morton 1990, p 48), cultural nationalists (Lattas 1990, p 52–3), and art lovers (Ryan 1989). Conservationists lionise Aborigines as the first conservationists because they 'took care of the country'; cultural nationalists value Aborigines as the original and primordial Australian, that is, the oldest living human civilisation; and Aboriginal art becomes considered as a major world art movement. These constructions present particular exploitable opportunities for Aborigines. But they also dispose Aborigines towards certain forms of self-recognition over others. These notions legitimate the congruence of Aboriginal and non-Aboriginal conservation values which have seen Aboriginal management and joint management of national parks, their employment as park rangers and greater Aboriginal access to those lands; and they have helped create a market for Aboriginal culture whether in tourism, music, art, theatre, design, or film. But, as Stephen Muecke notes, these cultural definitions also impose 'unnecessary limits on being Aboriginal' (1992, p 17). Muecke continues:

> While culture is not a natural endowment, it is treated as if it is, so that the only 'respectable' ways for Aboriginal people to find identity in this society tend to be through particular forms of culture, or through sport. Becoming a novelist or a painter can be a way of gaining 'legitimate' middle–class Aboriginal identity (and in any case there seems to be a market). (1992, p 17)

More local settler constructions of the Aboriginal urban and country town ghetto may be far more damaging. The Perth 'moral panics' which envisioned lawless Aboriginal youths terrorising non-Aborigines and their vehicles (see Mickler 1992b, pp 322–36) provoked interracial tensions from which the minority Aboriginal population suffered.

The forms of non-Aboriginal Australian knowledge about Aborigines and the structures which sustain such knowledges help determine the opportunities available to Aborigines and impact upon the ways in which they fashion their identity. If these include the spectacle of an anthropologist's ethnography including films telling Aborigines how to perform their rituals (Michaels 1986a, p 6), it is also that of a cadre of non-Aboriginal expertise that exists 'on the top' of Aboriginal purpose, favouring in the process particular ways of 'performing Aboriginality' (ethnographically, realistically, in relation to culture) (Hodge 1990, pp 290–1; Muecke 1992, p 17).

In this context it is worth noting that no segment of the Australian population has been more surveyed, monitored, regulated and targeted for reform. The value of knowledges about Aborigines can quickly change from being *enabling* to *disabling* of Aboriginal practice. Notions of the wealth of human civilisation in Aboriginal culture that informed the pathbreaking ethnographic films of the 1960s of Cecil Holmes, Roger Sandall and Ian Dunlop (such as *I the Aboriginal* (Holmes, 1964) and *Desert People* (Dunlop, 1965) were important in establishing respect and providing a record of ongoing Aboriginal cultural achievement (see Dunlop 1983, p 16; Leigh 1988, p 87). These helped make land rights claims a possibility by demonstrating the maintenance of a relationship with the land and a viable cultural practice. Today such ways of knowing Aborigines on film are not viable. As Aboriginal communities were themselves in transition, ethnographic filmmaking became concerned from the 1970s with 'societies in change' (Dunlop, 1983, p 16). Ethnographic and anthropological knowledges can be used to compromise living Aboriginal tradition, unnecessarily constraining its evolution by seeming to impose tests of Aboriginal cultural distinctiveness that cultures in transition—particularly urban 'fringe-dwellers'—cannot easily meet (Cowlishaw 1988, p 89). The popularisation of anthropological conceptions can thus inhibit Aboriginal political demands for the special rights of indigenous peoples by making these rights contingent on particular kinds of customary cultural values and practices.

Aboriginal tradition also poses its own strictures on modes and types of acceptable behaviour. Aboriginal culture is far more emergent than most. Obviously when 98 per cent of the people living on your land are foreigners, the pressure to change, adapt, adjust and 'emerge' is enormous, if not fundamental to basic survival. Aboriginal culture under these conditions is being constantly reinvented, with attendant uncertainties and confusions surrounding what it is to be Aboriginal. Additionally, Aboriginal life-ways and aspirations are in many cases bounded by a chronic social crisis manifested in alcoholism, violence, unemployment and homelessness, stemming from the ongoing effects of colonisation. In some contexts, Aboriginal participation in bureaucracy, commerce and the wider society are seen by Aborigines and non-Aborigines as 'selling out' their community and Aboriginality.

Prior to the settler invasion, tradition played an important role providing the terms and forms under which this culture could be transformed. After the invasion the external input of settler claims introduced an important new transformative element alongside traditionally available means for managing social and cultural change.

These external, principally European elements, modified, subverted or in extreme cases wiped out traditional forms of cultural management and transformation.

Within this mix there is no one pattern of Aboriginal life-ways or of symbolic ethnicity. Much of the Warlpiri 'Aboriginal invention of television' in central Australia as Eric Michaels (1986b) described it is concerned with finding ways of incorporating settler Australian media and technology into the traditional Warlpiri mechanisms for constituting social and cultural reproduction. Television and telecommunication systems are being used to reaffirm Aboriginal cultural identity and life-ways. Michaels (1985, pp 505–10) argues that as traditional Aboriginal society is an information-based society, television represents important means, in Francis Jupurrurla's words, to fight 'fire with fire' by reconstituting Aboriginal communication networks, and promoting an expansionist Aboriginal program reclaiming land, information and dreamings (Michaels 1987b, p 74). Television becomes opportunity, not threat. For Michaels, Aboriginal populations are predisposed to audiovisual media with its bypassing of literacy, its capacity to include an oral dimension, and its portability (1990, p 24). The diverse Aboriginal media practices of central and northern Australia attempt to use communication technologies to maintain, transform, extend and dynamically reinvent cultural practices. These include community television and videos (as videos circulate along Aboriginal communication tracks). The use of telecommunications in the Warlpiri TANAMI network in 1992 offers Warlpiri community interaction across the Tanami desert through video teleconferencing. The reconciliation between 'traditional ways' and the 'new ways of life' comes together in remote Aboriginal communities as the problem of two laws and their reconciliation according to the terms of Aboriginal culture.

In an urban and country town context, Aboriginal television issues involve a different kind of accommodation. Here the cultural mix is neither non-Aboriginal nor 'traditional' but a mixture of both. In this case the problem is to establish for non-Aboriginal authorities the existence of *any* tradition and attachment to place. This was a problem for Perth fringe-dwellers in their bitter dispute with the Western Australian state Labor government over the Old Swan brewery (Goonininup) and Rottnest Island burial grounds (Mickler 1991, pp 69–88). Part of Rottnest and the brewery site are now the subjects of mabo-style land claims. State and federal politicians often find it easier electorally to recognise some Aboriginal cultural rights in central and northern Australia while overlooking or actively opposing claims closer to home. The Alice Springs dam proposal and Coronation

Hill are further away from the centres of settler culture than is Perth's Old Swan brewery site, where stereotypes or tropes reducing 'real' Aboriginality to more traditional lifestyles persist in guiding both policy and thinking. The differences between remote Aborigines with secure land tenure and a Perth fringe-dweller is as much a political as a cultural matter.

But too much can be made of the division between remote and urban Aboriginal communities. All support to varying degrees the 'Aborigine as minority' imaginary, sometimes called pan-Aboriginalism, and its creation of national solidarities, connections and the management of potential conflict between linguistically and customarily fragmented populations. Both have in their sights a common need (although internally differentiated) to negotiate with settler culture on an ongoing basis.

Whatever their situation, Aboriginal television developments are enabling Aborigines to select and transform their culture, items and practices on their terms. This transformation is based not only upon the symbols and practices of Aboriginal culture but also those of the settler Australian culture. This constitution will not only transform Aboriginal politics, culture and society over the next decade but will also transform the settler culture's understanding of and relationship with Aborigines.

AN ABORIGINAL PUBLIC SPHERE

These political priorities, program developments, new conditions in television, broader developments in Aboriginal communities, and more sophisticated political and administrative structures are part of a sea change in which the recognition of Aboriginal cultural, political and social rights to participation and autonomy is replacing older protectionist, paternalist and social disadvantage (therefore welfarist) agendas. If the settler culture still imagines itself as donor, and therefore having certain rights over its Aboriginal recipients through that donation, these programs, strategies and Aboriginal expectation are based upon an emerging logic of Aboriginal political, cultural and social rights. Non-Aboriginal initiatives in the Aboriginal area are increasingly being queried. Previously, Aboriginal negotiation in relation both to welfare and to cultural institutions was informal, only partially transparent, and relatively unavailable to public scrutiny. Typically, Aboriginal actors were forced to act at one remove through non-Aboriginal agents (usually through white cultural brokers: anthropologists, Aboriginal affairs departments, ethnographic filmmakers, and current affairs and documentary producers). With the emerging ascendance of non-welfarist logics of cultural, economic and political rights by virtue of original inhabitance, Aboriginal spokespersons and representative structures have achieved a greater degree of formalisation. (Also, less univocal: with this formalisation has come a greater capacity for inter-Aboriginal differences to become publicly apparent.) In these circumstances Aboriginal voices can only be expected to become more strident and less accommodating of the existing Aboriginal social and cultural circumstances, including televisual arrangements.

Aboriginal television presents a multifaceted and heterogeneous mix of policy issues, practices and tactics. None of these elements is simply in the business of representing Aboriginal culture, but actively intervenes in Aboriginal and settler cultures. For example, within Aboriginal television the question of the processes of production, financing and staffing has definite and specific outcomes on the form of representation. This makes it unlike the typical film policy and film production process relationship where more mediated and less direct relationships hold. Here the processes of production impact upon the organisation of production and represent a tactical intervention into Aboriginal culture and identity.

These diverse points of engagement necessarily have a mixed character in that the contemporary Aboriginal community life-ways and the dominant settler culture are sometimes sharply different, at other times blurred. There is considerable tension between the different Aboriginal television projects. Should the priority be Aboriginal television? Should it be organisational control of television and program production? Should it be programs on mainstream television? Should it be the accommodation of Aboriginal concerns and priorities in mainstream news and current affairs, fiction and dramatic forms? These tensions turns on the diversity of purposes, aspirations and political priorities in Aboriginal Australia. Fuelling these tensions between projects is the issue of what is possible from government as television production facilities compete with power generators and adequate water supply within a limited funding scenario in ATSIC. As in all Aboriginal–settler negotiations, the negotiations are conducted on an unequal basis, with Aborigines being the dependent party (Perkins 1990, p 10).

Television is so immediately political because Aborigines are such a dispossessed and economically and socially disadvantaged group. They are the most deprived, imprisoned, harrassed, dependent, dispossessed group in Australia; and they are also the most intractable and embarrassing 'problem' group for government. As the Task Force on Aboriginal and Islander Broadcasting reported in 1984 'Aborigines are the most disadvantaged major segment of Australian society with respect to access to communications and the social and economic benefits which they provide' (pp 123–4). Given this often desperate situation, there is necessarily considerable dissension within Aboriginal Australia over tactics and interventions, as different groups and regions struggle for access to a limited though growing federal funding dollar (Willmot 1986, p 20). The greater disbursement of funding to the Northern Territory and to CAAMA draws criticism from TAIMA; while the BRACS scheme covers remote rather than regional and metropolitan Aboriginal groups.

Such political tensions are taking place in the context of a more organised Aboriginal public sphere than in the immediate past. ATSIC's representative structures, the formation of a self-proclaimed Aboriginal Provisional Government as a political vehicle for making the transition to self-determination, and the land councils across Australia are increasingly taking on an agenda setting, spokesperson, and political, cultural and social development role vis-a-vis the 'mainstream'. Aboriginal affairs programs and departments are increasingly being staffed by Aborigines, individual communities are taking over their own governance, and regional and state Aboriginal enterprise is developing (Bayles 1989). This includes an emerging politics of representative governance by Aborigines themselves, as the instruments of Aboriginal–state involvement shift from a relatively non-transparent welfare-based management of a subaltern and supposedly recalcitrant group in need of modernisation, towards self-management and representative governance. This makes Aboriginal television a site which is necessarily caught up in issues which are simultaneously local, regional, national and international (international at least partly in that Australia's reputation as an honest broker in international forums is at stake, as Australian diplomats and governments see themselves judged on their negotiations with Aboriginal peoples). Here are, necessarily, the same power politics, regional rivalries, and competition for limited resources that make federal and state politics a blood sport. Here too, are politically driven decisions on infrastructures, locations and funding which sees certain Aboriginal groups miss out while others are advantaged. And just as mainstream politics is internally divided—full of back-stabbing and internecine conflicts—agreement is often as difficult to manage in Aboriginal Australia. But just as mainstream politics is itself also a composite of political coalitions of a relatively enduring nature and capable of general political coordination, so too there are relatively enduring identities and priorities in Aboriginal Australia, despite the often desperate conditions and factionalism. This public sphere has very real limits; it is profoundly affected by interventions from without by virtue of its dependence upon government funding, which is provided predominantly as a welfare service provision and not, for example, as 'compensation payments for land lost' (Perkins 1990, p 11). Despite this fragility, this public sphere is nonetheless increasingly shaping the direction of the $1 billion (Perkins 1990, p 11) or more spent by the federal government on Aboriginal affairs as ATSIC's representative structures increasingly direct this Aboriginal funding. Also, there are the practical consequences of the various Land Rights Acts around the country, which are empowering Aboriginal communities and developing Aboriginal political, business and administrative skills (Bayles 1989, p 10). Both are slowly replacing the top-down policy practices of the past with more bottom-up policy development.

THE NON-ABORIGINAL PRESENCE IN ABORIGINAL TELEVISION

Many non-Aborigines are involved in the production and management of Aboriginal television just as non-Aboriginal involvement in many aspects of Aboriginal affairs is the norm. Almost all published commentary on Aboriginal television is by non-Aborigines, including this chapter (but see Langton 1993). As in community management and ATSIC, non-Aboriginal involvement in administrative and managerial positions in television is critical. Although Aboriginal organisations are ultimately controlled by an all Aboriginal committee or board, such organisations have become centres of non-Aboriginal employment and training. Aboriginal initiatives have also become the conduit for the financing of large regional infrastructural projects—such as the delivery of a commercial television service to the Central footprint through Imparja—which is beneficial to a mainly non-Aboriginal constituency. The provision of recession-proof 'Aboriginal industry' funding enables Alice Springs to enjoy the third highest per capita disposable income in Australia. These kinds of outcome lead activists such as Bryan Syron and Gary Foley to see non-Aboriginal involvement in television production as yet more non-Aborigines 'riding off the back of blacks' (Bell 1990, pp 35–9).

What is the impact of this non-Aboriginal involvement in producing Aboriginal television? Aboriginal television is not non-Aboriginal bricklayers building houses for Aboriginal people, it is non-Aborigines actively participating in the production and therefore definition of Aboriginal cultural artefacts as they are hired, in the 'interim', to direct, edit and write an 'Aboriginal' television program. To what extent is Aboriginal television a non-Aboriginal construction of what Aboriginal television should or might look like?

There are no simple solutions like: Aboriginalise everything, or get non-Aborigines out of Aboriginal affairs. It is policy in Aboriginal organisations to employ Aboriginal people where possible. But the necessary expertise is not as readily available in the Aboriginal community as it is in the non-Aboriginal community. This absence of expertise raises the question of the cultural and structural inhibitions against Aboriginal people acquiring certain kinds of skills and competences. The areas in which Aboriginal expertise is being developed are circumscribed: culture and the arts, welfare, policing, paramedical, paralegal and education. The critical areas of bureaucracy, commercial and administrative competences and qualifications, and the professions remain substantially off-limits. Yet these are all critical to television service delivery. Too often non-Aborigines are employed, particularly in management, with Aborigines tending not to gain the critical management and financial, administrative experience essential to running the organisation.

Aboriginal organisations typically rely on non-Aboriginal accountants, administrators, consultants, technicians, engineers, and, at times, senior management personnel to keep organisations going , with an Aboriginal board and lower level and unskilled Aboriginal employment in bottom positions in the organisation. Also there are real limits to the development of 'para' expertise which provide only some of the critical professional expertise needed. Twelve-week training courses and the experience of BRACS do not turn Aboriginal trainees into broadcast engineers. Training and on-the-job experience can only go so far. Non-Aboriginal involvement in Aboriginal television is not simply a consequence of the black–white divide but of the particularity of the film and television industries. These industries rely on networks of contacts, access to funding sources, and particular managerial and technical competences, and are characterised by intense competition for work and funding. It is difficult for an Alice Springs Aborigine or Torres Strait Islander to gain sufficient training, contacts, knowledge and competence to run production companies, organise off-shore production and co-financing and the like. It is difficult enough for non-Aborigines in the peripheral capital cities to organise their national and international contacts to good effect in the film and television industries. Not just anyone has the personality or talent to be successful with television production. Additionally, broadcasting technologies are constantly changing and interpersonal relations and competences require ongoing regeneration and replacement, usually with reference to the metropolitan core.

Given these clear limits to the Aboriginalising process in television, the political issue here is the nature, direction and priorities of non-Aboriginal involvement, and the extent to which it can realistically be Aboriginalised. The answers to this will vary depending on the job being done, the expertise required, and the circumstances. As part of this assessment of Aboriginalisation it is important to assert the right of Aboriginal groups and individuals to hire non-Aboriginal expertise. Aborigines have the right to non-Aboriginal professional legal counsel, Tracey Moffat and Frances Kelly to non-Aboriginal crews if they want them, Aborigines to work collaboratively on projects with non-Aborigines or simply to have non-Aborigines cover an Aboriginal story, Aboriginal groups to appoint non-Aboriginal administrators (without them the Aboriginal art market would collapse). Remote Aboriginal communities have a right to employ non-Aboriginal advisers to act for them, even when it is to act as a critical buffer between them and governments and, even in some cases, Aboriginal organisations. This Aboriginalisation is not only the placement of 'Aboriginal bodies' in staffing structures, it is also and importantly the right of Aborigines and their organisations to determine the most effective and appropriate mix of expertise and personnel.

THEORISING ABORIGINAL TELEVISION

The diverse sites of 'Aboriginal television' together make up a family of issues and sites which encompass different targets and agendas, policy issues and projects. Their diversity is a necessary consequence of the heterogeneity of television, Aboriginal aspiration, and government policy. Aboriginal television initiatives come about through Aboriginal negotiations with existing television services, structures, broadcast policy frameworks, and the kind of programming expectations these negotiations create in both Aboriginal and non-Aboriginal audiences. These initiatives also include Aboriginal negotiations with respect to the federal policy of self-determination with its separation of Aboriginal broadcasting policy from mainstream broadcast policy; and Aboriginal aspirations for culturally and politically appropriate television that is driven by proposals, initiatives and imaginings formed out of Aboriginal tradition, individual and collective entrepreneurial activity and political strategy.

Aboriginal television needs to be understood and placed within this context, as it simultaneously enables and circumscribes the form and direction of Aboriginal television: the actions taken, the plans developed, and the lobbying undertaken by Aborigines with respect to television. Aboriginal television is, as Michaels (1986b) suggests, a particular invention of television; but this invention is formed from the available materials, only some of which are Aboriginal and over which Aborigines have only limited control. Aboriginal television then is not just the televisual expression of Aboriginal culture and aspiration. It is also shaped by Aboriginal negotiation of the existing video and television industry with its mix of local and international elements, and of the policy (broadcasting and Aboriginal)—government-funding nexus.

Most of these initiatives are wholly or partly dependent upon government funding and/or policy. This dependence has consequences for the type of programming, its self-understanding, its positioning on Aboriginal and governmental horizons, and the kind of political lobbying that takes place with regard to it. The dependence upon policy and funding ensures a 'public service', non-commercial, community development orientation to these Aboriginal intitiatives. Just as dependence upon policy and funding gives a certain character to the ABC, SBS, the work of producers reliant upon AFC and FFC funding, and the arts organisations dependent upon Australia Council funding, so too dependence upon policy and funding gives a certain character to Aboriginal television. This public service character is both enabling of Aboriginal enterprise and disabling just as it is for these other organisations. Aboriginal thinking and initiative must translate itself through an existing policy framework, developed by both Aborigines and non-Aborigines. This makes for Aboriginal expertise in political lobbying, grant and submission applications, and an entrepreneurialism defined through a capacity to extract the most concessions and money from government bureaucracies, funding programs and politicians.

Aboriginal activity here is no different to that of non-Aboriginal recipients of governmental cultural and broadcasting policy initiatives. But what is perhaps critical with regard to Aboriginal television initiatives is that there is not much Aboriginal television initiative outside this governmental axis, unlike the case of the commerical networks and their infotainment and ongoing series programming in television, or the non-government supported ethnic press. That this is so is itself a consequence of Aboriginal social disadvantage. It means that Aboriginal thinking and purpose becomes directed at the public sector and therefore public broadcasting models: as community or public television for the Yuendumu and Ernabella 'pirate' stations or aspirations for a kind of Aboriginal SBS or ABC touted by Wayne Wharton and inscribed in the fully 'independent indigenous media sector within the Australian media' strategy of National Indigenous Media Association of Australia (NIMAA) formed in 1992

(Office of Evaluation and Audit 1992, p 1). The hand of government funding as the principal means of resourcing imposes itself on the form of television programming, program selection, film and television series funding, program innovation and overall policy construction. While commercial initiatives should emerge down the track, and private funding is already involved in some initiatives, public sector and community-oriented thinking and expenditure determine the shape and contours of Aboriginal television practice.

These developments and strategies of independence take place, then, within the context of public sector funding. The public and political interest of Aboriginal actors in this area is in expanding this general state provision for Aborigines and taking over responsibility for its distribution of funds. It is concentrating Aboriginal focus, skills and development into this area. But public sector funding necessarily defines and limits Aboriginal action to community interest, defined non-economically and politically. It presumes the continuation and extension of government funding, something which may prove difficult to achieve in times of economic recession and targetted spending.

This helps give self-determination its contradictory face. There is the basic contradiction of rights of self-determination being 'granted' to a colonised people by the government of the colonisers. And there is the policy of self-determination, itself a mixture of decolonisation and a continuation of the existing welfare colonialism, albeit in a reshaped form.

In response to an earlier draft of this chapter Mudrooroo put the problem like this:

> Aborigines should be aware that the issue is one of power, that to let or lease the representations of themselves to others means that they have only themselves to blame if they disagree with the representation. Then, the presentation of television images and the reading of them are part of culture. For Aborigines to be educated in this culture means that, too often, they learn how Europeans present images, and then re-present their own images according to this model.

CONCLUSION

Self-determination in Aboriginal television predominantly means a cross between an Aboriginal national broadcaster and public television (as per public radio): Aboriginal programming and organisation within mainstream television networks (particularly the national networks) and the aspiration of Aboriginal mainstreaming allowing Aboriginal access to existing film and television series subsidy arrangements, and the freedom to be an Aboriginal filmmaker, television producer and reporter, having the freedom to work on non-Aboriginal and Aboriginal issues alike. For many Aboriginal broadcasters, self-determination in Aboriginal television is an important component of the broader struggle for the power and right to determine Aboriginal cultural, political and economic futures.

With political and legal recognition inching towards formal recognition of the special claims of indigenous people, and with greater acceptance of Aboriginal economic and cultural self-determination among the broader population, the possibility of a number of kinds of Aboriginal autonomy within an overarching Australian territorial state is an increasing possibility. Aboriginal television is inevitably moving in this direction too.

Endnotes

INTRODUCTION

1 I agree with Yuri Lotman here when he suggests that a culture—in his terms a 'semiosphere'—is made up of rivalrous, incommensurable and simply adjacent elements (Lotman 1990, p 135). As he puts it: 'The languages which fill up the semiotic space are various, and they relate to each other along the spectrum which runs from complete mutual translatability to just as complete mutual untranslatability.' (Lotman 1990, p 125) This seems to me a reasonable way of thinking about the necessary heterogenity of a television service.
2 Ken Ruthven made these remarks as discussant for Sneja Gunew's paper on multiculturalism 'Cultural Studies: Pluralism and Theory' at the 1992 Cultural Studies Conference held at the University of Melbourne, 10–13 December.

1 AUSTRALIA'S TELEVISION CULTURE

1 In fact, the percentage of Australian households with the VCR tended to be a few percentage points higher than US, UK and Canadian figures over the 1980s.
2 Throughout this book the word American is used to indicate someone or something from the US. Although anyone from the Americas is an American, I felt I had to persist with this admittedly imperialist useage as it was the least misleading option. To use Yanks would be derogatory to (US) Americans; while North American includes Canada and Mexico whose experiences with television—not to mention their respective global position—are at some distance from the US.
3 The US imports concepts too, with the principal British impact upon US

television being through concept remakes. Australia is also an exporter of program concepts and television scheduling expertise through both the Grundy organisation and Rupert Murdoch's satellite television involvements in Europe with Australian television formats being most notably used to introduce Sky Channel in the UK.
4 The observations on ethnic communities here are drawn from the ethnographic work of Dona Kolar-Panov for her Murdoch University PhD in progress.

2 HIGH COMMUNICATIONS POLICY IN AUSTRALIA

1 Regional Television Australia, the buying consortium set up by the regional stations, was also involved in importing programs and in producing its own program segments for members. However, this was a limited operation geared more to securing the best price for the programming imported by the networks and for Australian-produced programming.

3 THE RISE AND FALL OF ENTREPRENEURIAL TELEVISION, 1986–92

1 Packer's Consolidated Press converted its $200m in preference shares owed by Bond Media and a further $25m in interests and dividends into 55 per cent of Bond Media. An additional $79m was to be raised to pay off debt to Bell Resources.
2 *Communications Update 85*, (February 1993, p 8) listed Ten's shareholders as follows: TNQ TV Ltd, 40 per cent, Can West Global Communications 15 per cent, John Singleton 10 per cent, Jack Cowin 10 per cent, Audant Investments (Robert Whyte) 15 per cent, Isi Leibler 6 per cent.
3 For an excellent discussion of the opportunities Australian cinema groups deliberately eschewed in the teens of this century, see Bertrand & Routt (1989, pp 3–28).

4 TELEVISION'S DOUBLE FACE: OF IMPORTED AND LOCAL PROGRAMMING

1 Percentages for program costs listed here are for overseas and local program expenditure by metropolitan commercial television stations as a proportion of costs identified by the ABT and the ABCB as being for local and overseas programs. This leaves out agent's commission and licence fees which apply equally to local and imported programming. Unless otherwise listed these figures are calculated from Brown 1986, p 134; the ABT's *Broadcasting in Australia,* Annual Reviews (1988–91) and *Broadcasting Financial Yearbook 1988/89* and *1989/90*. These figures should be approached with some caution. They are more indicative of trends than exact reportage.
2 But there could be no return to the cooperative buying practices of the

ENDNOTES

past—Trade Practices legislation had made them unlawful in the absence of Trade Practices Commission authorisation.
3 Television Business International's *World Guide' 90* (1990) p 506, suggests that the ABC was buying programs in the range US $7 500–$20 000, compared to the commercial range of US $40 000–$90 000. This suggests the ABC can pay as little as 22 per cent of the price the commecials pay for imports. Australian industry sources suggested that this figure was certainly higher for drama, with upwards of 80 per cent of the commercials price being paid by the ABC.
4 Pre-video, the feature film revival actually ensured a lagged presence of Australian movies on local television, with television screenings up to five years often local release (Jock Given, personal communication, 5 May 1993).
5 In the late 1980s and early 1990s producers were forced to actively seek export markets due to the increasing inability of the networks to fully find, through licence fees, an adequate level of after-tax return to production investors. Jock Given, an economist at the AFC, argues that the Film Finance Corporation provides 'a much more structured mechanism [than content regulations] to force producers of TV drama to seek exports markets' (Jock Given, Personal Communication, 5 May 1993).

5 TELEVISION AND NATIONAL CULTURE

1 Aboriginal Australia operates simultaneously on a local, regional, national and international level, whether in programming for Aboriginal audiences at each of these levels, in community and general governance, in the various regional Aboriginal identities (as Anaiwan and Koori, as Murri and Nyungar), and in their international identity as one among a number of indigenous people. This level is a special case formed largely outside the national cultural dynamics outlined here which predominatly relate to the settler culture. Its connections to and separation from the mainstream television culture will be dealt with separately in the last chapter.
2 The global level is often used to describe Hollywood and, to a lesser extent, British programming, the international television business's increasingly global reach (including its Australian reach), and a weak global culture formed in relation to the exhibition of transnational television programming and the transnationalisation of business operations.

9 AN ABORIGINAL TELEVISION CULTURE:
ISSUES, STRATEGIES, POLITICS

1 'Aboriginal' and 'Aborigine' are used throughout to refer to Aborigines and Torres Strait Islanders. As this chapter was written between Alice Springs and Perth, we were aware of the south-east Australian nature of the designation Kooris, and the Queensland nature of the alternative self-descriptor Murris, for all Aborigines in Australia. For a discussion of

Aboriginal television see CAAMA Production's *Satellite Dreaming* (1991), Meadows (1992) and Dutchak (1992). Michaels (1987a) provides a still pertinent discussion of issues for Aboriginal television and the difficulties involved in conceptualising it. Meadows and Rielander (1991) provide a comprehensive bibliography of writings on Aboriginal broadcasting.

Bibliography

Appleton, Gillian 1988, 'How Australia sees itself: The role of commercial television', in *The Price of Being Australian*, Australian Broadcasting Tribunal, Sydney, pp. 190–246

Arena, Franca 1985, 'The ethnic media: Issues and problems: A consumer's point of view', in *Immigration and ethnicity in the 1980s*, eds IH Burnley, S Encel and Grant McCall, Longman Cheshire, Melbourne, pp. 95–9

Armstrong, Mark 1974, 'Obstacles to sensible broadcasting regulation', *The Australian Quarterly* vol 46, no 4, pp. 7–21

—— 1988, 'Introduction', *Australian Communications Technology and Policy*, eds E More and G Lewis, AFTRS & Centre for Information Studies, Kuring-gai CAE, Sydney, pp. 3–12

Ashbolt, Allan 1985, 'Radio and television services for migrants: Problems and prospects', in *Immigration and ethnicity in the 1980s*, eds IH Burnley, et al, Melbourne; Longman Cheshire, pp. 104–10

ATSIC (Aboriginal and Torres Strait Islander Commission) and Department of Transport and Communication (DOTAC) 1991, *Aboriginal and Torres Strait Islander broadcasting policy review, a discussion paper prepared jointly by the Aboriginal and Torres Strait Islander Commissions and the Department of Transport and Communications*, July 1991, ATSIC and DOTAC, Canberra

Australian Broadcasting Tribunal (ABT) 1984, *Satellite Program Services* vol 1, Canberra, AGPS

——1985, *Remote Commercial Television Services Fourth Report Central Region*, AGPS, Canberra

——1988, *Broadcasting in Australia*, AGPS, Canberra

——1990, *Broadcasting Financial Yearbook 1988/89*, ABT, Sydney

——1991a, 'Arts programs on Australian television', *OZ Content* vol 3, ABT, Sydney, pp. 143–58

——1991b, *Broadcasting in Australia*, ABT, Sydney
——1992, *Broadcasting in Australia, Fourth Edition*, ABT, Sydney
Australian Broadcasting Corporation (ABC) 1985, *2nd Annual Report, 1 July 1984–30 June 1985*, ABC, Sydney
Australian Film Commission (AFC) 1975, *Report of the Interim Board of the Australian Film Commission*, Sydney, 14 February
Bailey, Julie James 1980, 'The road to ethnic television? Key dates and references', *Media Information Australia* no 15, pp. 12–14
Barker, Wayne 1984, *The Inuit broadcasting sysem: Some possibilities for Australia*, AGPS, Canberra
Barnouw, Erik 1975, *The Tube of Plenty*, Oxford University Press, New York
Barr, Trevor 1985, *The Electronic Estate*, Penguin, Ringwood
Barwise, Patrick & Andrew Ehrenberg 1988, *Television and its Audience*, Sage, London
Batty, Philip 1993, 'Singing the Electric', in *Channels of Resistence*, ed Tony Dowmunt, British Film Institute, London
Baughman, James L 1985, *Television's guardians: The FCC and the politics of programming, 1958–1967*, University of Tennessee Press, Knoxville
Bayles, Tiga 1989, 'We live with the problems, we know the solutions', *Frank Archibald memorial lecture series* no 4, University of New England, Armidale
Bednall, David HB 1988, 'Television use by Melbourne's Greek community', *Media Information Australia* no 47, pp. 44–8
Bell, Sharon 1990, 'Filming Radio Redfern: 'Riding to success on the backs of blacks'?', *Media Information Australia* no 56, pp. 35–9
Ben Bock, Alex 1988, 'Who is Christopher Skase', *Channels*, September, p. 46
Betts, Katharine 1991, 'Australia's distorted immigration policy', in *Multiculatural Australia: The challenges of change*, eds D Goodman, J O'Hearn and C Wallace-Crabbe, Scribe, Newham Vic, pp. 149–77
Blainey, Geoffrey 1984, *All for Australia*, Methuen Haynes, Sydney
Bostock, Lester 1983, 'Aboriginal broadcasting and training', *Media Information Australia* no 27, pp. 36–7
——1990, *The Greater perspective: Guidelines for the production of television and film about Aborigines and Torres Strait Islanders*, SBS, Sydney
Bostock, William W 1981, *Alternatives of Ethnicity*, Corvus Publishers, Melbourne
Bridges, James 1991, 'Letter to the Editor', *Sydney Morning Herald*, 18 March
Brisebois, Debbie 1990, 'Whiteout warning: Courtesy of the federal government', Inuit Broadcasting Corporation, Ottawa, October
Brown, Allan 1986, *Commercial Media in Australia*, University of Queensland Press, St Lucia
Brown, Allan 1988, 'Television equalisation: A case study of industry restructure', in *The Price of Being Australian*, ed ABT, ABT, Sydney, pp. 174–89
Burchill, Tony 1990, 'Saga of woe continues for the embattled television industry', *Financial Review*, 8 May 1990

BIBLIOGRAPHY

Bureau of Transport and Communications Economics 1991, *Economic Aspects of Broadcast Regulation*, AGPS, Canberra

Cantor, Muriel and Joel Cantor 1986, 'American television in the international market place', *Communication Research* vol 13, no 3, pp. 509-20

Carey, James 1981, 'Culture, geography, and communications: The work of Harold Innis in an American context', *Communication and dependency: The tradition of HA Innis*, eds W Melody and L Salter, Ablex Publishing Corporation, Norwood NJ, pp. 73-91

Carmichael, Helen 1991, *Seeing is believing: Scriptwriting in a multicultural society*, Office of Multicultural Affairs, Canberra, April

Carrington, Gerald 1983, 'The role of the media: Television', Paper presented at the Second Biennial Meeting of Members of the Australian Institute of Multicultural Affairs, 18 October

Cash, Nancy, 'Gerlach', *The Australian Way*, December 1990, pp. 8-10

Castles, Stephen, Mary Kalantzis, Bill Cope and Michael Morrissey 1988, *Mistaken Identity*, Pluto Press, Leichhardt (Sydney)

Castles, Stephen, Michael Morrissey and Brian Pinkstone 1989, 'Migrant employment and training and industry restructuring', in *The Challenge of Diversity*, ed J Jupp, AGPS, Canberra, pp. 127-40

Caughie, John 1990, 'Playing at being American: Games and tactics', in *Logics of Television*, ed Patricia Mellancamp, Indiana University Press, Bloomington, pp. 44-58

Central Australian Aboriginal Media Association (CAAMA) 1989, *The CAAMA Group*, CAAMA Group of Companies, Alice Springs

Chadwick, Paul 1989, *Media mates: Carving up Australia's media*, Macmillan, South Melbourne

Chicago Cultural Studies Group 1992, 'Critical multiculturalism', *Critical Inquiry* vol 18, no 3, pp. 530-55

Coftus, Jack 1987, 'International report', *Television/Radio Age*, 14 September 1987, p. 26

Collins, Richard 1990, *Television: Policy & Culture*, Unwin Hyman, London

——1991 'The tyranny of distance: Sentence increased or remitted?', *Metro Magazine*, no 86, Winter, pp. 13-19

Communications Law Centre (CLC) 1992, *The representation of non-English speaking background people in Australian television drama, discussion Paper*, Communications Law Centre, Kensington, (Sydney), March

Communications Update 1990, 'Whither AUSSAT?', *Communications Update* no 52, February, pp. 3-5

Connor Report 1985, also known as *Committee of Review of the Special Broadcasting Service, Serving multicultural Australia: The role of broadcasting, Part One*, AGPS, Canberra

Corker, John 1989, 'BRACS: Destined to fail', *Media Information Australia* no 51, pp. 43-4

Court, David 1991, 'Reforming Australia's film and TV industries, Review of *Cut*', *Entertainment Business Review* no 33, 22 August, p. 8

Cowlishaw, Gillian 1988, 'The materials for identity construction', in *Past* and present: The construction of Aboriginality, ed J. Beckett, Aboriginal Studies Press, Canberra, pp. 87–108

Crawford, Hector 1959, Commerical Television Programmes in Australia, privately published, Melbourne

Cunningham, Stuart 1987, 'Chauvel, the last decade', Continuum vol 1, no 1, pp. 26–46

——1989, 'Textual innovation in the Australian historical mini-series', in Australian Television: Programs, Pleasures and Politics, eds. G Turner and J Tulluch, Allen & Unwin, Sydney, pp. 39–51

——1992, Framing culture: Criticism and policy in Australia, Allen & Unwin, Sydney

Davidson, Jim 1979, 'The De-dominionisation of Australia', Meanjin vol 38, no 2, July, pp. 139–53

Davidson, Ken 1968, 'Profit—and loss', in Ten Years of Television, ed M MacCallum, Sun Books, Melbourne

Davies, Brian 1981, Those Fabulous Television Years, Cassell, Melbourne

Davies, Anne and Christina Spurgeon 1992, 'The Broadcasting Services Act: A reconciliation of public interest and market principle of regulation?', Media Information Australia no 66, pp. 85–92

Dell'oso, Anna Maria 1991, 'White man's dreaming', in TV Times, eds D Watson and D Corrigan, Museum of Contemporary Art, Sydney, pp. 18–22

Department of Aboriginal Affairs (DAA) 1984, Out of the silent land: Report of the Task Force on Aboriginal and Islander Broadcasting and Communications, AGPS, Canberra

Docker, John 1991, 'Popular culture versus the state: An argument against Australian content regulations for television', Media Information Australia, no 59, pp. 7–26

Donnelly, Austin 1990, 'No tax—no profit', The Independent Monthly, May, p. 19

DOTAC (Department of Transport and Communication) 1990, Review of Remote Area Television Services, Discussion Paper, AGPS, Canberra

Dunlop, Ian 1983, 'Ethnographic filmmaking in Australia: The first seventy years (1898–1968)', Studies in Visual Communication vol 9, no 1 (Winter), pp. 11–18

Dunnett, Peter 1990, The world television industry: An economic analysis, Routledge, London

Dutchak, Phillip 1992, 'Black screens: Aboriginal television', Cinema Papers no 87, pp. 48–53

Dwyer, Tim 1990, 'Emerging politics for pay-TV', Continuum vol 4, no 1, pp. 156–71

Dyson, Kenneth and Peter Humphreys 1988, 'Regulatory change in Western Europe: From national cultural regulation to international economic statecraft', in Broadcasting and New Media Policies in Western Europe, eds K Dyson, P Humphreys with Ralph Negrine, Routledge, London, pp. 92–160

Dyster, Barrie and David Meredith 1990, Australia in the International Economy, Cambridge University Press, Melbourne

EBR (Entertainment Business Review) 1991, 'Focus on the television industry:

How Seven, Nine and Ten are coping with the industry's transition to maturity', 4 November, pp. 1–3

Ethnic Communities' Council of NSW 1984, 'Submission to the Committeee of Review of the Special Broadcasting Service', Sydney, April

Ethnic Television Review Panel 1979, *Interim Report of Public Consultations on the Establishment of an Ethnic Television Service*, Melbourne

Evans, Huw 1987, 'Prospects for the SBS', *Media Information Australia* no 46, pp. 17–22

——1989, 'Achieving a qualitative diversity of choice in Australian television', *Media Information Australia* no 53, August, pp. 37–42

FACTS (Federation of Australian Commercial Television Stations) 1970, *Facts of Australian content in television programme schedules*, FACTS, Sydney, September

FACTS 1972, *1971/72 11th Annual Report*, FACTS, Sydney

Fields, Howard 1987, 'DC crowded as stations elbow in for news feeds', *Film & Radio Times*, 14 September, pp. 51–2, 84

Foster, Lois and Stockley, David 1988, *Australian multiculturalism: A documentary history and critique*, Multilingual Matters 37, Clevedon, Philadelphia

——1990, 'The construction of a new public culture: Multiculturalism in an Australian productive culture', *ANZJS* vol 26, no 3, pp. 307–28

Garnaut, Ross 1989, *Australian and the Northeast Asia ascendancy: A report to the Prime Minister and Minister for Foreign Affairs and Trade*, Canberra, AGPS

Geller, Henry 1990, 'Broadcast regulation in a changing environment', *TV 2000: Choices and challenges*, ed Elizabeth Moore, ABT, Sydney, pp. 113–24

Gellner, Ernest 1983, *Nations and nationalism*, Oxford, Blackwell

George, Sandy 1989, 'The other news', *Broadcast*, May, pp. 15–16

Given, Jock 1991, 'Television and the GATT, paper presented at the Television Industry Conference, Sydney, 30 September to 1 October

——1993, 'Australian production: the outlook', *Communications Update* 85, February, pp. 23–4

Gomery, Douglas 1984, 'Economic change in the US television industry', *Screen* vol 25, no 2, pp. 62–7

Grenard, Philip 1982, '"Ethnic" television: Massive funds but poor ratings', *Bulletin*, 3 August, pp. 51–2, 54

Hall, Ken 1991, 'Ken G Hall and Australia's fledgling television', in *TV Times*, eds D Watson and D Corrigan, Museum of Contemporary Art, Sydney, pp. 40–3

Hall, Sandra 1976, *Supertoy*, Sun Books, Melbourne.

——1981, *Turning on turning off: Australian television in the eighties*, Cassell, North Ryde

Harding, Richard 1979, *Outside interference: the politics of Australian broadcasting*, Sun Books, Melbourne

Harrison, Kate 1980, *The points system for Australian television content*, Royal Institute of Public Administration, Brisbane

Harrison, Kate and Henry Mayer 1984, 'Broadcasting regulation: Australia's dilemmas', *Studies of Broadcasting* no 20, pp. 58–90

Hartley, John 1992, *Tele-ology: Studies in Television*, Routledge, London

Hartley, John and Tom O'Regan 1992, 'Quoting not science but sideboards: Television in a new way of life', in *Tele-ology: Studies in Television*, pp. 202–17

Hazlehurst, Cameron 1990, 'The dawn of the satellite era in Australia', *Media Information Australia*, no 58, pp. 9–22

Head, Sydney and Christopher Sterling 1990, *Broadcasting in America* 6th Edition, Houghton Mifflin, Boston

Hobsbawm, Eric and Terence Ranger (eds) 1983, *The invention of tradition*, Cambridge University Press, Cambridge

Hodge, Bob and Vijay Mishra 1991, *The dark side of the dream*, Allen & Unwin, Sydney

Hodge, Robert 1990, 'Aboriginal truth and white media: Eric Michaels meets the spirit of Aboriginalism', *Continuum* vol 3, no 2, pp. 201–25

Holton, RJ 1989, 'Small business policy for a multicultural Australia', in *The Challenge of Diversity*, ed J Jupp, AGPS, Canberra, pp. 114–26

Holton, RJ and S Salagaras 1989, 'The participation of non-English-speaking persons in tertiary eduction', in *The Challenge of Diversity*, ed J Jupp, AGPS, Canberra, pp. 99–113

Industries Assistance Commission 1989, *International Trade in Services*, Report no 418, AGPS, Canberra

——1989a, *Assessing Barriers to International Trade in Services*, Inquiry into International Trade in Services, Discussion Paper no 2, AGPS, Canberra

——1989b, *International Initiatives to Liberalise Trade in Services*, Inquiry into International Trade in Services, Discussion Paper no 3, AGPS, Canberra

International Business 1990, 'The Stateless Corporation', *International Business*, 14 May 1990, p. 59

Jacka, Elizabeth 1988, 'Australian cinema: An anachronism in the '80s', in *The imaginary industry: Australian film in the late '80s*, eds Susan Dermody and Elizabeth Jacka, AFTRS, Sydney, pp. 117–30

——1991, *Global television—Internationalisation and Australasian audio-visual policy*, Communications Law Centre, Occasional Paper 5, Sydney

Jakubowicz, Andrew 1989, 'Speaking in tongues: Multicultural media and the constitution of the socially homogeneous Australian', in *Australian communications and the public sphere*, ed Helen Wilson, Macmillan, South Melbourne, pp. 105–27

Jayasuriya, Laksiri 1983, 'The facts, policies and rhetoric of multiculturalism', *Australian Society*, 1 July, pp. 23–7

——1988, 'Language and culture in Australian public policy: Some critical considerations', in *Occasional Papers, New Series* no 4, Department of Social Work and Social Administration, University of Western Australia, Perth, April

Johns, Brian 1991, 'SBS: Coping with a strange idea', *Multicultural Australia: The challenges of change*, eds D Goodman, D O'Hearn, C Wallace-Crabbe, Scribe, Newham (Vic.), pp. 13–20

BIBLIOGRAPHY

Jones, Ross 1991, *Cut! Protection of Australia's film and television industries*, Centre for Independent Studies, Sydney

Jupp, James 1989, 'The ethnic composition of Australian elites', in *The challenge of diversity: Policy options for a multicultural Australia*, ed J Jupp, AGPS, Canberra, pp. 33-43

Kapferer, Bruce 1988, *Legends of people, myths of state*, Washington, Smithsonian Institution Press

Kaufman, Tina 1989, 'SBS and independent filmmakers', *Filmnews*, September, pp. 2, 10

Kolar-Panov, Dona and Toby Miller 1991, 'Radio and civil war in Yugoslavia', *Media Information Australia* no 62, pp. 74-7

Lan Tran 1992, 'Vietnamese films and ethnic identity', Student Essay, Communication Studies, Murdoch University

Lange, Andre and Jean-Luc Renaud 1989, *The future of the European audio-visual industry*, European Institute for the Media, Manchester

Langton, Marcia 1993, *'Well I heard it on the radio and I saw it on the television...'* AFC, North Sydney

Lattas, Andrew 1990 'Aborigines and contemporary Australian nationalism: Primordiality and the cultural politics of otherness', in *Writing Australian culture*, ed Julie Marcus, *Social Analysis* no 27, 1990, pp. 50-69

Laurie, Victoria 1993, *'Exile and the Kingdom'*, *In the Picture*, Autumn, pp. 16-17

Lawson, Sylvia 1983, *The Archibald paradox: A strange case of authorship*, Allen Lane, Ringwood

Leigh, Michael 1988, 'Curiouser and curiouser', in *Back of beyond: Discovering Australian film and television*, ed Scott Murray, Australian Film Commission, Sydney, pp. 78-89

Lenti, Paul 1989, 'Bert Cohen', *Variety*, 19-25 April, pp. 48-9

Leong, Kathryn 1983, 'The emergence of multicultural TV in Australia', *Australian Journal of Communication* no 4, pp. 7-12

Lotman, Yuri M 1990, *Universe of the mind: A semiotic theory of culture*, trans Ann Shukman, Indiana University Press, Bloomington and Indianapolis

Mackinolty, Chips and Michael Duffy 1987, 'Guess who's coming to dinner in Arnhem Land?', Research and Communications Branch Bureau of the Northern Land Council, presented at National Film Documentary conference Adelaide, 17-18 October

Maher, Denis 1990, 'Big mob radio', *Filmnews*, March, p. 7

Mayrhofer, Debra 1992, 'Media briefs', *Media Information Australia* no 63, pp. 119-44

McAllister, Ian and Rhonda Moore 1991, 'The development of ethnic prejudice: An analysis of Australian immigrants', *Ethnic and Racial Studies* vol 14, no 2, pp. 127-51

McClelland, James 1974, 'The role of federal government in Australia's media', Paper presented to Seminar, 'The Media and Society', Adelaide, 22 February

McGuinness, Padraic 1990, *The media in crisis in Australia*, Schwartz and Wilkinson, Melbourne

McKay, Ian K. 1959, *Macquarie: The story of a network*, privately published

Meadows, Michael and Klaus Rielander 1991, 'Aboriginal and Torres Strait Islander broadcasting: A selected bibliography', *Media Information Australia* no 61, pp. 86-93

Meadows, Michael 1992, *A watering can in the desert: Issues in indigenous broadcasting policy in Australia*, Institute for Cultural Policy Studies, Griffith University

Michaels, Eric 1985, 'Constraints on knowledge in an economy of oral information', *Current Anthropology* vol 26, no 4, pp. 505-10

——1986a, 'Information management and disclosure: Warrumungu, the ruined ritual'. Unpubliched ms, July

——1986b, *The Aboriginal invention of television in central Australia, 1982-1985*, Australian Institute of Aboriginal Studies, Institute Report, Canberra

——1987a, 'Aboriginal content: Who's got it, who needs it?', *Art & Text* nos 23-24 1987, pp. 58-79

——1987b, *For a cultural future: Frances Jupurrurla makes TV at Yuendumu*, Artspace, Art and Criticism Monograph Series vol 3, Sydney

——1987c 'Hundreds shot in Aboriginal community: ABC makes TV documentary at Yuendumu', *Media Information Australia* no 45, pp. 7-17

——1990a, *Unbecoming: An Aids diary*, EM Press, Sydney

——1990b, 'A model of teleported texts', *Continuum* vol 3, no 2, pp. 8-31

Mickler, Steve 1991, 'The battle for Goonininup', *Arena* no 96, pp. 69-88

——1992a, *Gambling on the first race: racism and talk-back Radio*, Louis St John Johnson Memorial Trust, Perth

——1992b, 'Visions of disorder', *Cultural Studies* vol 6, no 3, pp. 322-36

Miller, JDB 1988, 'Australia in the world', in *Australian Society*, ed Keith Hancock Melbourne, Cambridge University Press, 228-43

Molnar, Helen 1990, 'The broadcasting for remote areas community scheme: Small vs big media', *Media Information Australia* no 58, pp. 147-54

Moran, Albert 1982, 'Localism and Australian Television', in *Nellie Melba, Ginger Meggs and friends: Essays in Australian cultural history*, eds S Dermody, J Docker and D Modjeska, Malmsbury, Victoria, Kibble Books, 89-102

——1985, *Images and Industry: Television Drama Production in Australia*, Currency Press, Sydney

——1987, 'King of the Coral Sea: An interview with Lee Robinson', *Continuum* vol 1, no 1, 100-10

——1989, 'Crime, romance, history: Television drama', in *The Australian Screen*, eds A Moran and T O'Regan, Penguin, Ringwood, pp. 236-55

Morris, Meaghan, 1988, 'Tooth and claw: Tales of survival and *Crocodile Dundee*', in *The Pirate's fiancee: Feminism, reading and postmodernism*, Verso, London, pp. 241-69

——1992, *Ecstasy and economics: American essays for John Forbes*, EM Press, Sydney

Morton, John 1990, 'Rednecks, 'roos and racism: Kangaroo shooting and the Australian way', in *Writing Australian Culture*, ed Julie Marcus, *Social Analysis*, Adelaide, pp. 30–49

Muecke, Stephen 1992, *Textual spaces: Aboriginality and cultural studies*, University of New South Wales Press, Kensington, Sydney

Norton, Suzanne Frentz 1985, 'Tea time on the "telly": British and Australian soap opera', *Journal of Popular Culture* vol 19, no 3, pp. 3–20

O'Connor, Cass 1989, 'Whose fault is it?', *B & T*, 29 September 1989, pp. 28, 30–1

Office of Evaluation and Audit 1992, *Evaluation of Broadcasting and Communications Sub-Program*, ATSIC, Canberra

Oram, James 1988, *Neighbours: Behind the scenes*, Angus and Robertson, North Ryde

O'Regan, Tom and Ulla Hiltula 1985, 'Perth commercial television since 1965', in *The Moving Image: the History of Film and Television in Western Australia*, eds T O'Regan and B Shoesmith, History and Film Association of Australia, WA, Perth, pp. 75–82

Patterson, Rosalind 1986, 'EA ethnic radio: Dilemmas of direction', *Media Information Australia* no 41, pp. 50–6

——1992, 'SBS-TV: Forerunner of the future', *Media Information Australia* no 66, pp. 85–92

Perkins, Charles N 1990, 'Welfare and Aboriginal people in Australia: Time for a new direction', *Frank Archibald memorial lecture series*, no 5, University of New England, Armidale

Price, Charles 1968, 'Migrants in Australian society', in *Anatomy of Australia*, Melbourne, Sun Books, pp. 95–112

Price, Charles A 1989, 'Ethnic groups in Australia', in *The Challenge of Diversity*, ed J Jupp, AGPS, Canberra, pp. 6–19

Pringle, John Douglas 1978, *Australian Accent*, Rigby, Adelaide

Reel, A Frank 1979, *The Networks: How they stole the show*, Charles Scribner's Sons, New York

Reid, Mary Anne 1991, 'SBS-TV: How Australia's smallest network plans to bring home the advertising dollar', *Entertainment Business Review*, 22 August, pp. 1–7

Reynolds, Henry 1987, *The Law of the Land*, Penguin, Ringwood

Riddell, Elizabeth 1968, 'Entertainment', in *Ten Years of Television*, ed Mungo MacCallum, Sun Books, Melbourne, pp. 27–43

Roddick, Nick 1985, 'Strewth! A beginner's guide to Australian TV', *Sight and Sound*, Winter, pp. 250–4.

Routt, William 1982, *Prolegemena to a theory of popular art*, PhD diss., Committee on Social Thought, University of Chicago

——1991 'New Lealand culture?', *Continuum* vol 4, no 2, pp. 218–24

Routt, William and Ina Bertrand 1989, 'The Big Bad Combine: Some aspects of national aspirations and international constraints in the Australian cinema, 1896-1929', in *The Australian Screen*, eds A Moran and T O'Regan, Penguin, Ringwood, pp. 3–27

Rowse, Tim 1985, *Arguing the Arts*, Ringwood, Penguin

Ryan, Judith 1989, *Mythscapes: Aboriginal art of the desert*, National Gallery of Victoria, Melbourne
Special Broadcasting Service (SBS) 1981, Special Broadcasting Service, *Annual Report 1980/81*, AGPS, Canberra
——1986, *Annual Report 1985/86*, AGPS, Canberra
——1987, *Annual Report 1986/87*, AGPS, Canberra
——1988, *Annual Report 1987/88*, AGPS, Canberra
——1989, *Annual Report 1988/89*, AGPS, Canberra
——1991, *Annual Report 1990/91*, AGPS, Canberra
——1992a, *Annual Report 1991/92*, AGPS, Canberra
——1992b, *New in '92*, SBS, Sydney
Schaffer, Kay 1989, *Women and the Bush: Forces of desire in the Australian cultural tradition*, Cambridge University Press, Sydney
Schlesinger, Philip 1991, 'Media, the political order and national identity', *Media, Culture and Society* vol 13, no 3, pp. 297–308
Schultz, Julianne 1989, 'Failing the public', in *Australian Communications and the Public Sphere*, ed Helen Wilson, Macmillan, Melbourne, pp. 68–84
Schwarz, Bill 1992, 'England in Europe: Reflections on national identity and cultural theory', *Cultural Studies* vol 6, no 2, pp. 198–206.
Semmler, Clement 1985, 'The SBS network: Innovative TV moves into a new era', *Bulletin*, 2 July, pp. 74–5
Seneviratne, Kalinga 1992, 'Multicultural television: Going beyond the rhetoric', *Media Information Australia* no 66, pp. 53–8
Sepstrup, Preben 1990, *Transnationalization of television in Western Europe*, John Libbey, London
Shaw, Sylvie 1992, 'The Asian screen test', *Cinema Papers* no 87, pp. 34–40
Shoebridge, Neil 1990, 'Ten: Now for the hard part', *Business Review Weekly*, 22 June, p. 23
Smith, Anthony D 1986, *The Ethnic Origins of Nations*, Oxford, Basil Blackwell
——1990, 'Towards a global culture?', *Theory, Culture & Society* vol 7, pp. 171–91
——1991, *National Identity*, Penguin, London
Smolowe, Jill with Carl Robinson 1982, 'Does anyone speak Lapp?', *Newsweek*, 19 July, p. 18
Souter, Gavin 1981, *A Company of Heralds*, Melbourne University Press, Melbourne
Spigel, Lynn 1990, 'Television in the family circle: The popular reception of a new medium', in *Logics of Television*, ed Patricia Mellancamp, Indiana University Press, Bloomington, pp. 73–97
Stern, Lesley 1982, 'The Australian cereal: Home grown television', in *Nellie Melba, Ginger Meggs and friends: Essays in Australian cultural history*, eds S Dermody, J Docker and D Modjeska, Kibble Books, Malmsbury, pp. 103–23
Summers, Anne 1975, *Damned whores and God's police: The colonisation of women in Australia*, Penguin, Ringwood

Summers, Robert E & R Harrison 1966, *Broadcasting and the public*, Wadsworth, Belmont

Sykes, Roberta B 1989, *Black majority*, Hudson Publishing, Hawthorn

Taft, Ronald 1962, 'The myth and migrants', in *Australian Civilization*, ed Peter Coleman, FW Cheshire, Melbourne, pp. 191-206

Tariff Board 1973, *Tariff Board report: Motion picture films and television programs*, AGPS, Canberra

Television Business International 1990, *TBI World Guide 1990*, Television Business International and ACT III Special Publishing, New York and London

Thomas, Tony 1990 'Regional television's woes', *Business Review Weekly*, 2 February, pp. 54-9

Thompson, Kristin 1985, *Exporting Entertainment*, British Film Institute, London

Treffry, Sally 1991, 'Beyond', *TV World*, October, p. 20

Tulich, Katherine 1986, 'Keeping SBS special', *TV World*, December, pp. 27-8

Tulloch, John and Graeme Turner (eds) 1989, *Australian television: Programs, pleasures and politics*, Allen & Unwin, Sydney

Turnbull, Susan (1992) 'The media and moral identity: Accounting for media practices in the lives of young women', PhD, La Trobe University

Turner, Graeme 1989, 'Transgressive TV: From *In Melbourne Tonight* to *Perfect Match*', in *Australian television: Programs, pleasure, politics*, eds J Tulloch and G Turner, Allen & Unwin, Sydney, pp. 25-37

Turner, Neil 1990, 'Pitchat and beyond', *Artlink* vol 10, nos 1 & 2, pp. 43-5

University of Technology, Sydney (UTS) 1990, *Racism, cultural pluralism and the media*, Office of Multicultural Affairs, November, Canberra

van der Weel, Adriaan 1990, 'Subtitling and the SBS audience', *Media Information Australia* no 56, pp. 22-6

Variety 1991, 'Global programming prices', *Variety*, 15 April 1991, M-107

Venner, Mary 1988, 'Broadcasting for Remote Aboriginal Communities Scheme', *Media Information Australia* no 47, pp. 37-43

Vincent Report 1964, 'The Vincent Report', *Overland* no 29, April, pp. 27-38. Its official title was: *Report from the Select Committee on the Encouragement of Australian Production for Television*, AGPS, Canberra, October

Walker, RR 1967, *Communications*, Landsdowne Press, Melbourne

Ward, Russell 1978, *The Australian legend*, Oxford University Press, Melbourne

White, Naomi Rush and Peter B White 1983, *Immigrants and the media*, Longman Cheshire, Melbourne

White, Patrick 1989, *Patrick White speaks*, Primavera, Sydney

Willmot, Eric 1986, 'Future pathways: Equity or isolation', *Frank Archibald memorial lecture series*, no 1, University of New England, Armidale

——1987, *Australia: The last experiment, 1986 Boyer Lectures*, ABC, Sydney

Wright, L 1989, 'TV incurs its first loss', *Sydney Morning Herald*, 22 May
Young, Christabel 1988, 'Ethnic media and ethnic groups', *Media Information Australia* no 40, pp. 49–55
Yuendumu Community Education Centre 1990a, *Communications in the Tanami: A report on a satellite-linked workshop held between Yuendumu, Lajamanu and Sydney*, October 24–26, Yuendumu Community Education Centre, Yuendumu
——1990b, *Communications in the Tanami: A proposal for the establishment of the Tanami Network*, December, Yuendumu Community Education Centre, Yuendumu

Index

Aboriginal affairs, government funding to 187
Aboriginal and Torres Strait Islander Commission (ATSIC) 169, 177, 179, 186
Aboriginal Australians 21, 26, 82, 94, 95, 105, 112, 113, 125; and discrimination 109; and non-Aborigines 173-5, 177-8, 179, 184, 187-9; participation/self-determination 175-80, 186, 191-2; urban 180, 183-4
Aboriginal cultures 92, 94, 175-6, 180-4; television representation of 178-9
Aboriginal issues xxiv-xxv, 33, 158-9, 161, 169-70, 174, 177, 178-9
Aboriginal television xix, xxiv, 2, 3, Chapter 9; Aboriginal initiatives/control 170-5, 178-80, 184-7; funding 186, 190; and non-Aborigines 173-5, 177-8, 179, 187-9; policy/strategies 177-80; political priorities 178-9; video networks 172, 176-7
Aboriginal-controlled production companies 173
accents on SBS-TV, ethnic 139, 150

Acropolis Now 113, 115
advertisers, multinational/foreign 55, 57-8
advertising: deregulation 58, 75; ethnic presence in 110; national 32, 33, 46; quotas 71; regulations 38, 41, 58, 71, 75; revenues 42, 46, 54, 57, 66; SBS-TV and 135; stereotypes in 80
affirmative action 105, 109
All in the Family 18
Allen, Dave 21
Alvin 104
Always Afternoon 161
America/Americans, Australian perception of 16; *see also* US
Americanisation 8
Angel at My Table 13
Anglophone culture 88-9, 105, 127, 134
ANZAC Day 95
ANZACS 80
Arena, Franca 135, 164
Armstrong, Mark 37
Ashbolt, Allan 153
Asia and Australian identity 95-6, 118-19
Asia and Australian national culture 95-6, 118
Asia Report 119, 122, 166

209

Asian–Australian integration 117, 118–19
Asian–Australian issues 166–7
Asian culture 118
Asian ethnicities and Australian-produced drama 119
Asian immigration 117–18
Asian migrants, English-speaking 127
Asian orientation and SBS-TV 163, 166–7
AsiaSat 167
assimilation policy 128
audience statistics 146, 148–9, 154–5, 162
audiences, Aboriginal 169, 177, 195n
audiences, SBS-TV 137, 138, 142–50, 154–5; and change to UHF frequency 162–3
Aunty Jack 113
AUSSAT 6, 25–6, 28–9, 39, 42, 138; *see also* satellite
Australian Broadcasting Authority (ABA) 36–7, 38
Australian Broadcasting Corporation (ABC) xix, xxi, xxiii, 2, 7, 9, 10, 50–1; Aboriginal programming 172–5; Aborigines, employment of 178; AUSSAT 6, 26; competition with commercial TV 7; and domestic satellite 27–8; and ethnic minorities 109; and imported programs 63–5, 76; and multiculturalism 108, 125, 131; programming 104, *see also* programming; and SBS-TV 136
Australian Broadcasting Tribunal (ABT) 36, 37, 38, 49, 50
Australian Film Commission (AFC) 51, 57, 174, 178, 190
Australian film industry, *see* film
Australian Film, Television and Radio School (AFTRS) 161, 173
Australian Football League 6, 30
Australian Mosaic 160, 161
Australian national culture xxiv, Chapter 5; and Anglophone culture 87–91, 120; and globalisation 98–105; and international culture 87–91; projects 92
Australian national identity 8, 75, 78, 93–7, 103, 116; and Asia 95–6, 118–19; and the bush 94; in geopolitical terms 116–20
Australian Shorts 160
Australian-made programs, *see* locally-produced

Backlash 170
Bali Hash 159
Bangkok Hilton 8
banks, and network ownership 43, 45, 49–50
BAPH (Brisbane, Adelaide, Perth, Hobart) stations 6, 26–7, 30, 34; and domestic satellite 28, 29
Barrett, Peter 151
Batty, Philip xxiv, 172
Beazley, Kim 49, 50, 55
Bellbird 8, 80, 104, 125
Beyond 2000 75
The Big Country 125
Bird on the Wire 13
Bjelke-Petersen, Joh 33
Black Out 169, 176, 177
Blainey, Geoffrey 95, 96
block buying of imported programs 67
Bodyline 8, 80
Bond, Alan 40, 43, 44, 45, 46
Bond Media group 40, 44, 48–9, 50
Bond University 45
The Bookshow 141
Bostock, Lester 171, 174, 179
Brides of Christ 51
Bridges, James 14, 15
Britain/British, Australian perception of 16
British Broadcasting Commission (BBC) 7, 65; news services 167; and non-English language programs 122
British Channel 4, *see* Channel 4, UK

INDEX

British television xx, xxi, 7, 10; compared with Australian television 10, 11, 14; regulations 7; see also British Broadcasting Commission
British television programming 1, 2, 17; and Anglophone culture 88–90; imports of 5, 63, 65, 68
Broadcasting in Remote Aboriginal Communities Scheme (BRACS) 169, 172, 175, 186; tape exchange system 176
Broadcasting Services Act 48, 75
Broadcasting Services Act (1992) 37, 38
Brown, Allan 63
Bureau of Transport and Communications Economics 57
Burke's Backyard 30

CAAMA Productions 173–4; see also Central Australian Aboriginal Media Association
cable television 6, 9, 24, 55; news services 167
CanWest 41
Canada, and US culture 105
Canadian public broadcasters 167
Canadian television xx, 1, 9, 10, 11, 13, 65, 66, 67, 68; and ethnic pay TV 136
capitalism, changes in 31–3
Carey, James 22–3, 39
Castles, Stephen 96
Caughie, John 86
Central Australian Aboriginal Media Association (CAAMA) 171, 172, 173, 176, 179, 186
Certain Women 8, 104
Chances 119
Chang, Victor 158
Changing Australia 159
Channel 4 (UK) 10, 65, 122, 123, 167
Chauvel, Charles 71
Children of the Dragon 119
Chinese-language programming 152
Chisholm, Sam 49
Cinema Classics 141

The Civil War 148, 159
CNN International news service 167
coaxial links 3, 4
Collins, Bob 55
comedy 18; ethnicity 113
Comedy Company 113
commercial power, shifts in 35–6; see also capitalism
commercial television xxi, 1, 6–8, 10, 24–5; and the ABC 8; British 7; and the entrepreneurs Chapter 2; and multiculturalism 108, 109; networking 29; regulations 3
commercial television networks 4, 47–8; cost-cutting 50–1, 56–7; costs 47–8; ownership, see ownership; and US programming 36, 47–8; see also by name of network
communications, mass 45–6
communications organisations, multinational 100
communications policy Chapter 2
companies, entrepreneurial Chapter 3; international integration 48–9; see also by name of company
competition: for local productions 73–4; in media ownership 35, see also ownership; for US programming 36, 72, 73–4
concentration, media 9
concepts, international trade in 18
Connections 158
Consider Your Verdict 113
Consolidated Press 35
content, Australian xxiii, 8, 55, 57, 61, 62–3, 70, 71, 72–7; rules 9–10; see also locally-produced programming
content regulations 55, 57, 62–3, 70, 71, 74, 75, 76, 77–8, 80, 81, 85, 102, 104
co-production, international 74–5
Cosser, Steve 40
cost: of current affairs programs 76; of imported programs 10, 12, 47–8, 60–1, 63, 64, 65–6,

211

69, 73, 74, 159; programming 47–8; of running networks 47–8; of running SBS-TV 159–63
cost-cutting, commercial network 50–1, 56–7
cost/value of television stations/networks 43–4, 50
Countdown 104
A Country Practice 8, 21, 72, 114
Cowra Breakout 80, 119, 124
Crawford, Hector 70, 78, 104
Crawford Productions 17, 41
criticism of Australian television 8–10, 13–14, 20–1, 104, 113, 155–6
Croatian-background Australians 165, 166
cross-media ownership, *see* ownership
cross-subsidisation in programming 59, 60–1, 62, 70, 72
cultural area identities, shared 104
cultural difference/similarity 109, 111, 127; *see also* ethnic identity
cultural diversity and SBS-TV 140–1; *see also* multiculturalism
cultural levels xxii–xxiii, 83–5
culture, Australian, *see* Australian national culture
culture, highbrow, *see* highbrow
A Current Affair xxii, 6, 30, 34
current affairs programs 6, 12, 18, 29, 30, 34, 59–60, 76; SBS-TV 156–9, 164
The Cutting Edge 157

Daily Mail General Trust 48
Darling, John 159
Dateline 60, 119, 164, 166, 167
Davies, Brian 69
Degrassi High 13
delivery systems, program, *see* program delivery
Dell'oso, Anna Maria 121, 146
demography, changing ethnic 114, 116
Department of Aboriginal Affairs 161

Department of Transport and Communications (DOTAC) 37
deregulation, financial sector 42
deregulation of television markets 100, 101, 102
derivative, Australian television as 13–17
Desert People 182
difference, cultural/ethnic, *see* cultural difference
disadvantaged groups 82, 127, 133, 185–6
discrimination 107, 109; issues 151; racial 127
The Dismissal 8, 80
distribution structures 4, 23
documentaries, SBS-TV 157, 161
documentary makers, Australian 71
Double Trouble 158
drama, Australian-produced 71, 72–3, 74, 75, 76–8; Asian ethnicities in 119; costs of 77; and ethnic cultures 113–15, 124; ethnic presence in 109–11; for international audiences 90; multicultural/multilingual 124, 131; and national culture/identity 81, 86; SBS-TV 161; *see also* serials/series
drama producers, Australian 63
drama programming: expenditure on 76; imported 70, 74–5, 76, 77, 123; quotas 71; regulations 75–8
The Dunera Boys 124
Dunlop, Ian 182
Dutch television 11, 12
Dyer, Bob 21
Dyson, Kenneth 102

E Street 80, 82
Eastenders 82
eastern European countries, disintegration of 164–5
Eat Carpet 141, 160
education level of ethnic minorities 112
Egyptian programming 151, 152
8-KIN network 171

INDEX

Embassy 104, 119
Empress Wu 82
English at Work 125
English language, migrant communities and 127–8
English language programming: imported xxii, *see also* imported programs; SBS-TV 139, 159, 163, 167
English language television 11, 12, 13; and national culture 87–90
Entertainment Business Review 56–7
entrepreneurs, media xxiii, Chapter 3
equal opportunity 105, 106, 109
equalisation policy, television 6–7, 27, 42, 51, 52, 74, 138
Ernabella television 172, 175, 190
ethnic communities xxii, 2, 9; disadvantaged 127, 133; and eastern European nationalism 164–6; and locally-produced programs 20, 109–16; political divisions in 132–3, 165, 166; and SBS-TV 129–30, 132–5, *see also* SBS-TV; sovereignty of 106, 108; and the television industry 109–16; *see also* migrants
Ethnic Communities Council of NSW 147
ethnic diversity and SBS-TV 139–41; *see also* cultural difference 139–41
ethnic identity 107, 112, 115–16, 140–1; defined 126–30; *see also* ethnicity
ethnic intermarriage 94, 110, 111, 112, 114, 126
ethnic television audiences 136
ethnicity 105, 107, 117; normalising 111; and SBS-TV 139–42; *see also* ethnic identity
Eureka Stockade 80
European migrant cultures 127–8
EVtelevision 171
Exile and the Kingdom 172
expenditure on television services, *see* funding

exported programs 11, 13, 68, 75, 77–8, 90, 162

Face the Press 164
Fairfax group 35, 51, 53
Federation of Australian Commercial Television Stations (FACTS) 72, 74
fibre optic cabling 28
Fields of Fire 115, 124
film classics on SBS-TV 155
Film Finance Corporation (FFC) 51, 57, 163, 178, 190
film industry, Australian 71, 75; and SBS-TV 131, 136–7, 160–1
film industry, international 101
filmmakers/filmmaking, Aboriginal 170, 171, 172, 173
financial state of television industry Chapter 3, 159–63
The First Australians 169, 176
First in Line 158, 161, 169
flag debate 92, 93
Flying Doctors 8, 82
Foley, Gary 187
food programming 159–60
Four Corners 60, 125
Fran 30
Fraser government and SBS-TV 131, 132
French Television 9, 10, 12
funding/subsidies 7, 13, 51, 73; to Aboriginal affairs 187; Aboriginal television 186, 190; production 73, 78, 80, 81; SBS-TV 135, 161, 163

Gardening Australia 30
Geller, Henry 7
geography, cultural xxi–xxii
geopolitical nation 116–20
Girl from Steel City 122, 161
Given, Jock 61–2, 195n
globalisation and national culture 98–105
Goddard, Trisha 21
Gomery, Douglas 42
Gorton, John 104

213

government funding/subsidies, *see* funding
GP 8, 21, 104, 119
Grant, Stan 21, 178
Greek Variety 125
Greek-background Australians 112, 113, 115, 125, 165
Greek-language programming 152
Grundy organisation 41, 194n
GTK 104
Gunew, Sneja 193n
Gyngell, Bruce 143

Hall, Ken 70
Hall, Sandra xxv
Hamilton, Ian 124
Hanlon, Tommy 21
Hartley, John 16, 143, 144, 168
Hawke, Bob 49
Hawke Labor government 33
Herald and Weekly Times 35, 51, 53
highbrow/elite: audiences 147; culture 123, 141, 155; programs 150
Hinch 6, 30, 34
Hines, Marcia 21
Hobart 24, 25
Hodge, Bob 95
Holiday 30
Hollywood imports 69, 70, 73
Holmes, Cecil 182
Home and Away 13, 41
Home Sweet Home 113
Homicide 9, 17, 63, 80, 104, 113
homosexual themes 158
Humphreys, Peter 102

I the Aboriginal 182
imitation or invention xx, xxi, Chapter 1; *see also* criticism
immigration 92, 105, 128; Asian 117–18; *see also* migrants; migration
Imparja Television 169, 171, 173, 176
import diversification, lack of 67–8
imported programming xxi, xxii, xxiii, 1, 4–5, 11, 12, 16; and Australian national culture 81; cost of 10, 12, 47–8, 60–1, 63, 64, 65–6, 69, 72, 73, 74, 159; and local programming Chapter 4; SBS-TV selection of 152–4; and sense of difference 86–7; US block booking of 67; *see also* non-English language programs
income levels of ethnic minorities 112
Income Tax Assessment Act 77
independence: informational 6; station 4, 6
Industries Assistance Commission 57
Industry Commission 57
information revolution 45–6
infotainment: ABC programming 75; costs 76; and national culture 86; and SBS-TV 164
integration policy 128
intermarriage, ethnic 94, 110, 111, 112, 114, 126
international events 80–1, 164–6
international programming xxii, xxiv, 74–5; and global culture 86; *see also* globalisation
international television system 36
internationalisation 102, 105, 117; of program sources 123; of television, *see* globalisation
invention or imitation xx, xxi, Chapter 1; *see also* criticism
investment, foreign 103
Islam in programming 151
Italian-background Australians 112, 113, 115, 140, 165

Jacka, Elizabeth xxi
Jackaroo 30
Japanese television 9
Johns, Brian 144, 156, 164
Jupurrurla, Francis 171, 183

Kalantzis, Mary 115, 116
Kamahl 21
Keating, Paul 54, 92
Kelly, Frances 189
Kerin, John 55

INDEX

Kingswood Country 18, 113
Kolar-Panov, Dona xxiv, 194n, 195n
Kooris, *see* Aboriginal Australians
Kostakidis, Mary 165

Land Rights Acts 187
Lane, Don 21
language strategy, SBS-TV 139–40, 155–6
language teaching, SBS-TV 137
languages on SBS-TV 151; *see also* Anglophone; multilingual; NESB 151
The Last Bastion 80
Lateline 6
Lattas, Andrew 94
Lawson, Henry 128
The Leaving of Liverpool 51
Let's Go Greek 125
licence ownership, *see* ownership
Limb, Bobby 104
Lloyd-James, Andy 144, 148
local content, *see* content; locally-produced programming
local/imported programming Chapter 4; *see also* imported programs
localism and national integration 30
locally-produced programming xxiii, 4–5, 8–9, 12, 18–19, 30, 69; and imported programs Chapter 4; and minority issues 108–9; and SBS-TV 123–4, 160, 163–4, 166; *see also* drama
Lotman, Yuri 193n
Lowy, Frank 40, 44, 45
Lusic, Vladimir 164, 165, 166

McAllister, Ian 111
McLelland, Doug 104
Macquarie network 3
Maltese-language programming 152
marketing strategy 32
marriage, inter-ethnic 94, 110, 111, 112, 114, 126
The Max Gillies Show 18

media groups, international 48–9; *see also by name*; network mergers 31
Metropolitan Cats 141
Michaels, Eric 15–16, 170–1, 172, 183, 189–90
microwave links 3, 4, 24, 25
The Midday Show 6, 30
migrants: and Australian television 19–21, *see also* SBS-TV; and discrimination 109; European 127, *see also by country of origin*; perception of Australia 19; *see also* immigration; ethnic communities; minorities; NESB communities
migration, global 101
Milbindi 169, 176
Miller, J.D.B. 88
Miller, Kennedy 8
mini-series 1; Australian 73; *see also* drama; serials/series
minorities xxii, xxiii, 3, 105; programming for 82, 124–6, 141–2, 148, 150; *see also* SBS-TV; ethnic communities
Mishra, Vijay 95
Mistaken Identity 116
Moffat, Tracey 171, 189
monopoly, media ownership 35
Moore, Rhonda 111
Mother and Son 7, 18, 113, 114
The Movie Show 155, 164
Moyle, John 159
Mudrooroo 191
Muecke, Stephen 181
Multicultural Affairs, Office for 161
multicultural media policy 106
multicultural television 2, 82; *see also* SBS-TV; multiculturalism; multilingual programming
multiculturalism xx, xxiv, xxv, 80, 92, 93–4, 98, 105–16, 128–30; and nation building 116–20; projects 106–7; and SBS-TV 132–5, 136, 138–42, 164, *see also* SBS-TV; in television 108–10, 121–6

215

multilingual programming xxii, 65, 82, 121-2, 123-4, 139, 150-6
multinational communications organisations 100
Murdoch, Rupert 6, 24, 44, 48, 51, 53, 194n
Murphy, Paul 164
Musca, Camelo 160

Namatjira, Albert 159
nation building 116-20
National Aboriginal Video Magazine 169, 176
National Basketball League 30
national culture, *see* Australian national culture
National Forum for Equal Access to Public Broadcasting 155
national identity, *see* Australian national identity
National Indigenous Media Association of Australia (NIMAA) 190-1
national integration: of advertising 46; of programming 27-31, 46-7
national political culture 81-2
nationalising of business and media 31-3
nationalist movements, eastern European 164-6
Nature of Australia 75
Neighbours xxi, 13, 41, 51, 72, 80, 82
NESB (non-English-speaking background) 89, 126; category 110-12; disadvantages 112; European communities/migrants 127-8; identity 110; intermarriage, *see* intermarriage; issues in SBS current affairs service 156; and the local television industry 110-16, *see also* SBS-TV; programming; ethnic communities
networking 4, 6, 23-4, 29-31, 32, 34, 39, 42; business 32-3; US 3-4, 6

networks, Australian 5, 6, 42-3; sale of 40, *see also* ownership; *see also by name of network*
networks, US 3-4, 5, 6
New Zealand TV 13, 49
News Corporation 48
news services 12, 18, 34, 59-60; costs 76; regional 6; SBS-TV 140, 156-9, 167
newsreaders/presenters and eastern European nationalism 164-6
Nganampa Anwernerkenhe 169, 176
Nine Network xxii, 4, 8, 24, 29, 36, 40, 43, 45, 48, 49, 56-7, 70
non-English-language programs, availability/selection of 152-4, *see also* imported programming
non-English-speaking background, *see* NESB
Norman Gunstan Show 18
Northern Star Holdings 48
Number 96 8, 72

Ohisson, Terry 41
One Australia? 115, 116
Optus group 29, 55
Oram, James xxi
overseas investors 48-9
ownership, cross-media 3, 22, 35, 38, 43, 51
ownership, media 3, 5, 7, 22, 24, 27, 29, 35-6, 42-9, 62, 73, 74; foreign 48, 49, 50, 81; regulations 75; US television 5

Packer, Frank 70
Packer, Kerry 24, 35, 40, 44, 50, 51, 53, 55, 130
The Paul Hogan Show 18
Pay TV 7, 13, 29, 37, 38, 41, 46, 55, 75
Perfect Match xxi
Perth Extra 32
Perth stations 25, 27, 30, 34, 35, 52, 69
pluralism in multicultural policy 107, 109
Police Rescue 51, 114

INDEX

policy, broadcast Chapter 2, 42; and content legislation, *see* content; development 36-9; *see also* ownership
political change in ethnic homelands 164-6
political divisions and SBS-TV 132-3
political issues in television programming 151-2, 153, 157-8
political priorities, Aboriginal 178-9
political tensions, Aboriginal 184-7
politics, nationalising 33-5
politics and SBS-TV 130-8
Price, Charles A. 88
prices for stations; *see* cost/value
production industry 40-1; *see also* locally-produced programming
production subsidies 73, 78, 80, 81
productions, co- 41
program delivery, pre-1986 24-5; costs 25
program delivery systems 78-9, 138
program scheduling xxiii, 15-16; SBS-TV 132-3; *see also* programming
programming: Aboriginal Chapter 9; by Aborigines 170-5, 178, 186; Australia-wide 30-1, 34; availability/selection of non-English 152-4; costs 47-8, 72, 194n; ethno-specific 151-2; international xxii, xxiv, 74-5, 86; regionally-produced 160; SBS-TV 144-56; simultaneous 27, 32, 46-7, 74
programs, Australian-made, *see* locally-produced
programs, imported, *see* imported programming
Public Broadcasting System, US 167
public service broadcasting/ television xxi, 1, 8, 10, 11

Qintex group 44, 48
quality television 8-9

quiz shows 17
quotas: advertising 71; Australian content 71; drama 71, 75-7

racism 106, 107; anti- 105, 109
ratings 51, 148, 162; commercial television 7; SBS-TV 145; *see also* audience
RCTS, *see* Remote Commercial Television Service
Real Life 6, 21, 178
recession, economic 41, 51, 54, 64
regional television xxi, xxii, 2, 6, 24, 47; and domestic satellite 25-8, 29, 30; and the recession 54
Regional Television Australia 6, 194n
regulations: advertising 41, 58, 71, 75; commercial television 3; content 55, 57, 62-3, 70, 71, 74, 75, 76, 77-8, 80, 81, 85, 102, 104; control 38; drama 75-8; new pattern in broadcast 36-9; ownership 75; *see also* ownership
Remote Commercial Television Service (RCTS) 26, 33, 169, 172
republicanism 92
Richardson, Graham 55
Riddell, Elizabeth 16
Rijavic, Frank 172
Roberts, Rhoda 158, 165
Robinson, Lee 71
Roddick, Nick 20
roots, tracing family 94-5
Rose Against the Odds 169-70
Rugby League 30
Ruthven, Ken xx, 193n

Sandall, Roger 182
satellite, domestic 2, 6, 7, 25, 27-9, 39
Satellite Dreaming 173-4
satellite links with US 36
SBS-TV (Special Broadcasting Service television) xix, xx, xxii, xxiii, xxiv, 2, 9, 10, 18, 20, 21, 27, 47, 51, 80, 82, 105,

217

Chapter 7; Aboriginal programming 172–5; attitude to/criticism of 130–1, 132–7, 155–6; audiences 137, 138, 142–50, 154–5; change in orientation 163–8; cost of operating 159–63; current affairs service 156–9, 164; and domestic satellite 28, 29; employment of Aborigines 178; English-language programs 159; funding 135, 161, 163; imported programs 64, 65, 122–3, 152–4; and locally-produced programs 164; and multiculturalism 107–8, 121–6, 132–6, 138–42, 164; and political change in eastern Europe 164–6; politics and 130–8; programming 121–2, 144–50; and regionally-produced programs 160; as a service Chapter 8; social and cultural issues 157–9; social policy 125, 126, 137, 145
SBS World News 140
scheduling, program xxiii, 15–16, 132–3; *see also* programming
Schlesinger, Philip 83
serials/series, Australian 74, 77–8; and ethnicity 114; multilingual 122; *see also by name*
serials/series, co-production of 74–5
settler culture 94, 95
Seven Network xxii, 4, 8, 32, 34, 36, 40, 41, 43, 48, 50, 54, 56–7
7:30 Report xxi, 166
Six Pack 122, 161
60 Minutes 6, 17, 18, 25, 32, 60
size of television services compared 10–13
Skase, Christopher 43, 44, 45, 46
Skippy 13
Sky Channel, UK 29, 45, 194n
Small, Frank 144
Smash Palace 13
SMBA (Sydney, Melbourne, Brisbane, Adelaide) television: competition for US programs 36;

local orientation 69; networking arrangements 4, 23–4, 25, 27–8, 71–2
Smith, A.D. 81, 91, 103
soap operas 18, 114; and national identity 86
social and cultural issues 157–9; *see also by name of issue*
social equity policies 82
social policy: and ethnic communities 127; of SBS-TV 125, 126, 137, 145
socialisation, popular 81
The Sound of Music 104
Soviet Union 165
Special Broadcasting Service, *see* SBS-TV
Spigel, Lynn 16
sporting programs 6, 18, 30, 59, 147, 148; costs 76; national identification in 80
Sports Report 147
Spyforce 13
State Affair 34
state-based programs 33–5
Stephensen, P.R. 128
stereotyping 109; in advertising 80
Stratton, David 155
subsidies, production 73, 78, 80, 81
subsidisation, *see* cross-subsidisation
subtitling 124, 137, 139, 162
The Sullivans 72, 80
Sunday 32
Sydney Extra 32
Sylvania Waters 51, 116
Syron, Bryan 187

Taft, Ronald 114
Tanami Network 170, 183
Task Force on Aboriginal and Islander Broadcasting 185–6
tax concessions 13, 73, 77
technologies, television 2, 78–9, 100
Telecom 28–9
telecommunications 6; policy 25; *see also* communications
television cultures compared 3–10

INDEX

Television New Zealand 49
television services/technologies 2, 78–9, 100
Ten Network xxii, 4, 7, 8, 24, 36, 40, 41, 44, 48, 50, 54–5, 125
Thames television 48
They're a Weird Mob 113
This Day Tonight 104
Till Death Us Do Part 18
Tonight Live 14, 18
Tour de France 147
A Town Like Alice 13
Townsville Aboriginal and Islander Media Association (TAIMA) 171, 176, 179, 186
trade, international 101–2
Trade Practices Commission (TPC) 38
The Traveller's Guide to the Orient 166
Tudawalli 170
Turkish programming 151, 152
Turner, Graeme xxi
Turner, Neil 170–1, 172

UHF frequency and SBS-TV 162–3
UK, *see* British
Uluru: An Anangu Story 158
United Artists 46
United States of America, *see* US; USA
The Untouchables 17
US television xx, xxi; ABC network 4; CBS network 4, 49; compared with Australian TV 3–7, 9–11, 14–17; and criticism 9; media groups 49; NBC network 4, 48; networking 3–4, 5; ownership regulations 3; PBS network 122; production houses 48
US television programming 1, 17; and Anglophone culture 88–90; competition for 36, 72, 73–4; cost of importing 65–6; imports of 62–3, 64, 65–8; and shared culture 88
USA: Australian cultural relationship with 104–5, *see also* Anglophone culture; Australian

identification with 19; communications policy 22–3
value/cost of television stations 43–4
VCR 2; in Australian households 1, 193n
Vicary, Pierre 166
Victorian Football League 6, 25
video, ethnic 167
Video and Audio Entertainment and Information Service (VAEIS) 29
videotape 2, 5–6, 25
Vietnam 119
Vietnamese-language programming 152
Vincent Report, 1963 70
violence, television 8
Vizard, Steve 14
Vox Populi 122, 146, 156, 164

Walsh, Max 44
Warlpiri community 183
Warlpiri Media Association 171, 183
Weekend Magazine 125
Wendt, Jana 21
Westfield group 44
Wharton, Wayne 171, 190
Wheel of Fortune xxi
White Australia Policy 106
Wide World of Sport 18, 59
Wogs out of Work 113
Women of the Sun 122, 158, 170
women's rights issues 151
World Cup soccer 147, 148
World News, SBS-TV 123–4, 146, 156, 167
World Series Cricket 6, 25, 32
World Sports 147, 164
world television 18

Yothu Yindi music video 178
Young, Christabel 156
Yuendumu 174
Yuendumu television 172, 175, 190
Yugoslavia in SBS-TV programming 151, 164–5

219

For Product Safety Concerns and Information please contact our EU representative GPSR@taylorandfrancis.com
Taylor & Francis Verlag GmbH, Kaufingerstraße 24, 80331 München, Germany

www.ingramcontent.com/pod-product-compliance
Lightning Source LLC
Chambersburg PA
CBHW051520230426
43668CB00012B/1681